THE MOUNTAIN BIKER'S GUIDE TO THE OZARKS

Dennis Coello's America by Mountain Bike Series

Missouri
Arkansas
Western Kentucky

Steve Henry

Foreword and Introduction by
Dennis Coello, Series Editor

MENASHA
RIDGE
PRESS

FALCON™

Library of Congress Cataloging-in-Publication Data

Henry, Steve.
    The mountain biker's guide to the Ozarks: Steve Henry;
foreword and introduction by Dennis Coello, series editor.
    p.   cm.
    —(Dennis Coello's America by mountain bike series)
    "A Falcon guide"—CIP galley.
    ISBN 1-56044-220-4
    1. All terrain cycling—Ozark Mountains Region—Guidebooks.
2. Ozark Mountains Region—Guidebooks.   I. Title.   II. Series:
America by mountain bike series.
GV1045.5.093H46   1993
796.6´4´097671—dc20   93-47051
                                                                        CIP

Maps by Tim Krasnansky

Menasha Ridge Press
3169 Cahaba Heights Road
Birmingham, Alabama 35243

Falcon Press
P.O. Box 1718
Helena, Montana 59624

 Text pages printed on recycled paper.

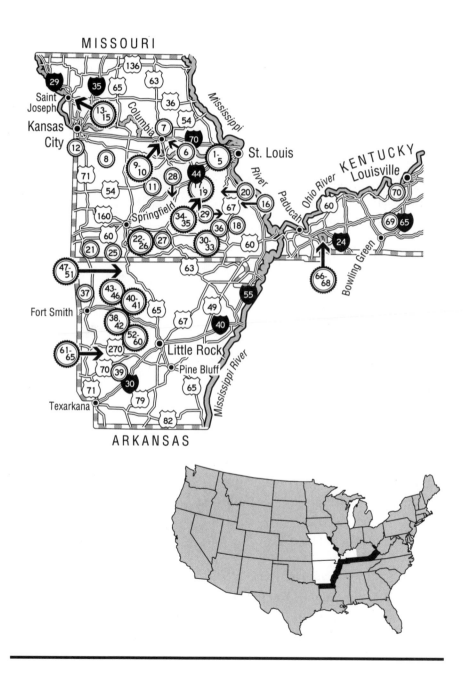

Table of Contents

List of Maps

AMERICA BY MOUNTAIN BIKE   *MAP LEGEND*

Ride trailhead

Steep grade

Primary bike trail | *Direction of travel* | *(arrows point downhill)* | *Optional bike trail and trailhead* | *Other trail* | *Hiking trail*

Interstate highways (with exit no.) | *U.S. routes* | *State routes* | Red Bridge Rd. *Other paved roads* | *Unpaved, gravel or dirt roads (may be 4WD only)*

U.S. Forest Service roads | Little Rock ⊙ St. Louis *Cities* | Mena ⊙ Hope *Towns or settlements* | *Dam* *Lake* | *River, stream or canal*

0   1/2   1 MILES *Approximate scale in miles* | **N** *True north* | MT. NEBO ST. PK. *Parklands* | *State border*

✈ Airport | 🗼 Fire tower or lookout | Museum

Archaeological or historical site | 🍴 Food | Observatory

Archery range | Gate | Park office or ranger station

▲ Campground (CG) | House or cabin | ↟ Picnic area

≡ Cattle guard | Lodging | Port of entry

Cemetery or gravesite | Mountain or butte | Power line or pipeline

Church | Mountain pass | Horse farm or stable

Cliff, escarpment or outcropping | △ 3312 Mountain summit (elevation in feet) | Swimming area

Drinking water or spring | Military test site | Transmission towers

| ✕ Mine or quarry | Tunnel or bridge

xi

Acknowledgments

Writing this trail guide would have been impossible without the help and support of many people and organizations. Special thanks go to the folks at The Alpine Shop in St. Louis, who let me use their computers, laser printer, and library, gave me a job with the flexible schedule I needed to do my trail research and writing, and gave me constant encouragement as I neared the end of this project. If you need any information on biking trails in the southern Missouri Ozarks, The Alpine Shop is the place.

Thanks also to The St. Louis Bicycle Touring Society and The Touring Cyclist, who gave me access to their computers and cycling information when I began the project two years ago. The Touring Cyclist and Touring Society marked the Lost Valley Trail, and have donated lots of time and money to the development of the Katy Trail.

I'm also indebted to the folks at the Pack Rat in Fayetteville, who helped me out on my very first research trip, showing me the trails in their area and giving me a list of contacts and information for other trails in the beautiful state of Arkansas.

I can't say enough good things about the personnel in the city, county, and state parks, the national forests, the Buffalo National River area, Tennessee Valley Authority, and any other land agency in which these trails are located. Busy as they were, they always took the time to talk with me and answer my questions. We all owe a debt of gratitude to these dedicated folks for their work in making possible our recreational experiences on public lands.

My heart and stomach both thank Jeff at Great Harvest Bread. Always greeting me with an animated "How's your book coming?," he often gave me an extra bag of whole wheat rolls or one of those great chocolate chip cookies of his, free of charge. Those rolls look great on the fanciest dinner table, and yet always travel perfectly in an overstuffed fanny pack.

Thanks also to all my friends, who constantly told me they couldn't wait to see the book—even the ones who don't ride mountain bikes. Thanks to all of you for encouraging me when I thought I'd never get finished. Thank you, Steve Patten, for letting me use the seclusion of your cabin at the confluence of the Meramec and Huzzah Rivers to hide from society while working on the book. Special thanks go to Kurt Leemann, for giving me a place to live while I wrote, and for insisting that I look for my car keys one more time on that cold crossing of the Buffalo.

I wish I had space to mention all those who helped me out, but that would require another entire chapter. Thanks so much for your support, and I'll see you on the trail!

The gang at The Alpine Shop knows the best mountain biking trails in eastern Missouri.

Foreword

Welcome to *America by Mountain Bike,* a twenty-book series designed to provide all-terrain bikers with the information necessary to find and ride the very best trails everywhere in the mainland United States. Whether you're new to the sport and don't know where to pedal, or an experienced mountain biker who wants to learn the classic trails in another region, this series is for you. Drop a few bucks for the book, spend an hour with the detailed maps and route descriptions, and you're prepared for the finest in off-road cycling.

My role as editor of this series was simple: first, find a mountain biker who knows the area and loves to ride. Second, ask that person to spend a year researching the most popular and very best rides around. And third, have that rider describe each trail in terms of difficulty, scenery, condition, elevation change, and all other categories of information which are important to trail riders. "Pretend you've just completed a ride and met up with fellow mountain bikers at the trailhead," I told each author. "Imagine their questions, be clear in your answers."

As I said, the *editorial* process—that of sending out riders and reading the submitted chapters—is a snap. But the work involved in finding, riding, and writing about each trail is enormous. In some instances our authors' tasks are made easier by the information contributed by local bike shops or cycling clubs, or even by the writers of local "where-to" guides. Credit for these contributions is provided in each chapter, and our sincere thanks go to all who have helped.

But the overwhelming majority of trails are discovered and pedaled by our authors themselves, then compared with dozens of other routes to determine if they qualify as "classic"—that area's best in scenery and cycling fun. If you've ever had the experience of pioneering a route from outdated topographic maps, or entering a bike shop to request information from local riders who would much prefer to keep their favorite trails secret, or know how it is to double- and triple-check data to be positive your trail info is correct, then you have an idea of how each of our authors has labored to bring about these books. You and I, and all the mountain bikers of America, are the richer for their efforts.

Dennis Coello
Salt Lake City

P.S. You'll get more out of this book if you take a moment to read the next few pages explaining the "Trail Description Outline." Newcomers to mountain biking might want to spend a minute as well with the Glossary, so that terms like *hardpack, single-track,* and *windfall* won't throw you when you come across them in the text. "Topographic Maps" will help you understand a biker's need for topos, and tell you where to find them. And the Afterword on the land-use controversy might help us all enjoy the trails a little more. Finally, though this is a "where-to," not a "how-to" guide, those of you who have not traveled the backcountry might find "Hitting the Trail" of particular value. All the best.

Preface

When the early French explorers first wandered the rugged hills and hollows of what is now southern Missouri and northern Arkansas, they referred to the area as "Aux Arcs," meaning "With bows." No one knows whether this name came from the winding streams of the area or the *bois d'arc* bows carried by the native Osage Indians, but the name stuck. English-speaking settlers that later moved into the area kept the name, but changed the spelling to Ozarks.

During the 1800s and early 1900s, the Ozarks took a beating at the hands of these pioneers. They saw the land only as a resource for their use. They decimated game populations for food and hides, logged the forests for timber, railroad ties, and firewood, and turned the plains of northern Missouri and southern Arkansas into farms. Farming worked well in the plains, but the rocky soils and steep, un-glaciated hillsides of the Ozarks eroded rapidly under the pressure of the ax and plow.

While the plains country of this region remains heavily developed to this day, much of the heart of the Ozarks and the neighboring Ouachita mountains to the south have been restored to their former beauty. Even so, the settlers who were forced to leave their hardscrabble farms in the early part of the twentieth century left fading evidence behind. Many of the trails you will ride follow traces of roads built and abandoned by farmers and loggers. Old stone chimneys stand silently above crumbling foundations, and jumbled piles of logs mark where pioneer cabins once stood. In other areas, the only signs of pioneer farmsteads are overgrown beds of iris and tulips.

Names on the maps evoke haunting images of the past. Sam's Throne, Wolf Pen Hollow, Buzzard Roost Rocks, and others have generated their share of folk tales. The Boom Hole is the site of an old log slide on the Eleven Point River. Logs cut from the surrounding forest were dropped from a high bluff to the river below, where they landed with a booming splash. Peckout Hollow was named by loggers who "pecked out" a hollow in a rock below a spring to collect drinking water. Flyblow Hollow memorializes a cache of fresh game that was ruined by flies. If you ask a few questions of a forest ranger, store clerk, or resident you meet in camp or on the trail, you might add a bit of local lore to your experience.

THE SEASONS

Upland forests in this region consist of white, post, and red oak, shagbark and butternut hickory, and scatterings of black walnut and maple. High ridges and dry, rocky, south-facing slopes are often covered with stands of pine. Lowland trees include bur oak, pin oak, sycamore, cottonwood, willow, and hackberry. Flowering trees decorate the forest in early spring. Dogwoods, serviceberry, and hawthornes paint the drab early spring forest with their white blooms. They contrast pleasantly with the bright pink-red hues of eastern redbud.

Hard on the heels of the dogwood and redbud blooms come spring wild-flowers, exploding into multi-color displays that race to gather the sunlight before it is blocked by the budding leaves of the forest. Among the blooms are wild sweet William, fire pink, bird's foot violet, Dutchman's breeches, spider-wort, spring beauties, and wild blue phlox.

Those of us who live in the region know that autumn is the most spectacular season for mountain biking in the Ozarks. For two weeks in late October, the hillsides are a palette of crimson, yellow, orange, and caramel as the forest sheds its foliage in preparation for winter. Temperatures moderate, insects disappear, the summer vacation crowd dwindles, and, as the leaves fall, scenic vistas open on the ridge tops.

Although spring and fall are the best seasons to ride in the Ozarks, don't discount the lure of summer and winter cycling. The warm days that sometimes break through during winter are rare gifts to mountain bikers stricken with cabin fever. Riding on chilly days can be interesting, too. When there has been a prolonged cold snap, ice sculptures surround the many springs, seeps, and streams that flow through the quiet hollows. I'll never forget finding ice columns three feet thick and 100 feet tall stretching down the side of a bluff to the creek bed below.

These springs and seeps really come into their own in summer, when Ozark temperatures and humidity reach ridiculous levels. When it's hot, look for those rides near lakes or rivers. Nothing feels better than a swim in a cool Ozark stream after a hot, muggy ride.

Better yet, camp out near your trail and combine your ride with a canoe trip on some of the 5,000 miles of floatable streams in the Ozarks. Outfitters are located along almost every stream, ready to shuttle you and their boats to put-ins and take-outs. After a day of roughing it over the trail on your bike, a gentle float down a quiet Ozark stream feels like heaven.

THE WILDLIFE

Wildlife, once nearly exterminated from the Ozarks by logging and hunting pressure, has recovered impressively. No animal is more ubiquitous than the white-tailed deer. Coyotes will serenade you as you camp, before or after your ride. Beaver and otters are making a comeback on Ozark streams, and a black bear population in northern Arkansas is moving into Missouri.

One of the smaller mammals common to the Ozarks is the bat. They make their homes in the hundreds of caves that dot the region. Bats can be spotted at dusk, flitting through the darkening sky as they feed on flying insects. You can distinguish them from birds by their erratic flight paths, juking and weaving as they nab their dinner from the evening sky. Certain caves inhabited by bats are closed during winter, since disturbing them only once or twice during hibernation can cause them to burn off their winter fat reserves and die before spring.

The end of winter in the Ozarks is heralded by spring peepers. These tiny frogs fill the woods with their high-pitched cries as soon as the weather is warm enough for them to come out of estivation. The peepers are followed by the return of songbirds that live in the forest and plains. Titmice, ovenbirds, cardinals, robins, orioles, and hundreds of other birds saturate the forest with their tunes. Many larger birds haunt the woods, too. Turkey vultures, hawks, and an occasional eagle ride the updrafts off the ridges. You'll hear several kinds of woodpeckers knocking in the woods. If you're lucky, you'll spot one of the huge pileated woodpeckers that live in some parts of the Ozarks. If you camp in the woods, barred owls, great horned owls, and screech owls haunt the night with their calls, and the raucous gobbling of wild turkeys will rouse you from your slumber. Expect to be serenaded to sleep by the calling of whippoorwills.

The insect life of the Midwest can be annoying; however, if you have the right attitude, these six-legged creatures can be captivating. You'll be amazed by the plethora of walking sticks mating in early fall, throwing caution to the wind as they strut their stuff. Brightly colored butterflies work the flowers in summer, and wasps build huge nests high in the trees. I'll never forget resting in my camp after a hard day of trail riding in the Boston Mountains, watching a praying mantis stalk and munch the smaller insects attracted to the light of my lantern.

Enjoy the creatures of the forest, but be aware when riding during hunting season. There are usually spring and fall turkey hunts, and a fall deer season in early November. Check with the land agency involved for seasons. If you can, avoid the national forests and conservation lands during hunting season. Ride in state parks, where hunting is not allowed. If you must ride during these seasons, don't wear anything white and don't sound like a turkey. Wear hunter's-orange. Most hardware stores in the Ozarks sell hunter's-orange vests.

THE TRAILS

I have tried to include something for everyone in this guide. Trail quality varies from rugged single-track to wide gravel and paved roads. Some rides encompass a little of everything. Skill levels required for each trail are noted, but my definitions of beginner and expert may differ from yours. Most trails will have short stretches that will require portages, so expect to occasionally walk or carry your bike. Bail-out points where trails intersect roads leading back to the trailhead are noted, and carrying a map will enable those of you who can't handle the trail to escape and pedal back to your car. Road loops are a little better. You won't have to walk any of these unless your physical condition requires it.

I can't let you hit the Ozark trails without a few words of caution about route finding. Markings are not always good. Some are defaced by vandals or squirrels, and others simply fade from age. Trail routes are sometimes changed, and there are many unmarked side trails. Carrying a map and compass is highly recommended. Without these you greatly improve your chances of getting lost. Be especially cautious when riding in winter, when short days can catch you out. I always carry fire starter, so at least I'll be warm if I get caught short by the sunset.

This is not a book of road rides, so don't expect everything to be laid out perfectly for you. Expect to sometimes have trouble finding your way in the woods. Rather than being intimidated, though, think of route finding as an adventure. After all, aren't you hitting the woods to get away from regimentation? Sometimes the price of adventure is a little uncertainty. If you get confused, hang in there, study your map, and don't be afraid to backtrack. Persevere and, believe it or not, you'll find your way out in fine shape and enjoy the rewarding feeling of self-sufficiency.

Steve Henry

Introduction

Information on each trail in this book begins with a general description which includes length, configuration, scenery, highlights, trail conditions, and difficulty. Additional description is contained in eleven individual categories. The following will help you to understand all of the information provided.

Trail name: Trail names are as designated on USGS (United States Geological Survey) or Forest Service or other maps, and/or by local custom.

Length: The overall length of a trail is described in miles, unless stated otherwise.

Configuration: This is a description of the shape of each trail—whether the trail is a loop, out-and-back (that is, along the same route), figure-eight, trapezoid, isosceles triangle . . . , or if it connects with another trail described in the book.

Difficulty: This provides at a glance a description of the degree of physical exertion required to complete the ride, and the technical skill required to pedal it. Authors were asked to keep in mind the fact that all riders are not equal, and thus to gauge the trail in terms of how the middle-of-the-road rider—someone between the newcomer and Ned Overend—could handle the route. Comments about the trail's length, condition, and elevation change will also assist you in determining the difficulty of any trail relative to your own abilities.

Condition: Trails are described in terms of being paved, unpaved, sandy, hard-packed, washboarded, two- or four-wheel-drive, single-track or double-track. All terms that might be unfamiliar to the first-time mountain biker are defined in the Glossary.

Scenery: Here you will find a general description of the natural surroundings during the seasons most riders pedal the trail, and a suggestion of what is to be found at special times (like great fall foliage or cactus in bloom).

Highlights: Towns, major water crossings, historical sites, etc., are listed.

General location: This category describes where the trail is located in reference to a nearby town or other landmark.

Elevation change: Unless stated otherwise, the figure provided is the total gain and loss of elevation along the trail. In regions where the elevation variation is not extreme, the route is described in a more general manner of flat, rolling, or as possessing short steep climbs or descents.

Season: This is the best time of year to pedal the route, taking into account trail condition (for example, when it will not be muddy), riding comfort (when the weather is too hot, cold, or wet), and local hunting seasons.

Note: Because the exact opening and closing dates of deer, elk, moose, and antelope seasons often change from year to year, it is suggested that riders check with the local Fish and Game department, or call a sporting goods store (or any place that sells hunting licenses) in a nearby town. Wear bright clothes in fall, and don't wear suede jackets while in the saddle. Hunter's-orange tape on the helmet is also a good idea.

Services: This category is of primary importance in guides for paved-road tourers, but is far less crucial to most mountain bike trail descriptions because there are usually no services whatsoever to be found. Authors have noted when water is available on desert or long mountain routes, and have listed the availability of food, lodging, campgrounds, and bike shops. If all these services are present, you will find only the words "All services available in . . ."

Hazards: Special hazards like steep cliffs, great amounts of deadfall, or barbed-wire fences very close to the trail are noted here.

Rescue index: Determining how far one is from help on any particular trail can be difficult due to the backcountry nature of most mountain bike rides. Authors therefore state the proximity of homes or Forest Service outposts, nearby roads where one might hitch a ride, or the likelihood of other bikers being encountered on the trail. Phone numbers of local sheriff departments or hospitals have not been provided because, again, phones are almost never available. Besides, if a phone is reached the local operator will connect you with emergency services.

Land status: This category provides information as to whether the trail crosses land operated by the Forest Service, Bureau of Land Management, a city, state, or national park, whether it crosses private land whose owner (at the time the author did the research) allowed mountain bikers right of passage, and so on.

Note: Authors have been extremely careful to offer only those routes that are open to bikers and are legal to ride. However, because land ownership changes over time, and because the land-use controversy created by mountain bikes still has not subsided totally, it is the duty of each cyclist to look for and to heed signs warning against trail use. Don't expect this book to get you off the hook when you're facing some small-town judge for pedaling past a "Biking Prohibited" sign erected the day before. Look for these signs, read them, and heed the advice. And remember, there's always another trail.

Maps: The maps in this book have been produced with great care, and in conjunction with the trail-following suggestions will help you stay on course. But as every experienced mountain biker knows, things can get tricky in the backcountry. It is therefore strongly suggested that you avail yourself of the detailed information found in the 7.5 minute series USGS (United States Geological Survey) topographical maps. In some cases, authors have found that specific Forest Service or other maps may be more useful than the USGS quads, and tell how to obtain them.

Finding the trail: Detailed information on how to reach the trailhead and where to park your car is provided here.

Sources of additional information: Here you will find the address and/or phone number of a bike shop, governmental agency, or other source from which trail information can be obtained.

Notes on the trail: This is where you are stepped carefully through any portions of the trail that are particularly difficult to follow. The author also may add information about the route that does not fit easily in the other categories.

ABBREVIATIONS

The following road-designation abbreviations are used in the *America by Mountain Bike* series:

CR	County Road
FR	Farm Route
FS	Forest Service road
I-	Interstate
IR	Indian Route
US	United States highway

State highways are designated with the appropriate two-letter state abbreviation, followed by the road number. *Example:* UT 6 = Utah State Highway 6

Postal Service two-letter state code:

AL	Alabama	KY	Kentucky
AK	Alaska	LA	Louisiana
AZ	Arizona	ME	Maine
AR	Arkansas	MD	Maryland
CA	California	MA	Massachusetts
CO	Colorado	MI	Michigan
CT	Connecticut	MN	Minnesota
DE	Delaware	MS	Mississippi
DC	District of Columbia	MO	Missouri
FL	Florida	MT	Montana
GA	Georgia	NE	Nebraska
HI	Hawaii	NV	Nevada
ID	Idaho	NH	New Hampshire
IL	Illinois	NJ	New Jersey
IN	Indiana	NM	New Mexico
IA	Iowa	NY	New York
KS	Kansas	NC	North Carolina

ND	North Dakota	TX	Texas
OH	Ohio	UT	Utah
OK	Oklahoma	VT	Vermont
OR	Oregon	VA	Virginia
PA	Pennsylvania	WA	Washington
RI	Rhode Island	WV	West Virginia
SC	South Carolina	WI	Wisconsin
SD	South Dakota	WY	Wyoming
TN	Tennessee		

TOPOGRAPHIC MAPS

The maps in this book, when used in conjunction with the route directions present in each chapter, will in most instances be sufficient to get you to the trail and keep you on it. However, these maps cannot begin to provide the detailed information found in the 7.5 minute series USGS (United States Geological Survey) topographic maps. Recognizing how indispensable these are to bikers and hikers alike, many bike shops and sporting goods stores now carry topos of the local area.

But if you're brand new to mountain biking you might be wondering, "What's a topographic map?" In short, these differ from standard "flat" maps because they indicate not only linear distance, but elevation as well. One glance at a topo will show you the difference, for "contour lines" are spread across the map like dozens of intricate spider webs. Each contour line represents a particular elevation, and each topo has written at its base a particular "contour interval" designation. Yes, it sounds confusing if you're new to the lingo, but it truly is a simple and wonderfully helpful system. Keep reading.

Let's assume that the 7.5 minute series topo before us says "Contour Interval 40 feet." And that the short trail we'll be pedaling is two inches in length on the map, and crosses five contour lines between its beginning and end. What do we know? Well, because the linear scale of this series is two thousand feet to the inch (roughly 2 3/4 inches representing a mile), we know our trail is approximately four-fifths of a mile long (2″ x 2,000′). But we also know we'll be climbing or descending two hundred vertical feet (5 contour lines x 40 feet each) over that distance. And the elevation designations written on occasional contour lines will tell us if we're heading up or down.

The authors of this series warn their readers of upcoming terrain, but only a detailed topo gives you the information that enables you to pinpoint your position exactly on a map, steer yourself toward optional trails and roads nearby, plus see at a glance if you'll be pedaling hard to take them. It's a lot of information for a very low cost. In fact, the only drawback with topos is their size— several feet square. I've tried rolling them into tubes, folding them carefully, even cutting them into blocks and photocopying the pieces. Any of these systems is a pain, but no matter how you pack the maps you'll be happy they're along. And you'll be even happier if you pack a compass as well.

Major universities and some public libraries also carry topos; you might try photocopying the ones you need to avoid the cost of buying them. But if you want your own and can't find them locally, write to:

USGS Map Sales
Box 25286
Denver, CO 80225

Ask for an index while you're at it, plus a price list and a copy of the booklet *Topographic Maps*. In minutes you'll be reading them like a pro.

A second excellent series of maps available to mountain bikers is that put out by the United States Forest Service. If your trail runs through an area designated as a national forest, look in the phone book (white pages) under the United States Government listings, find the Department of Agriculture heading, and then run your finger through that section until you find the Forest Service. Give them a call and they'll provide the address of the regional Forest Service office, from which you can obtain the appropriate map.

HITTING THE TRAIL

Once again, because this is a "where-to," not a "how-to" guide, the following will be brief. If you're a veteran trail rider these suggestions might serve to remind you of something you've forgotten to pack. If you're a newcomer, they might convince you to think twice before hitting the backcountry unprepared.

Water: I've heard the questions dozens of times. "How much is enough? One bottle? Two? Three?! But think of all that extra weight!" Well, one simple physiological fact should convince you to err on the side of excess when it comes to determining how much water to pack: a human working hard in ninety-degree temperature needs approximately ten quarts of fluids every day. Ten quarts. That's two and a half gallons—*twelve* large water bottles, or *sixteen* small ones. And with water weighing in at approximately eight pounds per gallon, a one-day supply comes to a whopping twenty pounds.

In other words, pack along two or three bottles even for short rides. And make sure you can purify the water found along the trail on longer routes. When writing of those routes where this could be of critical importance, each author has provided information on where water can be found near the trail—if it can be found at all. But drink it untreated and you run the risk of disease. (See *Giardia* in the Glossary.)

One sure way to kill both the bacteria and viruses in water is to boil it for ten minutes, plus one minute more for each one thousand feet of elevation above sea level. Right. That's just how you want to spend your time on a bike ride. Besides, who wants to carry a stove, or denude the countryside stoking bonfires to boil water?

Luckily, there is a better way. Many riders pack along the effective, inexpensive, and only slightly distasteful tetraglycine hydroperiodide tablets (sold under the names of Potable Aqua, Globaline, Coughlan's, and others). Some invest in portable, lightweight purifiers that filter out the crud. Yes, purifying water with tablets or filters is a bother. But catch a case of Giardia sometime and you'll understand why it's worth the trouble.

Tools: Ever since my first cross-country tour in '65 I've been kidded about the number of tools I pack on the trail. And so I will exit entirely from this discussion by providing a list compiled by two mechanic (and mountain biker) friends of mine. After all, since they make their livings fixing bikes, and get their kicks by riding them, who could be a better source?

The following is suggested as an absolute minimum:

    tire levers
    spare tube and patch kit
    air pump
    allen wrenches (3, 4, 5, and 6 mm)
    six-inch crescent (adjustable-end) wrench
    small flat-blade screwdriver
    chain rivet tool
    spoke wrench

But their personal tool pouches carried on the trail contain, in addition to the above:

    channel locks (small)
    air gauge
    tire valve cap (the metal kind, with a valve-stem remover)
    baling wire (ten or so inches, for temporary repairs)
    duct tape (small roll for temporary repairs or tire boot)
    boot material (small piece of old tire or a large tube patch)
    spare chain link
    rear derailleur pulley
    spare nuts and bolts
    paper towel and tube of waterless hand cleaner

First-Aid Kit: My personal kit contains the following, sealed inside double zip-lock bags:

    sunscreen
    aspirin
    butterfly closure bandages
    band-aids

gauze compress pads (a half-dozen 4″x4″)
gauze (1 roll)
ace bandages or Spenco joint wraps
Benadryl (an antihistamine to guard against possible allergic reactions)
water purification tablets
moleskin/Spenco "Second Skin"
hydrogen peroxide/iodine/Mercurochrome (some kind of antiseptic)
snakebite kit

Final Considerations: The authors of this series have done a good job in suggesting that specific items be packed for certain trails—like raingear in particular seasons, a hat and gloves for mountain passes, or shades for desert jaunts. Heed their warnings, and think ahead. Good luck.

Dennis Coello
Salt Lake City

MISSOURI RIDES

St. Louis Area Trails

RIDE 1   CASTLEWOOD STATE PARK

Castlewood State Park has nine miles of trails divided into three loops of three miles each. There's something for everyone here. The River Scene and Grotpeter trails begin near the picnic area nearest the park entrance. The Stinging Nettle Trail, the newest trail in Castlewood, begins near the westernmost portion of the River Scene Trail.

The Stinging Nettle Trail is flat and easy to ride. One side of this hard-packed single-track is next to the Meramec River, and the other through the woods a short distance from the Meramec.

The River Scene Trail climbs to the top of the bluff above the river, then descends to river level at the base of the bluffs. From there, it follows the stream as it returns to the picnic area. It is gravelly and rocky single-track on the bluff, and hardpack down near the river.

The Grotpeter is a combination of flat hard-packed single-track in the Keifer Creek bottomlands, single-track and abandoned road along the ridge traversing the park's northern boundary, and short-but-tough rock-strewn climb and descent on its eastern and western ends.

While all three trails are suitable for beginners, the Stinging Nettle Trail is the easiest, the River Scene Trail more difficult, and the Grotpeter most difficult.

Between the First and Second World Wars, the area that is now Castlewood State Park was a popular recreation area. Thousands used the beaches along the Meramec, and surreptitiously sipped Prohibition home brew at the private clubs scattered in the woods north of the river. Ruins of these clubs are still visible in the park.

Especially interesting are the overgrown and deteriorating steps at the west end of the park. Part of the River Scene Trail, these steps lead from a low point in the bluff down to the ruins of the train depot, store, and post office that served the thousands of weekend revelers who frequented the river in its pre-park era. An exhibit at the park office gives a good description of the park in its wilder days.

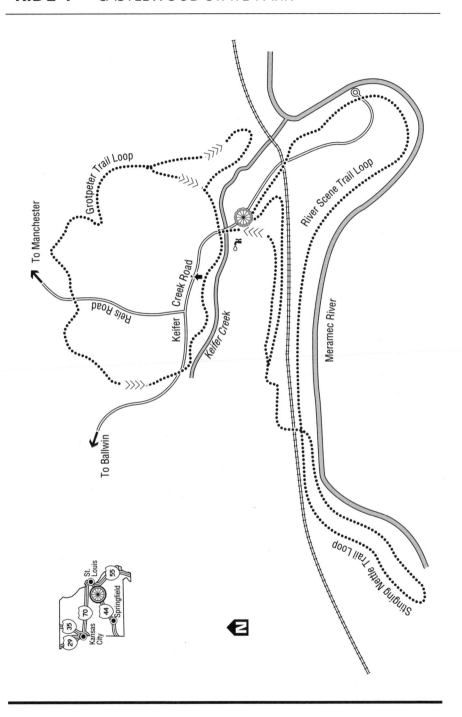

Today, Castlewood is an enclave of peace near the hustle of the city. Silver maple, black willow, and sycamore cover much of the bottomlands next to the river, and the slopes are covered with white and northern red oak, hickory, and redbud. Deer, coyotes, great blue herons, kingfishers, and numerous songbirds live in the area. It's the perfect place for a quick ride or commune with nature after a difficult day on the job.

General location: Western edge of the St. Louis metropolitan area, just south of Ballwin.

Elevation change: Elevations range from 400′ at Keifer Creek to a high of 700′ at the tops of the ridges. The River Scene Trail and the Grotpeter Trail each have one major climb and descent. The Stinging Nettle Trail is flat.

Season: Because of each trail's shortness and the park's proximity to the St. Louis area, Castlewood can be rewarding in any season. You can complete summer rides in the cool early morning or late evening, avoiding the heat and humidity. Winter rides can be finished before the cold takes too big a bite out of you.

Services: Water and restrooms are available in the park. All other services can be found in the nearby St. Louis metropolitan area.

Hazards: Watch for cars where the trail crosses Reis and Keifer Creek roads. Riding down the steps at the western end of the River Scene Trail is not recommended. Some pretty spectacular face-plants have been performed by those who have tried. Watch out for poison ivy next to the river.

Rescue index: Castlewood State Park is popular with both hikers and bikers, even on weekdays. If you get into trouble, you'll probably not wait long for help.

Land status: State park.

Maps: Trail maps for Castlewood State Park are available at the park office on Keifer Creek Road just inside the park. The 7.5 minute topo for the area is Manchester.

Finding the trail: Castlewood State Park is located just south of Ballwin, a suburb of St. Louis. To reach it, drive west on Big Bend Road from Interstate 270. Five miles west of I-270, turn south (left) on Reis Road. Go 1 mile to Keifer Creek Road. A left turn on Keifer Creek takes you into the park. Park at the picnic area.

Sources of additional information:

Castlewood State Park
Ballwin, MO 63021
(314) 527-6481

The Alpine Shop
601 East Lockwood
Webster Groves, MO 63119
(314) 962-7715

The St. Louis Bicycle Touring Society
c/o The Touring Cyclist
11816 St. Charles Rock Road
Bridgeton, MO 63044
(314) 739-5180

Notes on the trail: The River Scene and Stinging Nettle trails can be very muddy after rainfall. To keep these trails from becoming wide and rutted, stay off them when they are wet.

RIDE 2   *CHUBB TRAIL*

Nine miles long, the Chubb Trail is a versatile and popular point-to-point trail with a short loop on its eastern end. It connects West Tyson County Park to Lone Elk County Park, passing through the southern section of Castlewood State Park along the way. West Tyson is the recommended starting point. If you begin there, ride around the loop, and return, you will cover fourteen miles.

Well-maintained single-track is used for most of the trail, with a small amount of double-track in the eastern sections. The first three miles are somewhat technical, with steep, rocky climbs and descents. This is the part you will ride twice. The rest of the trail is mostly level hardpack, easy for beginners. Don't ride here when the trail is wet and muddy.

The Chubb Trail's excellent single-track makes it the most popular mountain bike trail in the St. Louis area. It has difficult sections, but is suitable for riders of all skill levels. Beginners can expect to portage for stretches in the western end of the ride, but don't let this discourage you. These unrideable sections will be short, and after three miles the trail levels out along the river.

Though you must pay for it by climbing, the long descent to the river is a thrill. It's followed by a level ride along the river, where the easy pedaling lets you pay less attention to the trail. Maybe you'll spot some deer, see a hawk soaring above the stream, or watch herons flapping just above the Meramec. In winter, the meadow along the river is prime feeding area for cardinals and other songbirds that stay north during the cold months.

General location: 15 miles southwest of St. Louis.
Elevation change: Elevation ranges from 400′ along the Meramec River to 750′ where the trail crosses the ridge in West Tyson County Park. There is one long half-mile climb, and then a descent of the same distance as you cross the ridge.
Season: Spring and fall are the best seasons, but the short Chubb Trail can be enjoyed year-round. Just beware of ice on the trail in winter. And be prepared to deal with ticks and chiggers during the hot summer months.

RIDE 2 *CHUBB TRAIL*

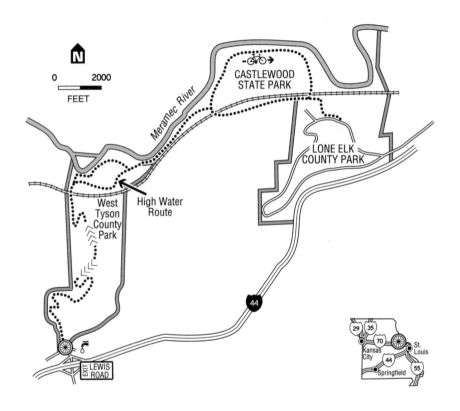

Services: Drinking water and camping are available in West Tyson County Park at the western end of the trail. All other services are available in the St. Louis metropolitan area 15 miles to the east.

Hazards: Parts of the eastern 3 miles of the trail are rocky, making it tough to control your bike. Especially hazardous is a set of step-like rock ledges on the descent to the river. You will have to ride over a couple of rock benches 10 inches high. They are hard to see in advance, and could surprise you. If you are ready for them, they'll be a fun challenge to your bike-handling skills. You should also expect to meet equestrians on the Chubb Trail. Dismount, move to the downhill side of the trail, and stand quietly while they pass.

Rescue index: The Chubb is heavily used by bikers, hikers, and equestrians, so it's likely you'll soon be found in an emergency.

Land status: County and state parks.

Maps: A map of the Chubb Trail is available from the County Department of Parks. Those using topos will need the Manchester 7.5 minute map.

Finding the trail: Drive west from St. Louis on Interstate 44 to Lewis Road. Turn right at the top of the exit ramp, and go 100 yards to the entrance to West Tyson County Park. Turn right into the park, and take the first left off the park entrance road. It will take you a short distance up a steep gravel road to the Chubb shelter and trailhead.

Sources of additional information:

St. Louis County Parks
41 South Central
Clayton, MO 63105
(314) 889-2863

The Alpine Shop
601 East Lockwood
Webster Groves, MO 63119
(314) 962-7715

The St. Louis Bicycle Touring Society
c/o The Touring Cyclist
11816 St. Charles Rock Road
Bridgeton, MO 63044
(314) 739-5180

Notes on the trail: The eastern portion of the trail can be a little confusing. Around 5 miles into the ride (starting from West Tyson), you'll come to an intersection and a sign reading "Castlewood Loop." Going left, you'll ride through an open grassland next to the river, and then into wooded bottomlands.

Just after you have looped around and are heading west, near the crossing of a small creek, the trail forks again. Take the left fork, which passes through a tunnel under the railroad tracks.

Just beyond the tracks is a trail running parallel to the railroad. Turning right will close the loop by taking you back to the main trail and on to the trailhead, a total of 14 miles. Turning left will take you one-half mile to the Lone Elk Park entrance road. Lone Elk is a great place for a mid-ride picnic, or to arrange a pickup for those not wishing to ride the trail back to West Tyson County Park.

RIDE 3   *GREENSFELDER COUNTY PARK*

Greensfelder County Park and the adjacent Rockwoods Reservation combined form a 5,000-acre tract of semi-wild public land in western St. Louis County. Oak-hickory forest covers the rocky hills and bluffs in the park. The forest is broken by several open glades, a scenic overlook, and some caves.

Greensfelder is a great haven when you want to escape the rush of the nearby St. Louis metropolitan area. The park's rugged trails offer a near-wilderness experience. They climb over rocky, wooded hills and pass through deep, quiet hollows. Park facilities include picnic shelters, primitive and developed campsites, and an orienteering course.

Greensfelder is a network of 25 miles of very challenging single-track. With its rocky trails and many steep climbs and descents, it is recommended for experienced riders only.

Of all the loops in the park, the Dogwood and De Clue trails are best suited to riding. Although they are steep and rocky, they can be ridden for most of their length. All other trails are open to cyclists, but pass over rough terrain requiring difficult portages.

General location: 30 miles southwest of St. Louis.

Elevation change: Elevation in Greensfelder ranges from 600′ to 900′. The area is very hilly, resulting in many ascents and descents on the trail network. Climbs vary in length from .1 to .5 mile.

Season: Spring and fall are the best seasons for riding in Greensfelder, with summer coming in third. Shorter trail choices help make winter cycling enjoyable.

Services: Drinking water and camping are available in Greensfelder Park. You'll find all other services in the St. Louis metropolitan area, immediately to the east of the park.

Hazards: The steep, rocky trails in Greensfelder can quickly throw your bike off line. Since the park is a popular equestrian area, be prepared for horses. Move to the downhill side of the trail, stand quietly, and wait for them to pass.

Rescue index: Greensfelder is a popular park for hiking, cycling, and horseback riding, so you should have no problem finding help.

Land status: County park.

Maps: Trail maps are available at the Visitor Center. The USGS topo for the area is the Eureka 7.5 minute map.

Finding the trail: Drive west from St. Louis on Interstate 44 to the Six Flags/Allenton exit, just west of Eureka. Exit I-44 and go north on Allenton Road. Parking is available at the Visitor Center, 2 miles north of I-44.

RIDE 3 *GREENSFELDER COUNTY PARK*

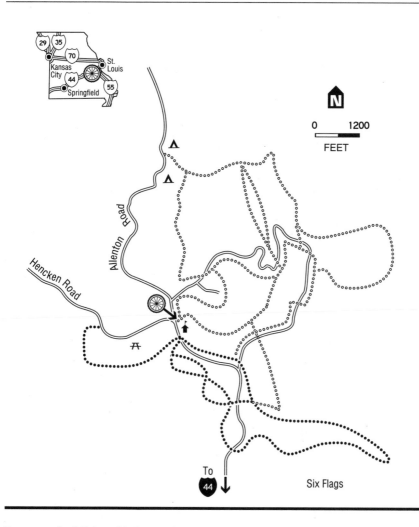

Sources of additional information:

St. Louis County Parks
41 South Central
Clayton, MO 63105
(314) 889-2863

The Alpine Shop
601 East Lockwood
Webster Groves, MO 63119
(314) 962-7715

The St. Louis Bicycle Touring Society
c/o The Touring Cyclist
11816 St. Charles Rock Road
Bridgeton, MO 63044
(314) 739-5180

Notes on the trail: If you ride the Green Rock Trail, you will find that it leaves the park and continues into Rockwoods Reservation. Since Rockwoods is off-limits to mountain bikes, turn around at the boundary and stay in Greensfelder Park.

RIDE 4   *KATY TRAIL*

In 1986, the Missouri, Kansas, and Texas Railroad, known as the Katy Line, abandoned its route from Machens to Sedalia. The state took over the old right-of-way and turned it into the longest rails-to-trails conversion in the United States. By the end of the summer of 1993, the trail had been completed all the way from St. Charles to Sedalia, a total of 200 miles. The trail surface is hard-packed gravel, and is suitable for riders of all skill levels.

The Katy Trail has a little of everything. You'll ride next to the muddy Missouri River, along towering sandstone bluffs, and through open prairie land. Two caves are accessible from the trail, between Rocheport and Jefferson City. Wildlife is abundant in the bottomlands next to the Missouri River.

Small towns along the way attract you with their relaxed charm. Wineries, bed-and-breakfasts, quaint restaurants, and old-fashioned country stores draw you off the trail when you're tired of riding. Shuttered train depots and concrete signal foundations remind you of the trail's history.

Planned additions call for extending the Katy to Machens in the east and Clinton in the west, bringing the total trail length to 233 miles. Trail organizations in Kansas City are proposing to link the Katy to their city via another abandoned rail line, making possible a cross-state trail ride.

General location: When completed, the Katy Trail will extend from St. Louis to Sedalia. The trail has numerous access points. Contact the Missouri Department of Natural Resources for maps showing the trail and its access points.

Elevation change: Because the Katy Trail follows an old railroad bed, there are no real climbs and elevation changes are virtually nil.

Season: Spring and fall are the best seasons for riding this trail.

Services: The trail passes through many small towns. Most of these have a store, restaurant, or tavern where you can get food, water, and access to restrooms. You'll find bed-and-breakfasts all along the route, and hotels in the

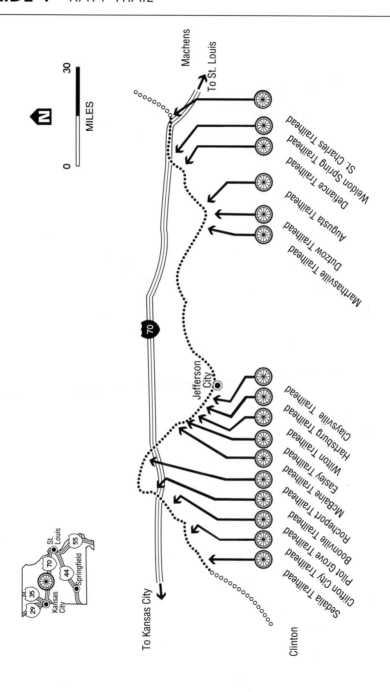

Kent Baker of The Touring Cyclist. The Touring Cyclist has two stores along the Katy Trail.

larger towns. No campgrounds are in place yet. The Department of Natural Resources may build several in the future. Bike shops are in St. Louis, St. Charles, Augusta, Jefferson City, and Sedalia.

Hazards: Don't let the lack of cars on the trail lull you into inattention at road crossings.

Rescue index: The Katy Trail is a popular and heavily used recreation site. If you have any trouble, you can count on being found quickly.

Land status: State park.

Maps: Maps of each section of the Katy Trail are usually available at trailheads. You can also contact the Missouri Department of Natural Resources at the address shown below.

Finding the trail: The Department of Natural Resources provides maps of the trail showing parking areas and other facilities. To get one, call (800) 334-6946.

Sources of additional information:

Missouri Department of Natural Resources
Post Office Box 176
Jefferson City, MO 65102-0176
(800) 334-6946

The St. Louis Bicycle Touring Society
c/o The Touring Cyclist
11816 St. Charles Rock Road
St. Louis, MO 63111
(314) 739-5180

The Touring Cyclist
301 Webster
Augusta, MO 63332
(314) 228-4882

Notes on the trail: Most of the land on either side of the trail is private. When this trail was proposed, long legal battles ensued with landowners who did not want it to pass through their property. Some of them still resent the trail's existence. Respect their property rights by staying on the trail, no matter how tempting off-trail exploration may be.

RIDE 5   *LOST VALLEY TRAIL*

The Lost Valley Trail in Weldon Spring Wildlife Area is a perfect ride for beginners. Eight miles long, it uses abandoned farm roads that later served as access to local ammunition stockpiles during World War II. These roads vary from double-tracks still used by Conservation Department patrols to abandoned paths through the woods.

With the exception of a couple of washed-out places, the hard-packed trail now known as Lost Valley Trail can be handled by novices. Riding the loop in a clockwise direction will make your climbs easier and your trail markings more visible. Several abandoned double-track roads lead off the loop, giving you the option of exploring even more of this interesting area.

Lost Valley was named in the days when farmers used to hide their stills in the hills and hollows of the area. On your ride you'll see an old chimney by the creek—all that's left of those early farming days. You may also see the remains of the U.S. government's ammunition storage bunkers and access roads from some of the side trails in Lost Valley.

After the military was finished with the property, it was taken over by the Missouri Department of Conservation. MDC has been gradually returning the area to its natural state while managing it as a wildlife hunting and study area. You are likely to spot deer as you ride the trail's first three miles along the creek on a relatively level double-track. There you'll pass through woods and open glades in the Lost Valley. After mile three, you'll begin the quarter-mile climb to the ridge above the valley. Once on the ridge, you'll ride around a large spring-fed lake. There you may spot waterfowl, or hear a deafening chorus of frogs in the spring.

RIDE 5 *LOST VALLEY TRAIL*

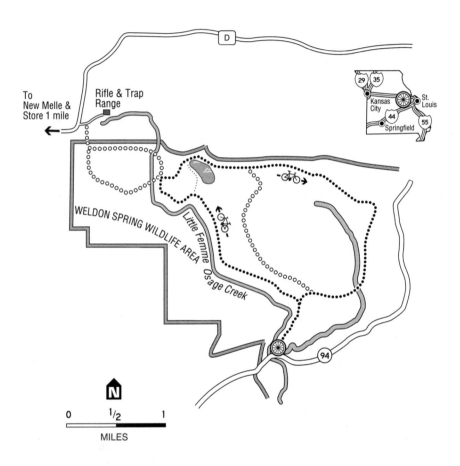

Many small streams lace the area in spring, and dogwoods, redbuds, and wild sweet Williams decorate the hillsides and valleys with shades of white, pink, and violet. With its combination of forest, open glades, and Missouri River riparian habitat, the area supports a wide variety of bird species. Weldon Spring Wildlife Area is a place where riders of any skill level can get away to the woods and enjoy the peace of the backcountry without driving hours to escape the city.

General location: Weldon Spring Wildlife Area, 30 miles west of St. Louis.
Elevation change: Elevation changes are not dramatic on this loop. They vary

Don't discount winter riding in the Midwest. Here riders on the Lost Valley Trail enjoy unbelievable traction on hard-packed sleet dumped by an unusual winter storm.

from 500′ along Little Femme Osage Creek to 700′ along the northern boundary of the wildlife area. There are only 2 climbs of any consequence on the loop, and they are not very steep.

Season: The Lost Valley Trail can be ridden year-round. Spring and fall are the best seasons. Summer may be hot and humid, and ticks can be a problem. Winter rides can be enjoyable on this easy and relatively short trail. Warm days may occur any month of the year in east-central Missouri.

Services: No drinking water is available along the Lost Valley Trail. Spring water should not be consumed under any circumstance; it may be contaminated by an ammunition plant that once operated nearby. The nearest water source is the Busch Wildlife Area headquarters, 2 miles west of MO 94 on County Road D. Those riding the optional loop to the intersection of county roads D and DD can obtain water, cold drinks, and food from a small store and a restaurant located there. All other services are available in the St. Louis metropolitan area, north and east of the wildlife area.

Hazards: Do not drink water from any streams or springs. They may be contaminated. Poison ivy is thick, so watch for it when riding this trail. Weldon Spring Wildlife Area is popular among hunters. Riding during the November deer season is strongly discouraged.

Rescue index: You are never far from a road while riding the Lost Valley Trail. The portion of the trail paralleling Little Femme Osage Creek is heavily used by hikers and bikers, so you'll have no trouble finding help there. The eastern portion of the loop is not far from MO 94. If you get into trouble there, work your way east to the highway.

Land status: Missouri Department of Conservation.

Maps: Maps of the Weldon Spring Wildlife Area can be picked up at Busch Wildlife Area headquarters, 2 miles west of MO 94 on CR D. The 7.5 minute topos covering the trail are Defiance and Weldon Spring.

Finding the trail: Exit US 40–61 at the St. Charles/Defiance exit. Drive south 7 miles on MO 94. Just before the bridge over Little Femme Osage Creek you'll see a parking area on the north side of the road. This is the trailhead for the Lost Valley Trail. It's directly across the road from a water treatment facility.

Sources of additional information:

Busch and Weldon Spring Wildlife Area
2360 Highway D
St. Charles, MO 63303
(314) 441-4554

The St. Louis Bicycle Touring Society
c/o The Touring Cyclist
11816 St. Charles Rock Road
Bridgeton, MO 63044
(314) 739-5180

Notes on the trail: Be sure you carry a map of the trail with you, because the loop is not well marked. There are markers every mile. Watch for these, and backtrack to the last one if you think you are lost. The wildlife area is fairly small, and is bounded by highways or fences. This makes it easy to find your way out if you get lost.

An unmarked optional loop off the northwest portion of the marked route will take you to the intersection of County Roads D and DD, where you'll find a small store and restaurant. This loop will add 5 miles to your ride. To find it while riding the loop clockwise, look for a road leading off to your left about 100 yards after you leave the creek and begin climbing. Bearing left on this faint road, you'll pass through an open wildlife food plot about 100 yards long. There will be a chain-link enclosure at its northern end. Next to the enclosure, you'll cross a creek and pick up a faint double-track heading west along a tumbledown fence. Follow it for three-fourths of a mile to a 4-way intersection with another old road. Turn right, and ride a quarter mile to CR D and a shooting range. Riding west (left) on D for 1 mile will take you to the store and restaurant.

To return, retrace your way back to the 4-way intersection. Instead of turning left to return the way you came, go straight (south). You'll make a sweeping turn to the east and descend to Little Femme Osage Creek, where you'll ford the stream and intersect the marked trail. Turning right will take you back to the trailhead; turning left lets you continue the loop.

Central Missouri Trails

RIDE 6 *CEDAR CREEK TRAIL*

Cedar Creek Trail passes through land that was depleted by intensive farming in the late 1800s and early 1900s. Although the area is now being reclaimed and managed as forest, evidence of its past shows in abandoned farmsteads, washed-out roads, and open fields with tumbledown fences. One mile into the ride you will pass the deteriorating Nevins farmstead, typical of the settlements that were once common in central Missouri. A signboard gives a brief historical review of the homestead.

The trail traverses the low ridges and tributaries of Cedar Creek, crossing that stream at two points. Total mileage of all loops is 33 miles, but only the first 8 miles north from Pine Ridge are really good for mountain biking. Seven of these miles are single-track, and the remainder follows a gravel county road. The trail is hardpack, and can be quite muddy after rainfall. Equestrians can make the trail really rough when it's wet.

With the exception of a few steep pitches, all of this trail can be handled by beginners. The remaining 25 miles are also open to mountain bikes, but use gravel roads or single-track when the trail is in poor condition. You will enjoy your ride more if you use the first eight miles of trail as an out-and-back ride.

General location: 18 miles southeast of Columbia.
Elevation change: Trail elevations range from 600′ to 800′. There are numerous climbs and descents, but most can easily be ridden. The exception is a very rocky, steep, and technical quarter-mile descent just east of the north crossing of Cedar Creek.
Season: While the trail can be ridden year-round, spring and fall offer the best riding conditions.
Services: Water and camping are available at the trailhead in Pine Ridge Recreation Area. All other services can be found in Columbia, 18 miles to the northwest.
Hazards: Be careful on the steep technical section of trail just east of the north crossing of Cedar Creek. Don't wade across Cedar Creek during high water.

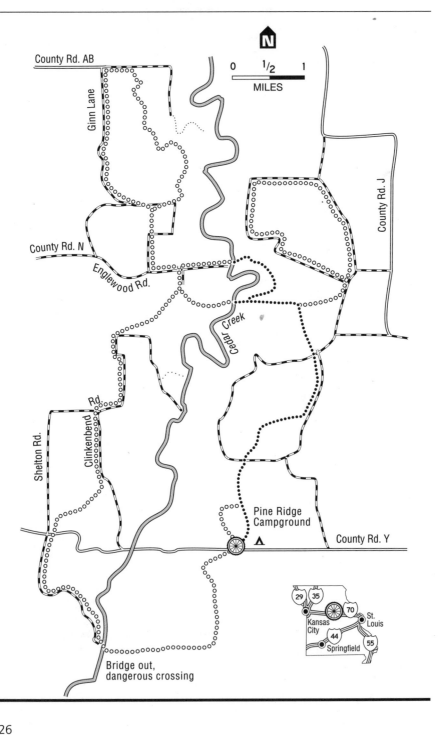

County Rd. AB

Ginn Lane

N

0   1/2   1
MILES

County Rd. J

County Rd. N

Englewood Rd.

Cedar Creek

Shelton Rd.

Clinkenbend Rd.

Pine Ridge
Campground

County Rd. Y

Bridge out,
dangerous crossing

29 35

70

Kansas
City

St.
Louis

44

Springfield

55

Instead, use the hiking/biking-only route, and cross the stream on Rutherford Bridge.

Rescue index: Since the trail sees plenty of use and crosses roads at many points, help is never far away.

Land status: Most of the trail is on national forest land. It occasionally crosses plots of private land. Be respectful of the property rights of owners.

Maps: Maps of the Cedar Creek Trail are available at the trailhead in Pine Ridge. If you want to use topos, you will need the 7.5 minute Millersburg SW, Jefferson City NW, and Guthrie maps.

Finding the trail: The trailhead at Pine Ridge Recreation Area is on County Road Y, approximately 7 miles east of Ashland, or 3 miles west of Guthrie. Park in the gravel lot across from the trailhead.

Sources of additional information:

Mark Twain National Forest
Cedar Creek Ranger District
1403 Airport Road

Mailing address:
4965 County Road 304
Fulton, MO 65251
(314) 642-6726

Notes on the trail: The first 8 miles of trail are well-marked with a combination of gray diamonds, yellow blazes, and bicycle symbols on trailside posts. This part of the trail is well used and easy to follow. Once past the 8-mile point, the trail becomes faint and markings are scarce. All of the trail is open to biking, but your ride will be more enjoyable if you stick with the first 8 miles. The Cedar Creek Trail Coalition maintains this trail. Parts of the remaining trail will some-day be improved, and become more suitable for mountain biking.

RIDE 7   *FINGER LAKES STATE PARK*

Most Ozark trails treat you to attractive natural landscapes. Finger Lakes State Park is different—it showcases a manmade one.

Between 1964 and 1967, 1.2 million tons of coal were removed from this area, leaving piles of earth around long, water-filled pits. The coal company reseeded much of the acreage, but left the rugged terrain created by the mining operation. Taken over by the state in 1974, this area is now an attractive set of long, deep lakes surrounded by grassy, shrub-covered hills, and laced with a 70-mile network of motorcycle trails.

Because Finger Lakes is also open to motorcycles, most of the trails are rough and loose with mudholes and washouts in many places. These trails carved out

RIDE 7 *FINGER LAKES STATE PARK*

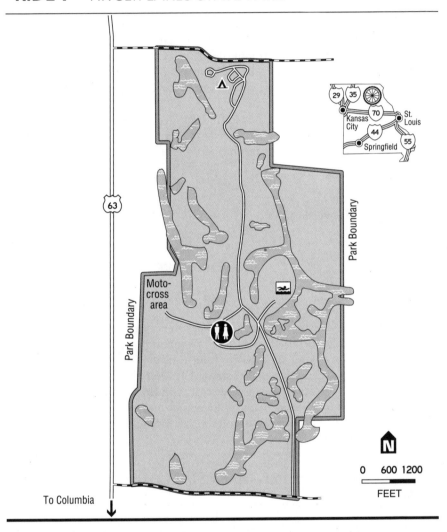

by motorcycles are often much steeper than those normally found in hiking and equestrian trails. The trails require well-developed bike-handling skills, and are not recommended for beginners.

General location: 10 miles north of Columbia.
Elevation change: Only minimal elevation changes occur at Finger Lakes. It is located in rolling plains country where elevations fluctuate little more than 75´. Still, there is little level riding. The mining operation left a landscape of small, steep hills, exposing you to continually challenging climbs and descents.

Finger Lakes State Park is named for long, narrow pools leftover from the time when the area was strip-mined for coal.

Season: Finger Lakes can be ridden year-round. Spring and fall are best. Summer heat can be offset by a dip at the swimming beach located near the center of the park. Since this is a trail network, winter riders can make their rides as short or long as the weather allows.

Services: Drinking water and campsites are located at the north end of the park road. All other services are available in Columbia, 10 miles to the south on US 65.

Hazards: Most of the trails are very steep, with washouts and mud after rain-fall. These conditions often result in face-plants by unprepared riders. Some of the trails come treacherously close to the steep lake embankments, so if you aren't attentive you could take an unexpected dip and lose your bicycle to the deeps. Since Finger Lakes is open to motorcyclists, be prepared to meet them at any time.

Rescue index: The park road bisects this long, narrow park from north to south, keeping you within 1 mile of the road at all times. Since the park sees a good amount of use, you should be able to find help quickly.

Land status: State park.

Maps: There are many trails in Finger Lakes, and the network is constantly being redeveloped by continued use. Because of this, there is no official trail or map. But that's the fun of this area. You are free to roam throughout most of the park.

Pick up one of the general park maps available at the entrance station and use it as a general guide, using the park road as a base. Though the long, finger-like lakes will sometimes make you feel caught in a maze, with a little perseverance you can easily find your way back to the road. The USGS 7.5 minute map for the area is Browns.

Finding the trail: Go 10 miles north of Columbia on US 63. Turn right onto a gravel road with a sign indicating the way to Finger Lakes State Park. The park entrance is 1 mile east on this road.

Sources of additional information:

Finger Lakes State Park
Columbia, MO 65202
(314) 443-5315

Notes on the trail: Finger Lakes has it all—miles of challenging trails, wildlife, camping, scenic lakes, and (after rainstorms) mudholes that would make a pig rub its hooves in anticipation. After the ride, a swim in the lake or a shower in the campground will wash off the mud and take the kinks out of your tired muscles.

For the well-rounded sportsman the lakes are stocked with fish, and canoeing and kayaking opportunities abound. Those camping at the park can enjoy a laid-back evening counting the stars, or head south to Columbia, home of the University of Missouri, and enjoy the nightlife.

RIDE 8 *MCADOO EQUESTRIAN TRAIL*

The McAdoo Equestrian Trail, a loop ride, is an excellent choice for a beginner's first single-track experience. With the exception of a one-mile stretch of old gravel road from the equestrian camp to the main loop, the entire trail is smooth single-track with a uniform hard-packed dirt surface.

The ride is eight miles if you start from the equestrian camp, and five miles if you start from the County Road DD access (see "Finding the trail"). The trail crosses Clear Fork Creek, and then parallels that stream for about a half mile. The creek passes through a prairie landscape bordered by a band of trees. The

RIDE 8 *MCADOO EQUESTRIAN TRAIL*

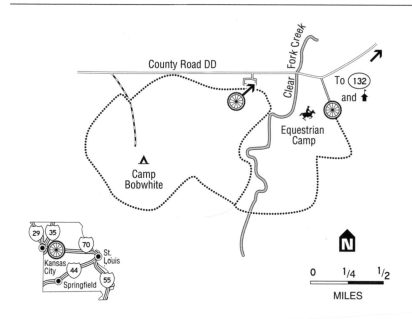

McAdoo winds through this wooded bottomland, entering one open prairie valley, and occasionally climbing to the tops of low hills along the Clear Fork.

The crossing of the Clear Fork is the most fascinating spot on the trail. After following an old abandoned road, you'll cross the fork on an aging steel bridge. One hundred yards south of the bridge is a heron rookery. Look for large, platform-like nests of sticks and twigs in the trees towering over the creek. The herons live here during the spring and summer, breeding and rearing their young. In early fall they migrate to warmer climates.

General location: Knob Noster State Park, 2 miles southwest of Knob Noster.
Elevation change: Elevation ranges from about 700´ to 800´. There are few climbs of any consequence on this trail. The longest climb or descent is around a quarter mile. There are many short ups and downs as the trail crosses the upper ends of small drainages. All can be handled by riders of any skill level.
Season: While spring and fall are the best seasons to ride this trail, it is a good experience year-round. Much of the trail is in the woods, making it cooler in the summer, and there are no water crossings to freeze your feet in winter.
Services: The park has an excellent campground, complete with showers, laundry facilities, and a telephone. While the campground may be used year-round,

From the iron bridge over Clear Fork Creek, riders on the McAdoo Equestrian Trail can view the heron rookery south of the crossing. Note the large, platform-like nests in the trees above the stream.

water and other services are turned off from November 1 to March 31. Water can still be obtained at the pumphouse behind the Visitor Center.

Restaurants, groceries, and gasoline are available in Knob Noster, 2 miles northeast of the park. Lodging and bicycle supplies are available in Warrensburg, 7 miles to the west, or in Sedalia, 20 miles to the east.

Hazards: The McAdoo Equestrian Trail offers no undue hazards, and is recommended for beginning mountain bike riders.

Rescue index: The trail sees moderate use by equestrians, hikers, and mountain bikers. The entire north portion of the loop parallels County Road DD, and the remainder of the ride is never more than 1.5 miles from that highway. If trouble arises, move north to intersect CR DD and await help.

Land status: State park.

Maps: Stop in at the park office to pick up a map of the McAdoo Trail. The topos for the area are the Knob Noster and Burtville 7.5 minute maps.

Finding the trail: Drive 1 mile west from Knob Noster on US 50 to MO 132. Go 1 mile south on MO 132 to the park entrance. The Visitor Center is just inside the park. Ask for maps and information here.

To reach the trail, take the park road leading south from the Visitor Center to CR DD. Turn west 1 mile on CR DD to the equestrian camp. Starting from here takes you on the 8-mile option. If you want the 5-mile option, continue west on CR DD an additional half mile to a parking area on the south side of the road. A spur trail from this lot leads you, after about one-tenth mile, to the main loop.

Sources of additional information:

Knob Noster State Park
Knob Noster, MO 65336
(314) 563-2463

Notes on the trail: Although the McAdoo Equestrian Trail is one of several trails in Knob Noster State Park, it is the only one open to mountain bikes. The others are steeper, and pass over highly erodable soil. The park appreciates your cooperation in staying off all trails other than the McAdoo.

The equestrian camp (trailhead for the 8-mile option) and the parking lot (trailhead for the 5-mile loop) are open year-round, but gates to these areas are sometimes closed. Just open the gates and close them behind you.

RIDE 9   *ROCK BRIDGE MEMORIAL STATE PARK*

This state park offers eight miles of riding on four loop trails over easy terrain. These rides are recommended for beginning mountain bikers. All the trails are in good condition, consisting mostly of hard-packed single-track on easy gradients.

The best ride is the Spring Brook Trail—it is most like a classic mountain bike ride. The Sinkhole Trail runs a close second. The Grassland Trail, a flat ride through open prairie, is easiest. The High Ridge Trail travels through open country like the Grassland, but contains two climbs and a short wooded stretch.

In contrast to the High Ridge and Grassland trails, the Spring Brook Trail leads you through wooded creek bottoms, makes two crossings of Little Bonne Femme Creek, climbs to the hilltop glades, and passes by the Rock Bridge. The Sinkhole Trail winds through the woods past the sinkholes for which it is named. The stream cascading through Rock Bridge still flows over an old mill dam at the southern opening of the Rock Bridge.

Rock Bridge Memorial State Park covers topography known as "karst." Karst was formed over millions of years by the action of water percolating

RIDE 9 *ROCK BRIDGE MEMORIAL STATE PARK*

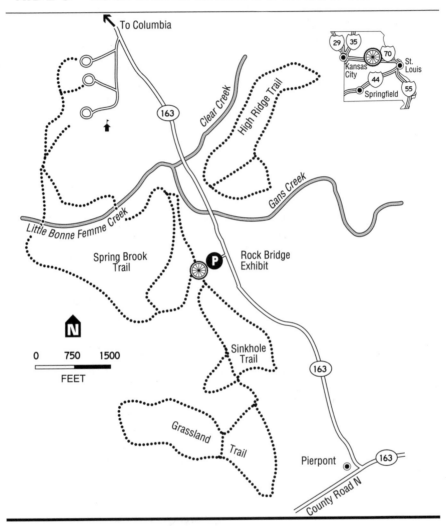

through the 300-million-year-old Burlington limestone in the park. The water dissolves the limestone as it moves through the rock, creating sinkholes, caves, underground streams, and springs. The sinkholes, which feed water into the park's underground cave system, are places where cave roofs have collapsed. The large natural bridge in the park is a portion of a cave roof that remained after surrounding portions fell.

South of the rock bridge you'll find Devil's Icebox, a huge double sinkhole that accesses the park's underground cave system. You can check out the cave

Part of the Spring Brook Trail in Rock Bridge Memorial State Park parallels one of the tributary streams feeding Little Femme Osage Creek.

entrance here, but only experienced cavers who have obtained permits at the park office may enter and explore the cave. The cave has been mapped for six miles of its length.

General location: 8 miles south of Columbia.
Elevation change: Elevation changes are minimal at Rock Bridge Memorial State Park. The peak is a little over 800′, and the low point is at 650′ along the creek. There are several short climbs on the Spring Brook Trail, one steep section on the Sinkhole Trail, and two short climbs on the High Ridge Trail. Most trails in the park are very easy.
Season: With its short trails, this park offers good riding any time of year. If you find it too hot or cold, you can bail out after only a short jaunt.

Services: Water is available at the picnic area in the park. All other services are available in Columbia, 8 miles to the north.

Hazards: There is one steep descent and ascent on the Sinkhole Trail, and a couple of rocky spots on the Spring Brook Trail where you should be careful.

Rescue index: All the park's trails see much use, so you should be found very soon if you get into a jam. You are never very far from the park headquarters, where help is available.

Land status: State park.

Maps: Rock Bridge Memorial State Park Trail Map shows all the trails in this park. If you want to use topos, get the 7.5 minute Columbia and Ashland maps.

Finding the trail: Drive south from Columbia on US 63 to MO 163. Turn right (west) on MO 163 to Pierpont. In Pierpont, 163 turns north toward the park. Follow it 1 mile north of Pierpont to a large asphalt parking area on the west side of the road. To reach the park office, continue one-half mile farther north on MO 163.

Sources of additional information:

Rock Bridge Memorial State Park
Columbia, MO 65201
(314) 449-7402

Notes on the trail: With its well-developed trails and few climbs, this is a great place for beginners or families to mountain bike. The routes are easy, and popular with hikers. Park management prefers that those of you who ride fast and wild go to Finger Lakes or other nearby trails better suited to experienced riders. All Rock Bridge trails are well marked by color-coded arrows on posts.

There is a confusing spot, however, on the Sinkhole Trail, where it approaches the rock bridge area. Just as you reach the boardwalk surrounding the bridge, the trail turns right and makes a steep descent. This turn is easy to miss. The Sinkhole Trail is best ridden clockwise, giving you a steep descent at the end of the ride rather than a steep climb at the beginning.

To start the Sinkhole Trail, ride to the far end of the grassy area south of the parking lot, where you will find the beginning of the loop.

The Grassland Trail was missing a few markings at the time of this writing, but because it passes through open prairie, you'll find it hard to get lost.

You should be aware that the park management here requests that you remain on designated trails. Let me underscore their request with special emphasis, for several reasons. Across the road from the main parking lot, just south of the High Ridge Trailhead, is the Gans Creek Wild Area. This portion of the park is designated wilderness, and bikes are not allowed within it. The trails in Rock Bridge are open to biking on a trial basis, and if we ride in prohibited areas, mountain bikes will be banned from the park. If we ruin the trails that could happen, too. So please, don't ride when conditions are wet and muddy.

RIDE 10 *THREE CREEKS STATE FOREST*

Three Creeks contains nine miles of trail that can be ridden in loops of various lengths. Distance options vary from 2.2 miles on the shortest possible loop to just over 10 miles for those riding every bit of trail in the forest. The riding is only moderately difficult, and offers a great opportunity for beginners to get that first taste of single-track. Nor should experienced riders fear it is too easy. Some fast downhills, lots of single-track, and numerous crossings of Turkey Creek make this a fun ride for cyclists of all skill levels.

Only about two miles of the trail follow double-track roads. The rest is hard-packed single-track, with a few rocky sections near creek crossings. Though it can be muddy after a rain, the trail is normally in excellent condition.

This 1,277-acre state forest takes its name from the three streams that flow through the area. Turkey, Bass, and Bonne Femme creeks drain an upland that has been carved by the combined erosive action of the streams and poor land use practices. Today, Three Creeks is marked by its peaceful creek bottoms and scenic bluffs, as well as the caves and sinkholes that are also common to Rock Bridge park.

The parking area is the beginning for the Turkey Creek Nature Trail, a 2.7-mile self-guided loop. One of the interpretive maps available at the trailhead will give you a better understanding of this state forest.

The stretch of single-track winding along Turkey Creek crosses the stream many times. You will pedal past tall bluffs that follow the meanders of the creek like huge amphitheaters. If you ride to the far south end of the forest, you will find an especially nice place to relax. As you climb the half-mile ascent from Bass Creek to the south parking area (see map), watch for a trail leading steeply down a slope to the east. Less than a quarter mile down this trail, Bass Creek flows over a flat rock bottom, with a bluff towering over its east side. In the bluff is a small cave. A stream gurgles from the mouth of the cave and empties into the creek. Continuing on toward the south parking area, you will enjoy a panoramic view of the valley of Turkey and Bass creeks.

General location: 10 miles south of Columbia.

Elevation change: Elevation changes are not drastic at Three Creeks. They vary from a minimum of 600′ to a maximum of 800′. The longest climb is just under one-half mile. None of the climbs are all that steep, and can be ridden by any rider in decent physical condition.

Season: Spring, summer, and fall are all good seasons to ride at Three Creeks. Winter riding can be fun, but wet feet from the many stream crossings on this trail could spell trouble for cold-weather riders.

RIDE 10   *THREE CREEKS STATE FOREST*

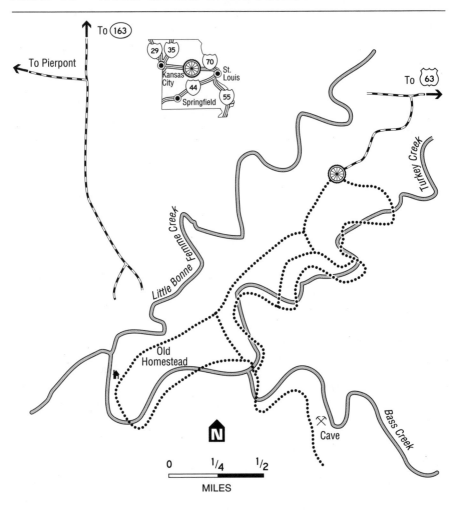

Services: Bring drinking water with you. None is available along the trail. The nearest source of water is the Deer Park Store at the junction of US 65, County Road AB, and Deer Park Road. The nearest camping is at Pine Ridge Campground in the Mark Twain National Forest, approximately 7 miles east of Ashland on CR Y. All other services are in Columbia, 10 miles to the north.

Hazards: Watch for slick rocks on the numerous crossings of Turkey Creek. Don't attempt any stream crossing when the creeks are in flood stage. Do not go into the cave at the south end of the forest without lights and a companion.

Crossing Turkey Creek numerous times, the trail in Three Creeks State Forest often follows the base of steep rock walls.

Rescue index: While there are 9 miles of trail in Three Creeks, they are all located within an area just over 2 miles square. You will never be far from your starting point. The trails see moderate use, making it likely you'll be found in case of an accident.

Land status: Missouri Department of Conservation.

Maps: Maps of Three Creeks State Forest are available in boxes at the trailhead. The USGS topo for the area is the 7.5 minute Ashland.

Finding the trail: From Columbia, go south 10 miles on US 65 to the Deer Park Store at the junction of US 65, CR AB, and Deer Park Road. Turn west on Deer Park Road, and follow it 2.5 miles to a sign pointing the way to Three Creeks State Forest. Turn left, and follow this road three-quarters of a mile until it dead ends in a small parking area.

Sources of additional information:

Three Creeks State Forest
Missouri Department of Conservation
1110 South College Avenue
Columbia, MO 65201
(314) 882-9880

Notes on the trail: Those riding the far southwest portion of the trail north of the junction of Turkey and Bass creeks may have trouble finding the way. The valley floor is wide and flat here, and the creek often floods and washes out the path. If you lose your way, just stay next to Turkey Creek.

The trail follows the southwest side of Turkey Creek from its junction with Bass Creek. As you curve around to the north along Turkey Creek, the trail will cross the stream. Your landmark is an old farmstead next to a large wildlife food plot on the east side of the creek. Go to the farmstead, and find an old double-track going east up the hill behind the buildings. This is the trail, and it will take you back to the parking area, 1.7 miles east of the farmstead.

RIDE 11 *TRAIL OF THE FOUR WINDS*

---

ocated on the edge of the Lake of the Ozarks, the Trail of the Four Winds is rfect for beginners. Most grades on this six-mile trail system are gentle. The il surface is a combination of single-track and old roads. Those who find the l too difficult can exit the system by following the bisecting trail, an easy-to-road, from the back of the system to the trailhead.

here is plenty for you to do here once you get off the trail. Nearby Lake of Ozarks offers swimming, fishing, water skiing, and camping. Ozark erns, located in this park, holds guided tours every day in season.

ou can also see a lot of wildlife in the area surrounding the lake. White-tailed are abundant, as are raccoons, squirrels, wild turkey, fox, and coyotes. rks soar on the lake breezes, and bald eagles nest in the park during winter. reat blue herons also live in the park, sharing the area with numerous song-s. Bats from the cavern cruise the sky at dusk and dawn, entertaining pers as they load up on airborne insects. And when the day is over, Osage h offers a wide choice of restaurants and nightlife.

ral location: Lake of the Ozarks State Park.

ition change: Elevations range from 600′ at the water's edge to 750′ at the lead. Most climbs and descents are moderately graded, and can be ridden vices.

n: Spring and fall are the best times to ride this trail. When followed by a h the nearby lake, summer riding can also be fun. In winter, with the ser crowds gone, you will have the trail to yourself, and there are no stream cngs to freeze your feet.

Sces: No drinking water is available on the trail, but it can be found at ot places in the park. The state park has campsites with showers. During the buseason, there is also a store at the marina. There is even an airport adja-cero the trailhead, just in case you want to fly your plane in for a quick jaunt on t bike. All other services are available in Osage Beach, 10 miles to the west on t 54.

RIDE 11 *TRAIL OF THE FOUR WINDS*

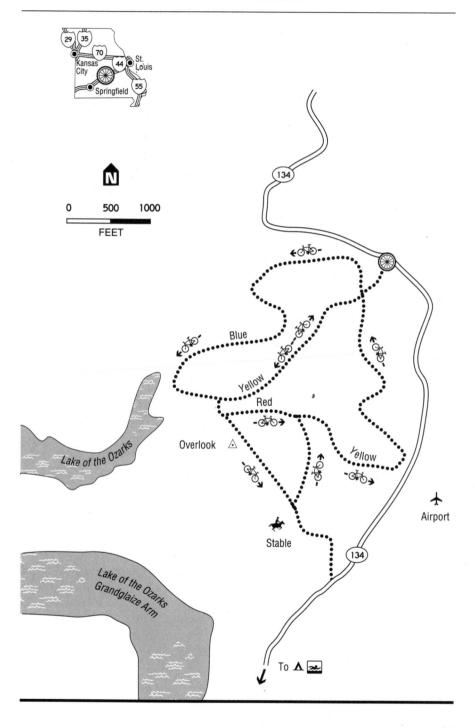

View from the trailhead of Trail of the Four Winds.

Hazards: The Trail of the Four Winds is used by equestrians. Be prepared to encounter horses at any time. Move to the downhill side of the trail, stand quietly, and wait for them to pass.

Rescue index: Since you are never more than 2 miles from the trailhead while riding the Trail of the Four Winds, help is never far away.

Land status: State park.

Maps: The state park publishes a Trail and Wild Area Guide. It is available at the park entrance or at the trail center along the entrance road. It is all the map you'll need. The topo map covering the area is the Toronto 7.5 minute map.

Finding the trail: From Osage Beach, drive east from US 54 on MO 134/42. After 4 miles turn south on 134 into the park. The trailhead is 2 miles down MO 134 from the park headquarters.

Sources of additional information:

Lake of the Ozarks State Park
Box C
Kaiser, MO 65047
(314) 348-2694

Notes on the trail: The trail is well marked with color-coded arrows on trailside trees. Riders are advised to follow the trail system counter-clockwise, as indicated on the trail guide, because the trail is marked only for cyclists riding in that direction. There are other trails in the park, but the Trail of the Four Winds is the only one open to mountain bikes. Do not ride on other park trails.

Kansas City/St. Joseph Area Trails

There are several good mountain bike trails in Kansas within a one-hour drive of Kansas City. The best are included here. For more rides in Kansas and the plains region, check out a copy of *The Mountain Biker's Guide to the Great Plains*.

RIDE 12 MINOR PARK

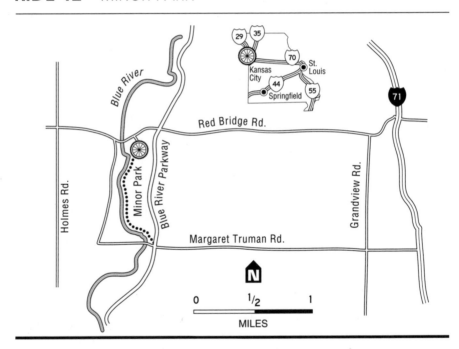

RIDE 12 MINOR PARK

This is a small city park in the Blue River Parkway greenway. Its trails, which parallel the river for approximately one mile, are all hard-pack, single-track. They can be muddy after a rain. There are no hills in Minor Park, so this is a perfect place for beginners and families. Although you can often hear traffic from the nearby city, the wooded riparian habitat through which the trail passes is a peaceful enclave in the midst of the big city.

General location: Southeast Kansas City.

Elevation change: Elevation changes on the trail in Minor Park are minimal. The route follows the edge of the Blue River through the park. There are no climbs.

Season: Since this trail is so short, it's fun any time of year. Much of the route takes you through the woods, keeping you cool in the heat of summer.

Services: All services are available in the surrounding Kansas City metropolitan area.

Hazards: There are no hazards on this easy trail.

Rescue index: You are in the heart of the Kansas City metropolitan area when riding this trail, and Blue River Road parallels the trail not far to the east. If you need help, make your way to Blue River Road and flag a passing motorist.

Land status: City park.

Maps: No official park map exists. Since the park is only about 1 mile long, it will be tough for you to get lost. This ride falls onto the Grandview 7.5 minute topo.

Finding the trail: From I-71, drive west 2 miles on Red Bridge Road. Just before crossing the Red Bridge, turn south into Minor Park. Drive to the parking area at the end of the road. The trail begins in the woods southwest of the parking lot.

Sources of additional information:

Kansas City Department of Parks
5605 East 63rd Street
Kansas City, MO 64132
(816) 444-3113

RIDE 13 *BLUFF WOODS HORSE TRAIL*

The Bluff Woods Horse Trail is a three-mile loop in the foothills east of the Missouri River. This 2,344-acre conservation area was purchased by the state in the 1970s to preserve one of the last forested areas in western Missouri. While most of the area is wooded, you will ride through an abandoned ridge-top pasture in the back of the loop. Here you'll be treated to wide-open views of the surrounding countryside.

The entire trail is single-track. Parts of it are pretty difficult, and will require portages. On some of the grades, the trail has been cut deeply into the ground from the combined pressures of horse hooves and erosion. Only experienced cyclists should ride here.

The western side of this triangle-shaped loop is the easiest. If you don't like the tough stuff, pedal this section of single-track as an out-and-back ride.

RIDE 13   *BLUFF WOODS HORSE TRAIL*

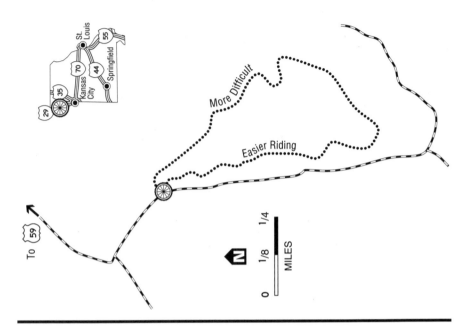

General location: 9 miles south of St. Joseph.

Elevation change: Elevations range from 825′ at the trailhead to 1,050′ on the ridge along the southern leg of the trail. There are 3 climbs and descents of a quarter mile each.

Season: Spring and fall are the best seasons to ride the Bluff Woods Horse Trail.

Services: No drinking water is available on the trail. All services can be found in St. Joseph, 9 miles to the northeast.

Hazards: Parts of the trail are eroded, exposing rocks at the bottom of horse-worn ruts. Be careful on these, and on the steep descent into the hollow halfway through the loop.

Rescue index: Because this trail is fairly short, you can get out quickly if you find yourself in trouble. On weekends, chances are good that you could get help from another trail user.

Land status: Conservation area, owned by Missouri Department of Conservation.

Maps: The Department of Conservation produces a good map of the area. You can get it by contacting the office listed below. The topos for Bluff Woods Conservation Area are the Halls and DeKalb 7.5 minute maps.

Finding the trail: Drive 9 miles south of St. Joseph on US 59. Look for a sign pointing to the entrance of Bluff Woods Conservation Area. Turn left onto a gravel road, and follow it one-half mile to an intersection. Turn right, and follow another gravel road around three-fourths of a mile to a fork.

Follow the left fork one-fourth mile to a parking area on the left side of the road. It should have a sign for Bluff Woods Conservation Area. The trail starts a little farther east on the road, just past the creek crossing.

Sources of additional information:

Missouri Department of Conservation
701 Northeast College Drive
St. Joseph, MO 64507
(816) 271-3100

Notes on the trail: There are other trails in the Bluff Woods Conservation Area, but they are not open to mountain bikes. Please cooperate with the Department of Conservation by staying off the other trails.

RIDE 14 *KRUG PARK*

Krug Park, located in a wooded area on the northwest edge of the city of St. Joseph, now contains about a mile of single-track trail. Local bike clubs are working with St. Joseph to expand the trail network in this beautiful city park, and hope to extend it into some surrounding public land. Plans call for a five-mile network of mountain bike trails. For now, you will have to settle for the mile of excellent hard-packed single-track that laces this hollow on the edge of the city. It's a good ride for cyclists of all skill levels.

One of the highlights of this ride is the waterfall in the center of the area. You'll have a great view where one of the trails crosses the stream just above the pour-off. Just before the waterfall, the trail forks. One fork crosses the stream as mentioned above, and then climbs to the ridge on the western edge of the park. The other fork bears to the right, climbs the hill to the east, and intersects the main trail coming down from the park.

The park itself is a beautiful site to hang out after your ride. There are picnic shelters, restrooms, a small lake, and an amphitheater for summer concerts. It's a great place for a family outing!

General location: St. Joseph.
Elevation change: Elevations range from 900′ along the creek to 1,050′ at the trailhead. Only a few of the relatively short climbs on this trail will require portaging, and only for very short distances. Most grades can be ridden by cyclists of all skill levels.
Season: This trail is a good ride any time of year. Much of the path is shaded,

RIDE 14   *KRUG PARK*

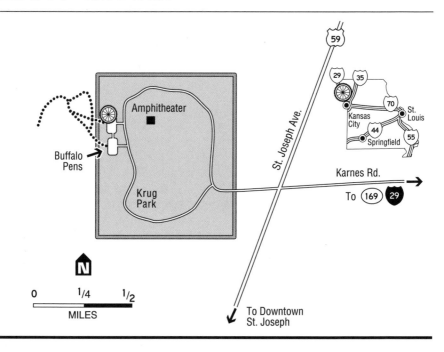

so it won't be too hot in summer. You can finish winter rides on this short trail before the cold gets to you.

Services: Water is available in the park. All services can be found in St. Joseph.

Hazards: There are a few very short steep sections that you should portage. Otherwise, there are no hazards in Krug Park.

Rescue index: Krug Park is located in the city of St. Joseph. There is a phone in the park, and you are never more than a mile from the trailhead while riding there.

Land status: City park.

Maps: There is no trail map for Krug Park. If you wish to use a topo, get the St. Joseph North 7.5 minute map.

Finding the trail: Krug Park is located in the northwest part of St. Joseph, near the intersection of Karnes Road and Northwest Parkway. The trailhead is in the back of the park, just north of the buffalo pens. Drive to the western end of the large parking lot, and look for a gate with a cable across it. This is the beginning of the trail.

Sources of additional information:

St. Joseph Department of Parks
Post Office Box 5116
St. Joseph, MO 64505
(816) 271-5500

Ride Bicycles
1109 South Belt Highway
St. Joseph, MO 64507
(816) 233-1718

Notes on the trail: The trail expansion mentioned in the introduction is being pursued by local bike clubs and bike shops. For further information about the expansion, call the park or Ride Bicycles at the numbers listed above.

RIDE 15 *SOUTHWEST PARKWAY TRAILS*

This network of trails is located in a small wild area in southwest St. Joseph that has become a playground for mountain bikes, horses, and ATVs. There are about five miles of single-track on a forested hillside. Although you'll run into a few short steep areas that will have to be portaged, most of the trails can be managed by beginners.

These trails are largely hardpack, and will be quite muddy after a rainfall. So stay off them when they are soft.

General location: St. Joseph.
Elevation change: Elevations vary from 850′ to 1,000′. Most climbs are rideable by cyclists in good physical condition.
Season: This trail is a good ride any time of year. Much of it is shaded, and there are no stream crossings to freeze your feet in winter.
Services: No water is available along the trail. All services are available in St. Joseph.
Hazards: Other than a few short, steep washouts, you'll find no hazards here.
Rescue index: You are never more than one-half mile from Southwest Parkway while riding this trail system. If you get into trouble, make your way east to the Parkway.
Land status: City park.
Maps: No map is available for this trail network. If you want to use a topo, you will need the St. Joseph South 7.5 minute map.
Finding the trail: From Hyde Park, drive north on Southwest Parkway. Park on the side of the road just south of the Interstate 229 underpass. The trail system stretches for about a mile south of here on the west side of the Parkway.

RIDE 15 *SOUTHWEST PARKWAY TRAILS*

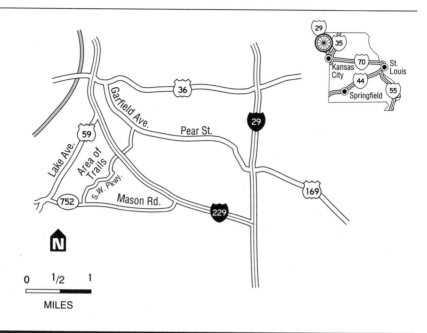

Sources of additional information:

St. Joseph Department of Parks
Post Office Box 5116
St. Joseph, MO 64505
(816) 271-5500

Ride Bicycles
1109 South Belt Highway
St. Joseph, MO 64507
(816) 233-1718

Mark Twain National Forest Trails

The Mark Twain National Forest, 1.5 million acres of wooded public land, straddles the Ozark Plateau in southern Missouri. Divided into nine tracts of different sizes, the forest provides a wealth of recreational opportunities.

Wildlife abounds: 175 species of birds inhabit the forest, along with 50 different mammals and 70 reptiles and amphibians. Scenic rivers meander through the area, framed in many places by tall bluffs of Ozark Mountain limestone. Some of the springs that feed the forest's rivers rank among the largest in the country.

It wasn't always this way. When the French first explored southern Missouri in the early 1700s they found lead, silver, and iron deposits. They logged the then-virgin forest to provide charcoal for smelting these ores. Intensive logging for timber began before the Civil War. Trees were heavily harvested for railroad ties, flooring, and whiskey barrels. In the early 1900s the largest pine mill in the world, located near Grandin, roared into production to meet the booming demand for lumber.

By the 1930s, the natural resources of southern Missouri were depleted. The national forest was formed to protect and restore the area, and the woods began to recover. Today, they show only minimal scarring. Hundreds of miles of trails, 29 campgrounds, picnic sites, and numerous river accesses are in place to help you enjoy your national forest.

Don't limit yourself to mountain biking in this Ozark wonderland. Combine your ride with a float trip on one of the scenic rivers that lace the area. The Eleven Point National Scenic River is a gem, located in the Eleven Point Ranger District; and the Ozark National Scenic Riverways are just to the north. The fishing is great in these streams, too.

More angling opportunities can be found in the lakes scattered throughout the Mark Twain. If you don't mind leaving your bike behind now and then, wilderness hiking awaits you. Over 63,000 acres in seven wilderness areas offer miles of trails to explore on foot.

As you ride the forest trails and roads, remember that many tracts of private land are interspersed with this public forest. Forest maps available at each ranger district show which areas are public and which are private. You are responsible for any trespass that may occur. Under Missouri's strict trespass laws, ignorance is no defense.

Some trails and roads cross private land with permission of the landowner. Others cross land leased from the Forest Service for grazing. You may pass through gates as you ride across these areas. Leave the gates open or closed as you find them.

In order to group the trails in this book geographically, a few liberties were taken. The Cedar Creek Trail, part of the Mark Twain, is included in the section on Central Missouri. Lake Wappapello and St. Joe state parks, while not part of the Mark Twain, are included with the trails in Mark Twain Southeast. Busiek and Huckleberry Ridge state forests are included with Mark Twain Southwest.

RIDE 16 *MARK TWAIN SOUTHEAST: AUDUBON TRAIL*

This 13-mile loop is very difficult in some places, and is not recommended for beginners. Some short unrideable sections will require portages. These are usually the steeper sections, where the trail runs straight downhill without switchbacks. Erosion and trail use have turned these steep pitches into loose rock, making ascents and descents fairly technical. But don't worry about this ride being all sweat and no fun. In addition to the tougher single-track, the loop makes use of abandoned logging roads that are a little more sedate.

Traveling clockwise, the trail crosses Bidwell Creek twice in the first three-quarters mile. After that you face your first long climb. The trail alternates between ridge-tops and valleys, with steep ascents and descents in between. Mountain bikers eager for a test of their bike-handling skills will love this trail. Nobody will clean the Audubon. Some of the climbs are simply too technical or too steep to ride.

And after getting yourself all heated up on the tough ride, you'll enjoy the stream crossings over Bidwell and Coldwater creeks. Near the crossings these streams flow over wide rock ledges, forming cascades that are perfect for a cooling splash or recharging your tired muscles as you lie back in the sun.

General location: 5 miles north of Womack.

Elevation change: Altitudes on the Audubon Trail range from 700′ at the trailhead on Bidwell Creek to just over 1,000′ at several points along the loop. There are 5 major climbs and descents, varying in length from one-quarter to one-half mile.

Season: Spring and fall are the best seasons to ride the Audubon Trail. Summer riding can be fun when combined with dips in Bidwell and Coldwater creeks, but insects and ticks may be a problem.

Services: Drinking water is not available anywhere along the trail. Water, food, and hotels can be found in Fredericktown, 15 miles to the southwest, or Farmington, 15 miles to the north. The nearest developed campsites are at St. Joe State Park, just west of Farmington, and at Silver Mines Campground in the Mark Twain National Forest, west of Fredericktown on MO 72 and CR D.

Hazards: Some sections of the trail are very rocky—stay alert and aware of your potential to lose control. Do not cross Bidwell or Coldwater creeks during high water.

Rescue index: On weekends, other trail users are likely to find you if you get

RIDE 16   *MARK TWAIN SOUTHEAST: AUDUBON TRAIL*

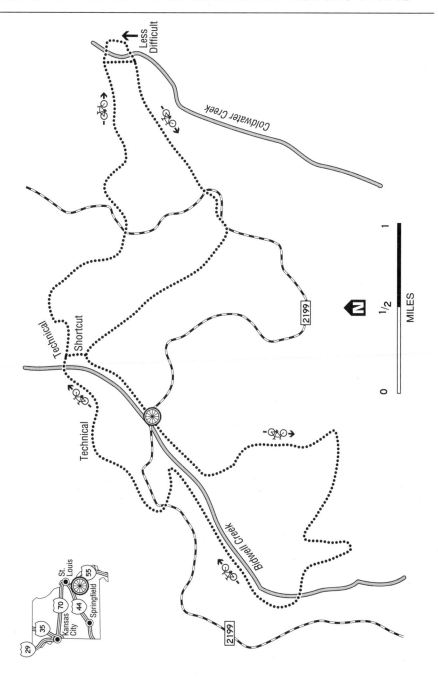

into trouble. The trail also crosses Forest Service Road 2199 four times. If you get into trouble, try to make your way to the road and wait for a passing motorist.

Land status: National forest.

Maps: The Forest Service produces a map of the trail, available at the office listed below. The USGS topo for the Audubon Trail is the Womack 7.5 minute map.

Finding the trail: The trailhead is on FS 2199 at the Bidwell Creek ford. To reach it from US 67, turn east off US 67 onto County Road DD at Knob Lick. Follow CR DD to CR OO, turn right (south), and follow CR OO to CR T. Drive left (east) 5 miles on CR T to FS 2199. This road is also marked Bidwell Creek Road. Follow it north 5 miles to the Bidwell Creek ford. There is a small parking area next to the ford.

Sources of additional information:

Mark Twain National Forest
Route 2, Highway 72 and OO
Fredericktown, MO 63645
(314) 783-7225

The Alpine Shop
601 East Lockwood
Webster Groves, MO 63119
(314) 962-7715

Notes on the trail: Follow this trail clockwise. That way the trail markings, white paint blazes on trees, are more visible.

Leave the parking area southbound. Halfway through the ride, the 2 sides of the loop come within 100 feet of each other. There is a cut-off trail bridging the gap between the 2 sides of the trail, giving you the option of returning to the parking area by following Bidwell Creek. This will shorten the loop to 8 miles. Those continuing on the longer option will continue along the creek another mile, cross it, and begin a steep climb.

Another possible deviation from the route occurs around 10 miles into the ride, shortly after crossing FS 2199. Just as you finish a long descent on an old logging road, the trail turns right to avoid the creek, crosses several swells on rough single-track, and rejoins the road a quarter mile away. If you would rather have the fun of splashing through the stream, ignore the trail markings and follow the road. You'll immediately cross the creek and hit another road. Turn right, and follow this road a quarter mile, where you'll rejoin the marked trail.

RIDE 17 *MARK TWAIN SOUTHEAST: BERRYMAN TRAIL*

Put the 24-mile-long Berryman Trail on your must-ride list: it offers one of the best mountain bike experiences in Ozark Country. Almost all of this scenic loop ride is on single-track—parts are rough and rocky, but are rarely so difficult that

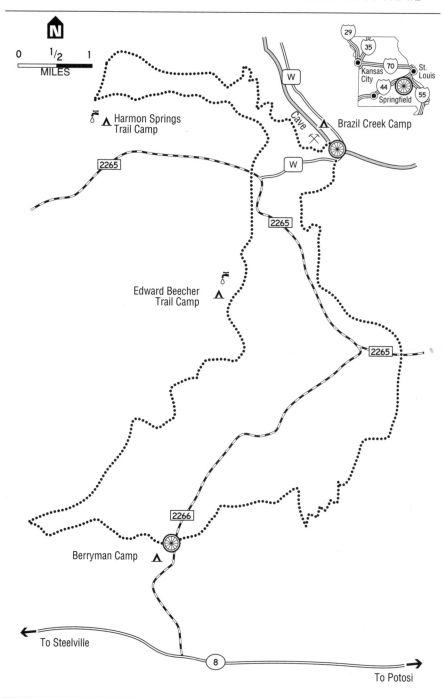

you will have to portage your bike. With its many climbs, rock-strewn technical sections, and satisfying length, the Berryman is ideal for the experienced rider, but probably a bit much for the beginner. Still, an inexperienced rider with a good attitude can enjoy riding a short section of the trail, using one of the roads that bisect the loop to create a shorter, less intimidating ride.

Because the trail alternates between ridge-tops and creek bottoms, the scenery includes both pleasant meandering streams and beautiful views from the tops of the climbs. Many stretches of the trail are carved out of the shoulders of ridges, skirting deep, quiet hollows in the forest. Your ride will swoop you around the tops of hollows, plunge you to valley floors, and take you past two natural springs.

These springs are great spots for lunch or rest stops. Near Brazil Creek Campground, there's a cave that's open to the public. It is rumored that Jesse James and his gang often camped at the cave entrance. For modern-day scalawags, the site offers a naturally air-conditioned retreat on a hot day.

General location: 17 miles west of Potosi.

Elevation change: The Berryman Trail climbs from a low of 800′ in the valleys to 1,200′ along the ridge-tops. There are numerous climbs along the trail, varying in length from one-quarter to three-quarters of a mile. With the exception of a few rocky stretches, all climbs are rideable. Good use of switchbacks has kept the grades manageable.

Season: Spring and fall are the best seasons to ride the Berryman. Summer can be very hot, and there are no good swimming holes along the way. Winter, while cold, offers scenic ridge-top views that are obscured by foliage during warmer times.

Services: No drinking water is available along the trail. There are springs at Edward Beecher Trail Camp and Harmon Springs Trail Camp, but the Forest Service doesn't recommend drinking from these sources without treating the water first. Camping is allowed anywhere in the national forest. Developed sites along the trail are located at Brazil Creek Campground along the northeast portion of the loop, and at Berryman Campground on the south. You'll find restaurants, hotels, and grocery stores in Potosi, 17 miles to the east of the campground, and in Steelville, 19 miles to the west. The nearest bike shops are in St. Louis, 90 miles to the north.

Hazards: The shortage of available drinking water could be a problem on a hot day. Bring purification tablets, and use them with spring water.

Some stretches of trail are covered with loose rocks. This can make bike control difficult, especially in fall when the rocks are covered with leaves.

Be very careful while negotiating the switchbacks above Brazil Creek. The trail bed is shored up by log retaining walls held in place by iron spikes. The spikes stick up 6 inches on the downhill side of the trail. A fall onto one of these could take some of the fun out of your ride.

Rescue index: For a trail with such a wilderness feel, the rescue index is excel-

Splashing through a creek on the northwest part of the Berryman Trail, just east of Harmon Springs Trail Camp.

lent. There are 5 road crossings to which you can make your way and await help. On weekend days during the warmer months the trail is regularly used by hikers, bikers, or equestrians who could give you a hand.

Land status: National forest.

Maps: The most useful map of the Berryman Trail is produced by the Forest Service. It is available in the Potosi Ranger District office at the address below. Topos covering the trail are the Berryman and Anthonies Mill 7.5 minute maps.

Finding the trail: The trail can be accessed at either Berryman or Brazil Creek campgrounds. To reach the Berryman Camp, drive 17 miles west of Potosi, or 19 miles east of Steelville, on MO 8. Look for Forest Service Road 2266, just east of the small town of Berryman. Go north 1 mile on FS 2266 to the camp. There is a paved parking lot at the trailhead. To reach Brazil Creek Camp, drive 17 miles south from Sullivan on MO 185 to County Road N. Go west on N approximately 8 miles to CR W. Turn south on W and drive approximately 9 miles to Brazil Creek Camp. If the pavement on W ends, you've gone 1 mile too far.

Sources of additional information:

Mark Twain National Forest
Post Office Box 188
Potosi, MO 63664
(314) 438-5427

The Alpine Shop
601 East Lockwood
Webster Groves, MO 63119
(314) 962-7715

The St. Louis Bicycle Touring Society
c/o The Touring Cyclist
11816 St. Charles Rock Road
Bridgeton, MO 63044
(314) 739-5180

Notes on the trail: The trail is marked by gray or white plastic diamonds nailed to trees. Most of the trail is well marked by blazes every 100 yards, but there are a few stretches where markings are scarce. The trail itself is well worn, making it tough to lose your way in any case.

This ride offers one of the best, most uniform single-track experiences described in this book. Beginners should be aware that the ride can be difficult. It can be handled by those with a positive attitude, though, especially when the ride is cut short at road intersections as mentioned in the introduction. The trail can be covered in 1 long day, or broken up into a 2-day experience by camping at a forest camp along the way. Non-riders who come along won't be bored, because the trail camps are great places to relax and get away from it all.

RIDE 18 *MARK TWAIN SOUTHEAST: LAKE WAPPAPELLO TRAIL*

Climbs and deadfall on the trail make this 15-mile loop in Lake Wappapello State Park challenging. The trail is recommended for experienced riders and beginners with positive attitudes. Your ride crosses the road at three points, giving you an opportunity to bail out if you find the going too difficult.

This trail is single-track, except for short sections where it follows abandoned double-tracks through the forest. Most of the ride is hard-packed dirt or gravel.

The western half of the loop passes through a typical Missouri hardwood forest. You'll cross several streams as you climb and descend between the ridges and drainages. The eastern part of the loop is even better, alternating between lakeside single-track and hilltop panoramas of Lake Wappapello.

In addition to the wildlife normally spotted in Missouri forests, you will see geese, ducks, herons, and gulls cruising the lake and feeding in its shallows. A backpacker camp on the northeast part of the loop provides a perfect rest stop at the water's edge, and a great place for a mid-ride dip in Lake Wappapello.

RIDE 18 *MARK TWAIN SOUTHEAST: LAKE WAPPAPELLO TRAIL*

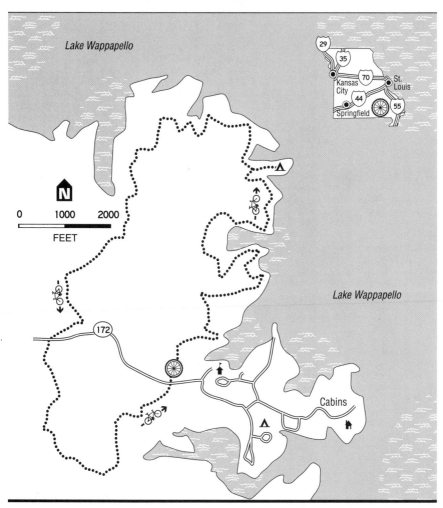

General location: 25 miles northeast of Poplar Bluff.

Elevation change: Elevation varies from 360′ at the lake level to 550′ at several points on the back side of the loop. The trail has numerous climbs and descents, with the most difficult along the stretch next to Lake Wappapello.

Season: All seasons are fine for riding this trail. The heat of summer can be quenched by dips in the lake after you are done pedaling, or during your ride at the backpacker camp 5 miles from the end of the trail. Winter riding can be wonderful. The bugs and humidity are gone, and the views are not obscured by foliage.

Hopping over the deadfall in the eastern reaches of the Lake Wappapello Trail.

Services: No water is available on the trail, but you can get it one-half mile from the trailhead in Lake Wappapello State Park. Camping, showers, and cabins are also available in the park. You'll find food and gas at a convenience store on MO 172 near the park entrance. All other services can be found in Poplar Bluff, 25 miles to the southwest.

Hazards: Other than occasional troublesome deadfall, you'll find no hazards on the Lake Wappapello Trail.

Rescue index: The trail crosses the road 3 times, so you'll never be far from an escape point. The park headquarters is only one-quarter mile from the trailhead. You could also work your way to the water's edge and flag one of the fishing boats that frequent the lake year-round.

Land status: The eastern half of the trail is located on state park land. The rest is on land owned by the Missouri Conservation Department.

Maps: The Lake Wappapello State Park Trail Map is perfect for following this

WHERE TO RIDE

Dennis Coello's *America by Mountain Bike series* presents classic fat tire rides. Published jointly by Menasha Ridge and Falcon Press, the 6 x 9" guides are written by local biking experts. Twenty regional books will blanket the country when the series is complete. So if you're wondering where the best rides are in your area, check out our mountain bike guides and then hit the trail for safe and memorable adventures.

GUIDES INCLUDE:

- Trail and route descriptions
- Area mountain bike shop listings
- Interesting facts on area history
- Trail difficulty, scenery, condition, length, and elevation change
- Trail hazards, nearby services and ranger stations
- Water and gear information
- Trail etiquette and conservation

FOR BOOKS AVAILABLE IN THE SERIES, WRITE FOR FALCON'S FREE CATALOG OR CALL TOLL-FREE.

NAME

ADDRESS

CITY_____STATE_____

ZIP

1-800-582-2665

FALCON

NO POSTAGE
NECESSARY
IF MAILED
IN THE
UNITED STATES

BUSINESS REPLY MAIL
FIRST-CLASS MAIL PERMIT NO 80 HELENA MT

POSTAGE WILL BE PAID BY ADDRESSEE

FALCON PRESS PUBLISHING CO
PO BOX 1718
HELENA MT 59624-9948

trail. It shows contour lines and location of park facilities. Topo maps are not necessary, but if you want to use one, you'll need the 7.5 minute Wappapello map. **Finding the trail:** Drive 8 miles east from US 67 on MO 172 to Lake Wappapello State Park. The trailhead and parking area for this loop are just east of the park headquarters on MO 172.

Sources of additional information:

Lake Wappapello State Park
Williamsville, MO 63967
(314) 297-3232

The Alpine Shop
601 East Lockwood
Webster Groves, MO 63119
(314) 962-7715

Notes on the trail: The Lake Wappapello Trail is marked in a counter-clockwise direction by yellow arrows and blazes. There are 3 other trails in the park, but the Lake Wappapello Trail is the only one open to mountain bikes.

RIDE 19 *MARK TWAIN SOUTHEAST: MOSES AUSTIN TRAIL*

The 14-mile Moses Austin Trail is named for the founder of Potosi, author of the plan for the American settlement of Texas. Moses Austin also had a distinguished son, Stephen Austin, who is known as the "Father of Texas."

Located in the northern part of the Missouri Ozarks, this loop ride winds through a country of low, wooded mountains that rise above valleys filled with small creeks and springs. Many of the valleys were farmed in the early part of the century, and still have open fields or pastures with an occasional tumble-down homestead.

Early in the ride, there are several crossings of Scott Branch. From the ridge-tops, you'll be treated to panoramic views of the surrounding countryside. The trail is easy to moderately difficult, but there are several short, steep, rocky sections that will require portages for most riders. Since there are only two of these, each less than a quarter mile, they don't present big problems.

Most of the trail takes you down abandoned logging roads interspersed with short stretches of single-track and gravel roads. This trail is great for both beginning and experienced riders.

General location: 15 miles west of Potosi.
Elevation change: The lowest point on the Moses Austin is one mile into the ride at the crossing of Scott Branch. From this low of 920′, the trail climbs to nearly 1,200′ at several points on the ridge-tops. There are no climbs longer than a quarter mile, but several of the short, technical climbs will push most riders to their limits or force portages.
Season: Spring and fall are the best seasons to ride the Moses Austin. In those

RIDE 19 *MARK TWAIN SOUTHEAST: MOSES AUSTIN TRAIL*

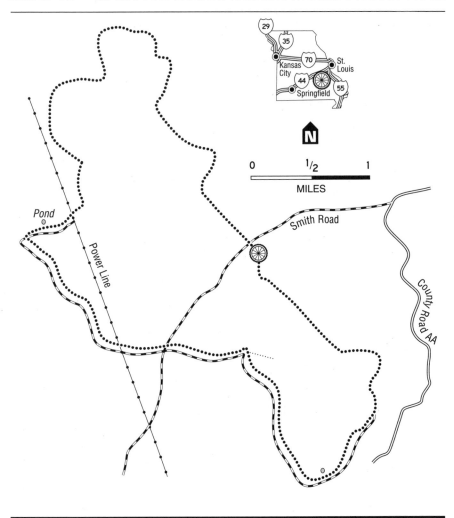

seasons, you'll enjoy the cooler temperatures, spring wildflowers, blazing fall colors—and experience fewer ticks and insects.

Services: No drinking water is available along the trail. Camping is allowed anywhere in the national forest. The nearest developed campsites are at the Berryman Trail Camp, 17 miles west of Potosi on MO 8, then 1 mile north on Forest Service Road 2266. The nearest lodging is in Steelville, 25 miles to the west. Groceries and restaurants are in Potosi, 15 miles to the east. The nearest bike shops are in St. Louis, 80 miles to the north.

Hazards: The few rocky and technical climbs and descents mentioned previously present a hazard to those without good bike-handling skills. Otherwise, the Moses Austin is very safe.

Rescue index: Although the trail does not see a lot of use, it does cross or follow gravel roads at several points. This gives you the opportunity to bail out and ride back to the trailhead, or await help by the roadside. While riding this loop, you are never more than 5 miles from the trailhead.

Land status: National forest.

Maps: A map of the Moses Austin Trail is available at the Forest Service office in Potosi. The USGS topo covering the trail is the Shirley 7.5 minute map.

Finding the trail: From Potosi, go west 11 miles on MO 8 to County Road AA. Go north on AA 3.3 miles, and turn left on Smith Road, a gravel road going west. Follow it 1.5 miles to the trailhead. The trailhead is easy to miss, since there are no signs. Look for a double-track crossing the gravel road, marked by white paint blazes. This faint road is the trail. There is a small parking area on the north side of the gravel road.

Sources of additional information:

Mark Twain National Forest
Post Office Box 188
Potosi, MO 63664
(314) 438-5427

The Alpine Shop
601 East Lockwood
Webster Groves, MO 63119
(314) 962-7715

Notes on the trail: This is a great trail for beginners, though some of the technical sections mentioned earlier may make you doubt that statement. The trail is well marked, Appalachian Trail–style, by white rectangular blazes on trees along the way. A double blaze indicates an intersection or abrupt change of direction. The trail markings are easier to follow if you ride counter-clockwise.

RIDE 20 *MARK TWAIN SOUTHEAST:*
ST. JOE STATE PARK

Developed on the tailings of mines belonging to the St. Joe Lead Company, St. Joe State Park has something for everyone, with a superb 40-mile network of maintained trails. There are also many more miles of unofficial trails open to mountain bikes. You could spend a weekend there riding the maintained trails and exploring the unmarked routes and never see them all.

While some of the trails in the network at St. Joe are difficult for beginners, most of the maintained trails can be ridden by novices. The unofficial trails that traverse the park are more technical, and better suited to experienced riders who enjoy testing their bike-handling skills. The trails include an 11-mile paved bike path for those who prefer an easy ride, very rugged and unmarked motorcycle trails, and a set of marked equestrian trails.

RIDE 20 *MARK TWAIN SOUTHEAST: ST. JOE STATE PARK*

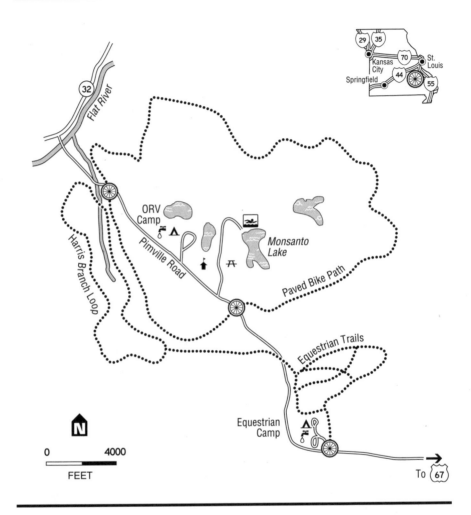

The horse trails are not extremely difficult, but do have a few washouts and steep sections. One of these rough spots is the northeastern stretch of the Harris Branch Trail. This is the trail marked by red arrows. It extends to the northwest part of the park. The western side of the loop is wide and easily ridden, but the east leg has some very difficult sections.

At its northernmost point, the trail passes within a quarter mile of Pimville Road, the asphalt highway bisecting the park. After riding to this point on the south and west sides of the Harris Branch Trail, inexperienced cyclists can avoid

Slickrock stream crossing of Harris Branch on the northwest part of the Harris Branch Trail, St. Joe State Park.

the technical section by following a side trail to Pimville Road and riding back to the starting point.

From the late 1800s to the 1950s, the entire 8,561 acres of St. Joe were part of a working lead mine. Approximately 25 percent of the park is honeycombed by underground mines. The old mine milling complex is still standing at the north end of the park. Some of its buildings date back to the turn of the century. They are being restored, and will become a major mining museum.

St. Joe State Park's recreational possibilities are as diverse as its trails. The wooded portions of the area have a wilderness feel. And, when you're overheated after a hot summer ride, a swim at the sandy beach at Monsanto Lake is a great way to cool off. Another cool spot awaits those who ride the rough northeastern section of the Harris Branch Trail. Here the trail crosses the creek where it flows for 100 yards over smooth rock layers. This is a perfect spot for splashing in the water.

There is a primitive trail camp along the Harris Branch Trail for those who would like to do some backcountry camping, and a secluded picnic shelter along the paved bike path for less adventurous souls.

General location: 5 miles west of Farmington.
Elevation change: Elevations in St. Joe State Park range from 800′ to 1,100′. The park is hilly. All trails will have challenging climbs and a few white-knuckle descents. Those looking for an easier ride should try the paved bike path. It has

several steep hills, but is level with short rollers for the remainder of its length.

Season: Riding in St. Joe State Park is good year-round, but spring and fall are the best seasons. Summer can be hot and humid, but you can beat the heat with a dip in Monsanto Lake.

Services: Drinking water is available at both campgrounds in the park, in Pim Day Use Area, and at both bike trailheads. The ATV campground has showers and laundry facilities. Hotels, restaurants, gasoline, and grocery stores are available in Farmington, 5 miles east of the park. The nearest bike shops are in St. Louis, 80 miles to the north.

Hazards: Some of the steep and rocky descents can make bike handling difficult. You may also encounter horses while riding the equestrian trails. Dismount, stand to the downhill side of the trail, and wait quietly for them to pass.

Rescue index: St. Joe is a popular park among cyclists, hikers, equestrians, and ATV riders. There is a good chance you will be found if you run into problems. If you can, make your way to the bike path or park road and await help.

Land status: State park.

Maps: Trail maps of St. Joe State Park are available at the park entrance station. They show only the maintained trails. Those wishing to explore unmarked trails may want to purchase the 7.5 minute topos for Farmington and Flat River.

Finding the trail: Follow US 67 to the southern Farmington exit (County Road W). There will be signs directing you to St. Joe State Park. Go west from US 67, following these signs 4 miles to the park. Parking is available at the equestrian camp, at Pim Day Use Area, and at the 2 trailheads for the paved bike path.

Sources of additional information:

St. Joe State Park
Flat River, MO 63601
(314) 431-1069

The Alpine Shop
601 East Lockwood
Webster Groves, MO 63119
(314) 962-7715

The St. Louis Bicycle Touring Society
c/o The Touring Cyclist
11816 St. Charles Rock Road
Bridgeton, MO 63044
(314) 739-5180

Notes on the trail: You can choose between 2 campgrounds if you are overnighting it in the park. The campground in the western end of the park has more facilities, but is closest to the designated ATV area. It can be very noisy. The equestrian camp at the park's eastern end has more limited facilities, but it is quiet and peaceful.

The park has everything from paved bike paths to bone-rattling single-track. Most of the trails are well marked by colored blazes. The equestrian trails can be confusing at times, but carrying and consulting maps will keep you from getting lost. Most riders find the Harris Branch Trail easy to follow.

A good way to check out the park is to ride the Harris Branch Trail and the paved bike path to get a feel for the layout of the area. Then, using these 2 trails as reference points, you can explore other trails in the park. Whether you follow marked trails or blaze your way on the many unofficial ones that lace the area, riding in St. Joe is mountain biking at its best.

RIDE 21 *MARK TWAIN SOUTHWEST: HUCKLEBERRY RIDGE STATE FOREST*

Huckleberry Ridge State Forest is a network of approximately 14 miles of trail. The network will take you over single-track, rough double-track, and narrow gravel roads. The single-track is the toughest riding in the forest, and is only recommended for experts. The most difficult of the single-track follows a horse trail, part of which is overgrown and lost.

The double-track and gravel trails are less difficult and can be easily ridden by beginners, but there will be several long climbs. Scenic vistas will reward you for the ascents to ridges in this forest. But you don't have to climb to enjoy a view; part of the trail follows Greer Creek, which you will cross twice, then parallel for a mile.

General location: 40 miles southeast of Joplin.
Elevation change: Elevations range from 900′ in the bottomlands to near 1,200′ on the ridge-tops. There are many climbs and descents as the trail passes over and along the ridges and valleys of Huckleberry Ridge.
Season: Spring and fall, with their moderate temperatures, are the best times to ride in Huckleberry Ridge State Forest.
Services: No drinking water is available in the forest. Primitive camping is allowed. All other services can be found in Neosho, 25 miles to the north, or in Joplin, 40 miles to the north.
Hazards: Be careful on the steep and loose sections of the single-track foot trails and horse trails.
Rescue index: You are never more than 1.5 miles from County Road K while riding in Huckleberry Ridge. Try to make your way to this road if you get into trouble.
Land status: State forest, owned by the Missouri Department of Conservation.
Maps: The Missouri Department of Conservation produces a good map of the area, available by writing the address below. The topo for the area is the Jane 7.5 minute map.
Finding the trail: From Pineville on US 71, drive 4 miles east on County Road K to Huckleberry Ridge State Forest. There are 2 parking areas and a primitive campsite. Park your car in one of these and hit the trail.

RIDE 21 *MARK TWAIN SOUTHWEST: HUCKLEBERRY RIDGE STATE FOREST*

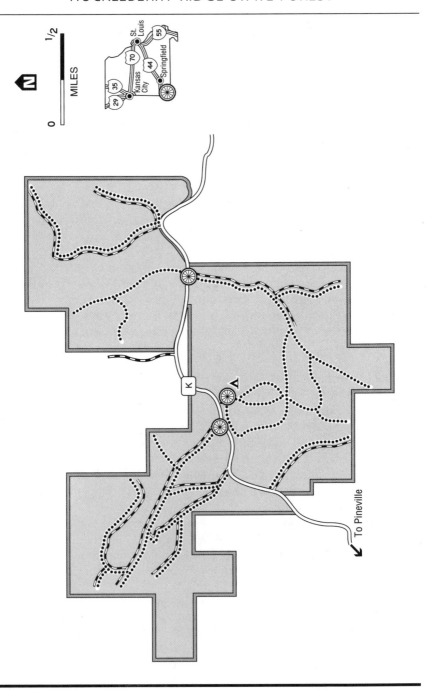

Rugged road in Huckleberry Ridge State Forest.

Sources of additional information:

Missouri Department of Conservation
Post Office Box 157
Neosho, MO 64850
(417) 451-4158

Notes on the trail: None of the trails in the forest are marked, so you will have to find your own way. Because this is a small area, it will be tough to get seriously lost. Paint marks on trees, supplemented by signs in the forest, mark the boundaries of Huckleberry Ridge State Forest, keeping you from straying too far. Carry a map and check it now and then, and you should be able to quickly ascertain your location.

RIDE 22 *MARK TWAIN SOUTHWEST: BUSIEK STATE FOREST*

This state forest's 15-mile network of trails winds through 2,505 acres of rugged Ozark topography. Beginners will enjoy riding along the roads paralleling Woods Fork and Camp Creek. Adventurous beginners looking for more rugged stuff could try the two trail loops north of Camp Creek in the western end of the

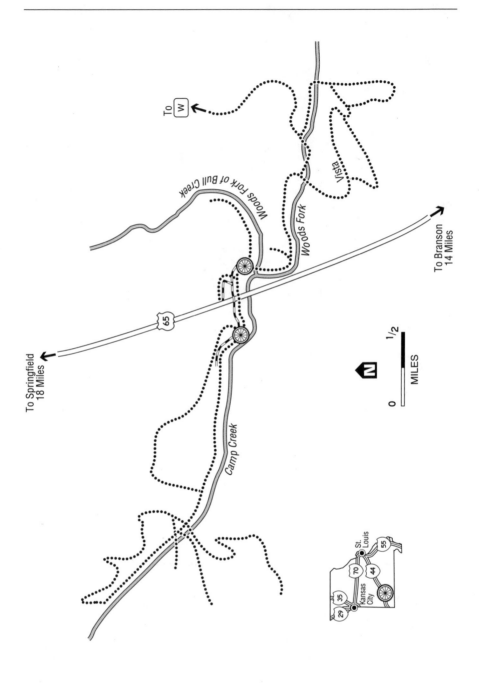

Scenic single-track in the eastern half of the Busiek, just east of the scenic vista.

forest. Some short portages will be required, but these loops can be handled by inexperienced riders willing to stick with it.

Trails in the hills east of US 65 tend to be more technical and rugged. They will force even the experts to portage many times.

Trail surfaces include gravel road near the highway, double-track roads along the creek in the western part, abandoned woods road in the hills above the creeks, and plenty of single-track.

On the lower trails in the eastern half of the Busiek State Forest you will cross Woods Fork three times. It feels great on a hot summer day, and is a fun way to introduce beginners to mountain biking on the easy creekside trails.

On the east side of the forest, you'll enjoy a great view where the trail tops out on a ridge. To reach this vista, take the trail south from the first crossing of Woods Fork.

In the western end of the forest, one of the trails skirts an abandoned quarry near US 65, giving you an interesting look into its canyon-like remains.

General location: 20 miles south of Springfield.

Elevation change: From a low of 950′ at the parking area, you will reach a peak of 1,200′ on the trails west of US 65. As a general rule, the trails east of US 65 have the steepest and most technical climbs, while those west of the highway are a little less difficult.

Season: Spring and fall are best. With the choices available for shorter loops, winter riding can be fun. You can finish your ride before the cold bites you too hard. If you bike here in summer, you will want to ride in the early morning or late evening when heat and humidity aren't as intense. Look out for ticks and chiggers.

Services: No drinking water is available in this state forest. All services are available in Springfield, 20 miles to the north on US 65.

Hazards: Parts of the climbs and descents are very steep and technical, perfect for those of you who like to break rocks with your teeth and knees. Be careful on these. Don't cross Woods Fork and Camp Creek during high water.

Rescue index: This is a popular mountain biking area for riders out of Springfield. Every trail will probably see some use on weekends, so you will be quickly found if you get into a jam. You will never be more than 2 miles from US 65. If all else fails, try to make your way to US 65 and flag a passing motorist.

Land status: State forest, owned by the Missouri Department of Conservation.

Maps: The Department of Conservation has an excellent map of the Busiek State Forest, showing many of the area's trails. It also shows contour lines, and is available at the address below. The topo for most of the forest is the Day 7.5 minute map. A small portion of the west half falls onto Spokane.

Finding the trail: Drive 20 miles south from Springfield on US 65. There will be a small brown sign marking the turnoff. Watch for it. You'll be descending a long hill, and it will be tough to get slowed down to make the left turn on this busy highway. Follow the gravel road into the forest to a T intersection with another gravel road. Turn left, and follow this road to a parking area.

Sources of additional information:

Missouri Department of Conservation
2630 North Mayfair Road
Springfield, MO 65803
(417) 864-8224

Sunshine Bicycles and Fitness
1926 East Sunshine
Springfield, MO 65803
(417) 883-1113

A & B Cycles
220 West Walnut
Springfield, MO 65806
(417) 866-6621
or
3201 South Campbell
Springfield, MO 65807
(417) 881-5940

Notes on the trail: The trail along Woods Fork in the eastern part of the forest is a fun one for beginners. The climb up to the ridge and the resulting panorama can be difficult, but worth the effort. Many of the remaining trails in the eastern end of the forest are very technical, and are best left to experts.

The western part of the forest is much better for beginning riders. The trail along Camp Creek is flat, with a few interesting stream fords when there is water in the creek. Riding the gravel road to the western boundary of the forest, then riding back on the two loops north of the road, is the best way to enjoy the west half of the Busiek. Though the climbs on these 2 loops may be steep in places, the grades are better handled as downhills eastbound than climbs westbound.

RIDE 23 *MARK TWAIN SOUTHWEST: CHADWICK MOTORCYCLE USE AREA*

Chadwick Motorcycle Use Area networks more than 100 miles of trail in a 12-square-mile area of the Mark Twain National Forest. It offers something for every mountain biker: potential loops of almost any distance, and rides to match the skills of any cyclist.

If you want something easy, the trails that follow ridges and drainages are fairly gentle, and are well suited to beginning riders.

Climbs and descents between the ridges and bottoms will challenge the more experienced riders. If you don't like rough portages, though, you should probably go somewhere else. The steeper grades will be very loose and washed out by ATVs. All cyclists should expect to carry their bikes on some of the tougher climbs and descents.

But don't let the presence of ATVs and rough trail sections keep you from experiencing Chadwick. There is some spectacular riding here. You could camp in the area and ride for two or three days without covering many trails twice. Loops as short as one-half mile and as long as 30 miles can be ridden. There are two areas, Sawdust Pile Rally Point and the Trial Bike Area, where off-trail riding is allowed, giving you an opportunity to test your trials skills.

RIDE 23 *MARK TWAIN SOUTHWEST:*
CHADWICK MOTORCYCLE USE AREA

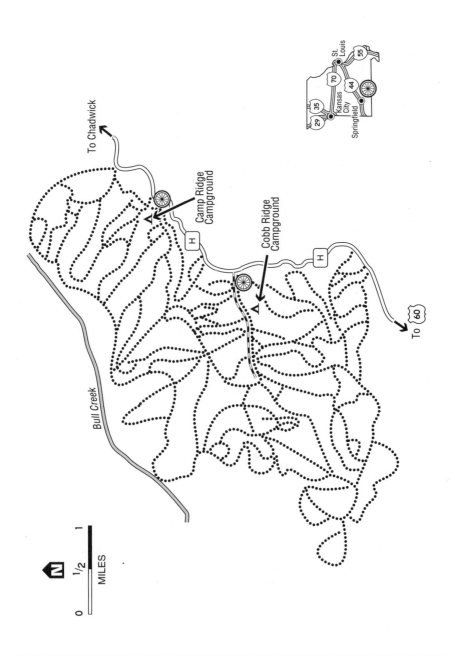

Riders sticking to bottomlands and ridge-tops will find excellent single-track in the Chadwick Motorcycle Use Area.

General location: 25 miles southeast of Springfield.

Elevation change: Elevation ranges from 960´ along Bull Creek to 1,350´ at the Cobb Ridge and Camp Ridge campgrounds trailheads. There are many climbs and descents of varying difficulty. Maps of the area show contour lines, so you can choose the trails that match your abilities.

Season: While spring and fall are the best seasons to ride in Chadwick, the area is well suited to year-round use. There are few stream crossings to freeze your feet in winter. The many trails in this small area let you choose shorter loops, keeping you close to the trailhead in cold weather. You should consider riding in the off-season, since fewer ATVs use the area during the heat of summer and the dead of winter.

Services: No drinking water is available anywhere on the trail system, even at the campsites. The area's 2 campgrounds, Camp Ridge and Cobb Ridge, are located on County Road H on the eastern edge of the area. These also serve as trailheads for Chadwick. A small store in Chadwick, 2 miles north of the trail system, has fuel and limited food. All other services are available in Springfield, 25 miles to the northwest.

Hazards: Since ATVs and motorcycles also use the area, some of the climbs and descents are washed-out and treacherous, presenting wonderful opportunities for riders to do some facial soil sampling. Take it easy on these.

Watch out for the ATVs, which will be especially thick on weekends in summer. If you meet one ascending while you are descending, give it the right-of-way. ATVs will have a tough time getting underway again if you force them to halt on a climb.

Rescue index: Though you may get tired of riding with noisy ATVs, their presence ensures that you will get immediate help in case of an emergency. Even on weekdays, Chadwick sees regular use in fair weather.

Land status: National forest.

Maps: The Forest Service has an excellent map of the area. It is usually available at the trailheads. The map shows contour lines, so topos aren't necessary. If you want to use a topo anyway, you will need the Chadwick 7.5 minute map.

Finding the trail: From Springfield, drive east on US 60 to MO 125. Turn south on MO 125 and follow it 20 miles to County Road H, just past the town of Chadwick. Turn right on CR H and follow it a short distance to the trailheads at Camp Ridge and Cobb Ridge.

Sources of additional information:

Mark Twain National Forest
Post Office Box 188
Business Route 5 South
Ava, MO 65608
(417) 683-4428

Sunshine Bicycles and Fitness
1926 East Sunshine
Springfield, MO 65804
(417) 883-1113

A & B Cycles
220 West Walnut
Springfield, MO 65806
(417) 866-6621
or
3201 South Campbell
Springfield, MO 65807
(417) 881-5940

Notes on the trail: Many trail networks this large are a confusing mess. Not so at Chadwick. All trails are numbered, and all intersections are marked. These markings correspond well with the map provided by the Forest Service. The contour lines shown on the map are a great help in choosing trail loops that best match your ability. If you are looking for easier rides, follow trails that travel along ridge-tops or creek bottoms, and you will only have to deal with climbs on the connectors.

If you want to get a good look at the entire area, take the loop that begins at Camp Ridge. Follow Trail 113 around the perimeter. Begin it by following

Strawberry Ridge, then descend to the valley of Bull Creek. Continuing along the perimeter, 113 parallels an open pasture, then turns south into Yount Hollow.

Halfway up Yount Hollow, bear right on Trail 106, and follow it to Forest Service Road 171. Follow FS 171 to the right to Trail 101, which descends into Flyblow Hollow. Continue along 101 through Flyblow Hollow and Peckout Hollow, and then up to FS 171 near Cobb Ridge. From there, you can jump on CR H and follow it back to Camp Ridge, or find your way back on the trail network.

RIDE 24 *MARK TWAIN SOUTHWEST: DEVREAUX RIDGE*

Are you always trying to get a mountain bike outing together with a bunch of your friends, but can't find a place suited to everyone's abilities? This ride is the answer. Hammerheads looking for rough and difficult trails can ride at nearby Chadwick Motorcycle Use Area, while those of you looking for a more sedate ride can still enjoy getting away from it all on Devreaux Ridge. You can all get together afterward at Cobb Ridge or Camp Ridge to brag about your trail exploits.

Devreaux Ridge is a great ride for beginners and experts alike. Inexperienced riders will enjoy the manageable grades and relatively smooth double-track roads on this route. Stronger riders can have fun blasting up and down the long grade between Devreaux Ridge and splashing through the crossings of Garrison Branch. There is just enough rough stuff to make the ride a fun mountain bike excursion, but not so much that first-timers will be intimidated.

Beginning from the junction of Devreaux Ridge and Garrison Ridge roads, the distance is 11 miles round trip. About a third of the double-track on this route is gravel, passable by normal cars. The rest is more rugged, following unmaintained double-track forest roads.

As I've mentioned, this ride is a great alternative to the rough single-track in nearby Chadwick Motorcycle Use Area. When I checked out the trail, there was a great swimming hole in Garrison Branch. Be sure to take a splash if you are doing the ride in the heat of summer.

General location: 6 miles south of Chadwick.
Elevation change: Elevations vary from 900′ along Garrison Branch to 1,300′ along Devreaux Ridge. The descent from Devreaux Ridge is around 1 mile in length, with a corresponding climb when the time comes to return to the ridge. The climb can be handled by riders of any skill level as long as they are in good condition. There are also several smaller climbs along the spine of Devreaux Ridge.

RIDE 24   *MARK TWAIN SOUTHWEST: DEVREAUX RIDGE*

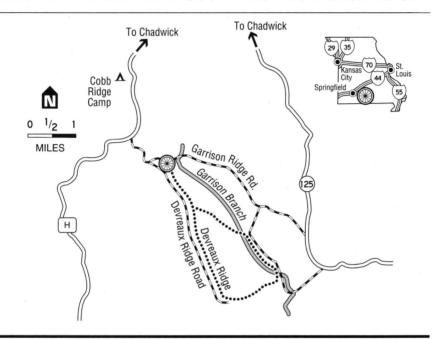

Season: Devreaux Ridge is a good ride in any season. Spring and fall, with their cooler temperatures, are best. Spring is the ultimate choice, when the ridge is painted white by one of the biggest concentrations of dogwoods I've ever seen, with a scattering of redbuds setting them off. If you do ride in summer, you can beat the summer heat by swimming in Garrison Branch, as mentioned in the introduction. It has several good swimming holes along its length. Winter riding, when leaves are off the trees, treats you to scenic vistas of the national forest from Devreaux Ridge.

Services: No drinking water is available along the trail. You can camp at Camp Ridge and Cobb Ridge recreation areas near the Chadwick Motorcycle Use Area, 2 miles north of Garrison Ridge Road on CR H. If you want to get away from motorcycle noise while you camp, drive 30 miles south on MO 125 to the trailhead at Hercules Glades Wilderness and camp there.

Food and gasoline can be found at a convenience store in Chadwick, 6 miles to the north. All other services are available in Springfield, 25 miles to the northwest.

Hazards: This double-track trail is a pretty safe ride. Just don't attempt either of the 2 crossings of Garrison Branch during high water.

Rescue index: The farthest you'll be from a paved highway is only 3 miles. If you get into trouble, work your way east to MO 125 or west to CR H, and wait

Devreaux Ridge Road sports one of the thick stands of dogwoods that make spring a spectacular season in Missouri.

for help there. You may even see an occasional four-wheel-drive vehicle on this double-track trail.

Land status: National forest.

Maps: The Garrison 7.5 minute topo covers this whole loop. This entire double-track ride is also shown on the Forest Service map of the Ava Ranger District of the Mark Twain National Forest.

Finding the trail: Good starting points for this ride are Camp Ridge and Cobb Ridge campgrounds, located on the eastern edge of Chadwick Motorcycle Use Area. Both are located around 2 miles south of Chadwick on County Road H. From either campground, ride south several miles on CR H to Garrison Ridge Road, a gravel road leading east. Follow it 1.5 miles to Devreaux Ridge Road, which leads to the southeast.

Both Garrison Ridge and Devreaux Ridge roads are marked. Their intersection is the starting point for your ride. You could drive your car easily to this point and start the ride from the intersection, but there is no parking area. You will have to park off to the side of the road. Start the ride heading southeast on Devreaux Ridge Road.

Sources of additional information:

Mark Twain National Forest
Post Office Box 188
Business Route 5 South
Ava, MO 65608
(417) 683-4428

Sunshine Bicycles and Fitness
1926 East Sunshine
Springfield, MO 65804
(417) 883-1113

A & B Cycles
220 West Walnut
Springfield, MO 65806
(417) 866-6621
or
3201 South Campbell
Springfield, MO 65807
(417) 881-5940

Notes on the trail: Though the difficulty of this ride is about the same no matter which way you ride the loop, it is easiest to follow when you ride clockwise. Riding southeast on Devreaux Ridge Road from the junction of Devreaux Ridge and Garrison Ridge roads, you'll reach a fork around a mile and a half from the junction. The road to the left is not as well maintained. Take it to begin the loop.

Just as the road begins to descend, there will be another fork. Bear right at this fork, and you will continue the long descent to Garrison Branch. When you reach the end of the descent, the road crosses the branch and hits a T intersection. Turn right, and follow Garrison Branch. Shortly after you cross the branch a second time, look for a road going south up the hill to the right. This road will climb up onto Devreaux Ridge, and follow it back to close the loop.

RIDE 25 *MARK TWAIN SOUTHWEST: THE MECCA*

This area was discovered by several mountain bikers out of Springfield, who called the place The Mecca because "You end up praying, one way or the other." Although a few spots are a little difficult, after riding the base eight miles of the network, I decided they meant praying in thanks for such a good riding area.

The main route through the area, Forest Service Road 1002, is a double-track road that can easily be ridden by beginners. When riding southbound on FS

RIDE 25 *MARK TWAIN SOUTHWEST: THE MECCA*

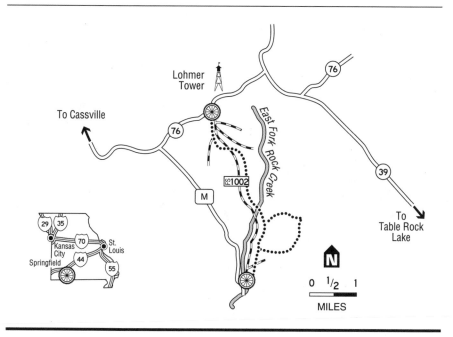

1002 just after crossing the east fork of Rock Creek, a side road bears left, offering additional miles of riding for inexperienced cyclists.

Another 100 yards south of the crossing of the creek is the beginning of a side loop that climbs high up onto the ridge overlooking the area, and then drops down a steep and technical descent back to the Rock Creek Valley, where it rejoins FS 1002. Look for a faint ATV track going to the left.

The main route along FS 1002 crosses Rock Creek twice, and several smaller streams are forded on the side trails leading off the main loop. These side traces offer some fun and challenging riding for those of you who want a little more than a double-track road.

Get off the trail and explore, using FS 1002 as a base. Along the central part of the main trail you will pass through a large forest burn, opening up great vistas of the surrounding Ozark ridges. Wildflowers grow in the open area left by the burn, and in spring, dogwoods scatter patches of white on the surrounding wooded hillsides.

General location: 10 miles west of Cassville.
Elevation change: Elevations range from 1,570′ at Lohmer Tower to 1,000′ along the East Fork of Rock Creek. There is a 1.5-mile climb or descent on the main trail along Forest Service Road 1002, depending on the direction you

FS 1002 winding through the forest burn in The Mecca, just south of the turn-off for the side loop.

travel, and a 1-mile ascent on the side loop if you ride it in the suggested direction. You'll ride many other hills if you take other side trails off the main trail and side loop.

Season: Spring and fall are the best seasons to ride The Mecca. Summer brings heat, humidity, ticks, and chiggers. Part of the ride passes through an old forest burn, where you will be exposed to the sun. While this makes summer riding uncomfortable, it can help warm a winter ride, and the views will be better when the leaves are gone.

Services: No drinking water is available along the trail. Cassville, 10 miles to the west, has groceries, gas, restaurants, and hotels. Camping is available at Roaring River State Park, 6 miles south of Cassville, and at several national forest and Corps of Engineers sites on the shores of Table Rock Lake just to the southeast on MO 39. All other services are available in Springfield, around 50 miles to the northeast.

Hazards: There are some big ledges on the side loop off the main trail. Be cautious on these, and on the rough stretches of other side trails. Be careful when crossing the East Fork of Rock Creek during high water.

Rescue index: Not many people venture into this area. Weekends may see some mountain bike and four-wheel-drive use, but the area is otherwise fairly remote. If you get into trouble, try to make your way north to MO 76 or south to County Road M.

Land status: National forest.

Maps: The topos for the area are the Golden and Shell Knob 7.5 minute maps. The main double-track followed by the ride is shown on the Cassville ranger district map of the Mark Twain National Forest.

Finding the trail: The ride starts at the Lohmer Lookout Tower, 10 miles east of Cassville on MO 76. Park at the tower, and ride one-half mile west to FS 1002. Turn south on FS 1002, and enter The Mecca.

There is also access to the southern end of the area from CR M, where M crosses the east fork of Rock Creek. To reach it, drive 8 miles east of Cassville to CR M. Go south 4 miles to the bridge. Park in the open field a quarter mile north of the bridge.

Sources of additional information:

Mark Twain National Forest
Highway 248 West
Cassville, MO 65625
(417) 847-2144

Sunshine Bicycles and Fitness
1926 East Sunshine
Springfield, MO 65804
(417) 883-1113

A & B Cycles
220 West Walnut
Springfield, MO 65806
(417) 866-6621
or
3201 South Campbell
Springfield, MO 65807
(417) 881-5940

Notes on the trail: The Mecca is a fun place for group rides with cyclists of differing skill levels. The beginners can ride the easy FS 1002 along the valley, while those looking for a little tougher ride could pedal the side trails that offer bigger challenges.

Be aware, though, that none of this trail is marked for you to follow. Route finding, while not that difficult, will be up to you. If you doubt your skills in the woods, do not venture off the double-track of FS 1002. This main road is an obvious landmark, paralleling Rock Creek in its lower reaches. It is hard to get lost if you stick to this main double-track through the area.

The Mecca is best explored north to south. When you have had your fill of mountain biking, you can ride on down FS 1002 to CR M, and ride north on M and east on MO 76 back to Lohmer Tower. Traveling south, you will begin on the highest point along the trail.

Around 100 yards south of the crossing of Rock Creek, near the top of a short climb, there will be a faint trail to the east (left). This is the side loop, which will take you on a 1-mile climb to the top of the ridge to the east. It will follow the ridge for one-half mile, and then drop back down to FS 1002 on an extremely rough descent. At the bottom of that descent, you'll reach a fork, where you should bear west (right) back to the main trail.

You could ride the side loop in the opposite direction if you don't like long climbs. To do this, continue past the first turn-off just after the crossing, and ride until you reach a fork. There, a more rugged road bears to the left, deep into the forest burn. Follow this to the east. As you near a small creek, there will be another fork. Turn left and begin climbing. The climb is much shorter when riding the side loop this way, but plan on portaging.

In fact, no matter which way you ride the loop, you will have to portage this steep grade, either up or down, with its 2-foot rock ledges and rugged surface. Suit yourself, and have fun!

RIDE 26 *MARK TWAIN SOUTHWEST: SWAN CREEK HORSE TRAILS*

When I first began to check out this system of over 50 miles of horse trails, I found myself wondering how the trail builders had developed such an extensive network. According to the Forest Service, this set of trails had been laid out by a couple of equestrians, with no help from the national forest. The only map I had was a hand-drawn guide the ranger had given me. He said it was made by the folks who built the trail system. Yet that crude map guided me through this spaghetti bowl of trails like something from Rand McNally.

Just before sundown, I broke out of the woods near the Bar K Wrangler Camp and blundered into an equestrian camp, spooking their mules. After they calmed their stock, Larry and Marian Jackson introduced themselves, offered me a beer, and asked where I had ridden. I said I didn't know for sure, and pulled out the map to show them. Larry looked at it in surprise, pointed at Marian, and said, "That's her map!" I'd stumbled into the two people who had designed and laid out this trail system.

In 1978, Larry and Marian began exploring the Swan Creek drainage with their horses and mules. Trails were few then, so they followed abandoned roads that laced the area. Not satisfied with so few choices, they began to expand the trail network, sometimes with the help of their friends, but usually on their own.

Because of their hard work, Swan Creek grew from a relatively unknown part of the forest, accessed only by a rutted double-track road, to one of the more popular riding areas in southwestern Missouri. Now a graded access road leads to the newly constructed Bar K Wrangler Camp. Larry and Marian have cut about 50 miles of trail in this wild area, almost all single-track, with a small amount following old roads.

As Larry and Marian built up the trail system and other riders began to use it, the Forest Service began to take an interest. They built the Bar K Wrangler Camp in 1992. By the end of 1994, they hope to have marked over 19 miles of the trails in the system as official Forest Service routes.

At the time of this writing, the trails in the area are marked and named by the Jacksons, with titles you'll not find on any map. The Moonshine Hollow Trail is named for the foundations of old stills Marian found nearby when she was cutting that trail. Horseshoe Falls is named for a curving cascade in Swan Creek near the trailhead. Beer Can Alley follows an old road that was used by four-wheel-drives before the area was declared a non-motorized area. Larry and Marian carried out mountains of the beer cans the revelers left behind. Larry and Marian are in Swan Creek often. If you're lucky, you'll run into them, and can hear more of the area's history.

Swan Creek is a great riding area for experts or for less experienced riders who don't mind some portages. Many of the trails offer easy riding, but almost all have stretches of rocky, steep, technical single-track that will require portages. You just can't plan to ride every inch of any loop you choose.

Nor is the trail system marked in the traditional way. White-painted can lids mark most intersections, bearing the name of each trail, but these have sometimes been destroyed. Even the map is only a guide, since no official map of the trail system exists. The one in this book was made from a hand-drawn copy made by the Jacksons. Still, it is fairly easy to find your way around. If you get lost, following any drainage will take you west to Swan Creek.

Don't let these factors keep you from enjoying this challenging trail system. You're in for stream crossings, scenic vistas, challenging climbs, cruises through ridge-top pine forests, and a dip in Swan Creek at the end of your ride. Try to remember what I told you in the introduction. Uncertainty is an adventure, so get out to Swan Creek and have one!

General location: 6 miles southeast of Chadwick.

Elevation change: Elevations vary from around 900´ along Swan Creek to over 1,300´ along the ridge in the eastern part of the trail system. There are many climbs and descents. While most of these are short, some extend for nearly a mile.

Season: Spring and fall are the best seasons to ride this trail system. Ticks and chiggers take over by July. Winter riding can be tough: the first thing you do after leaving the trailhead is ford Swan Creek.

Services: No drinking water is available at the trailhead. Water, food, gasoline, and limited groceries are available at a convenience store in Chadwick, 6 miles to the north.

Bar K Wrangler Camp is at the trailhead, and additional campsites can be found at Cobb Ridge and Camp Ridge campgrounds, just south of Chadwick

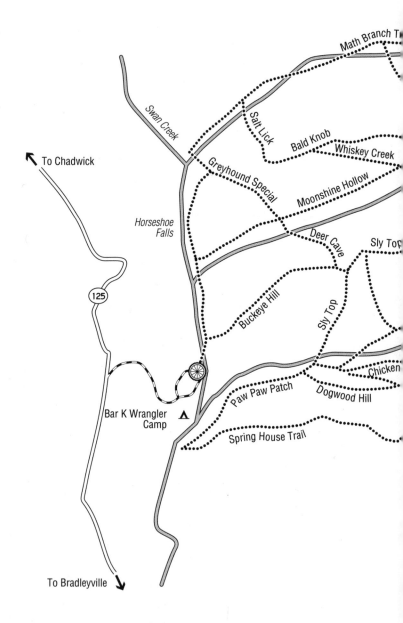

To Chadwick

Swan Creek

Math Branch T

Salt Lick

Bald Knob

Whiskey Creek

Greyhound Special

Moonshine Hollow

Horseshoe
Falls

Deer Cave

Sly Top

125

Buckeye Hill

Sly Top

Chicken

Paw Paw Patch

Dogwood Hill

Bar K Wrangler
Camp

Spring House Trail

To Bradleyville

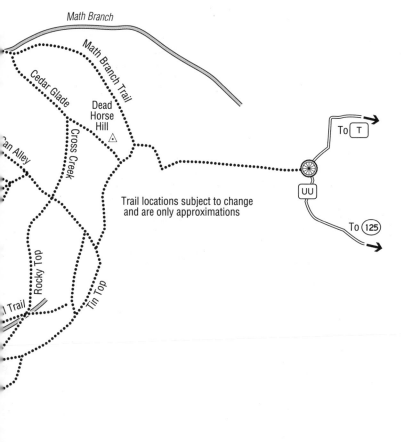

Math Branch

Math Branch Trail

Cedar Glade

Dead
Horse
Hill

Cross Creek

an Alley

Rocky Top

Tin Top

Trail

Trail locations subject to change
and are only approximations

To T

UU

To 125

N

0   1
MILES

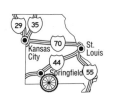

29 35

Kansas
City

70

St.
Louis

44

Springfield

55

Spring House Trail, central area of the Swan Creek Horse Trails.

on County Road H. All services are available in Springfield, about 30 miles to the north.

Hazards: Swan Creek can rise quickly during rainstorms. Don't cross it when it is deep—it can easily sweep you off your feet.

There are many short, rocky, and technical sections scattered throughout this trail system. Be very careful on these.

Be prepared to encounter horses at any time. Dismount, move to the down-hill side of the trail, and let them pass.

Rescue index: While these trails see heavy use by equestrians, the sheer number of miles in the system means you're unlikely to meet anyone on the trails. You should plan to take care of yourself if you get into a jam.

In the eastern part of the system, work your way east to CR UU. In the west, find your way west to Swan Creek, then work your way down the creek to Bar K.

Horseshoe Falls on Swan Creek, one-half mile north of Bar K Wrangler Camp.

Land status: National forest.

Maps: Most of the trail system falls onto the Bradleyville and Keltner 7.5 minute topos. A sliver of territory on the western edge falls onto Garrison and Chadwick.

Finding the trail: The main trailhead is at Bar K Wrangler Camp. To reach it, drive south from Chadwick on MO 125 for 6 miles. You will see a sign for Bar K Wrangler Camp on the left. Turn left onto this dirt road, and follow it one-half mile to the camp. The trails start on the far side of Swan Creek.

Sources of additional information:

Mark Twain National Forest
Business Route 5 South
Post Office Box 188
Ava, MO 65608
(417) 683-4428

Sunshine Bicycles and Fitness
1926 East Sunshine
Springfield, MO 65804
(417) 883-1113

A & B Cycles
220 West Walnut
Springfield, MO 65806
(417) 866-6621
or
3201 South Campbell
Springfield, MO 65807
(417) 881-5940

Notes on the trail: Sometimes Swan Creek is too deep to cross, preventing access to the trails from the trailhead. Or worse, if you are riding the trails when heavy rains occur, the creek can rise and prevent you from getting back to your car. Not to worry. You can reach County Road UU from the eastern end of the trail system.

To reach CR UU, bushwhack straight east from any point until you strike the road. It is easiest, though, if you find the junction of Tin Top and Math Branch trails. From there, a sign points down an abandoned double-track to CR UU. Follow it for 1 mile, and you'll strike the highway one-half mile south of a dirt road marked UU 11. From here, ride south to MO 125, and then north on MO 125 to Bar K.

You could also access the trail system from CR UU, saving you from crossing Swan Creek. The access point is 5 miles south of the intersection of CR T and UU, or 5 miles north of the intersection of MO 125 and CR UU. There are no markings. Look for an old double-track on the outside of a curve in UU, just south of CR UU 11. Park your car here and ride down the old double-track. After a short distance, you'll come to a gate. Ride around it, take a right at the first fork, and 1 mile later you'll be at the intersection of the Math Branch and Tin Top trails.

RIDE 27 *MARK TWAIN SOUTHWEST: RIDGE RUNNER TRAIL*

If you like challenging mountain biking in a wilderness setting, you'll love the Ridge Runner Trail. Divided into two loops, the Noblett Loop to the north and the North Fork Loop to the south, this entire 38-mile trail is narrow single-track and abandoned logging roads. Long climbs are followed by fast, cooling descents. Stream crossings on the Noblett Loop make that ride bearable on hot summer days.

Because there are steep and technical sections scattered throughout the trail, the Ridge Runner is not recommended for beginners. All riders should occasionally expect to portage their bikes, especially on the more difficult Noblett Loop of the Ridge Runner, where parts of the climbs are too rugged to ride and the stream crossings can be waist-deep.

RIDE 27 *MARK TWAIN SOUTHWEST: RIDGE RUNNER TRAIL*

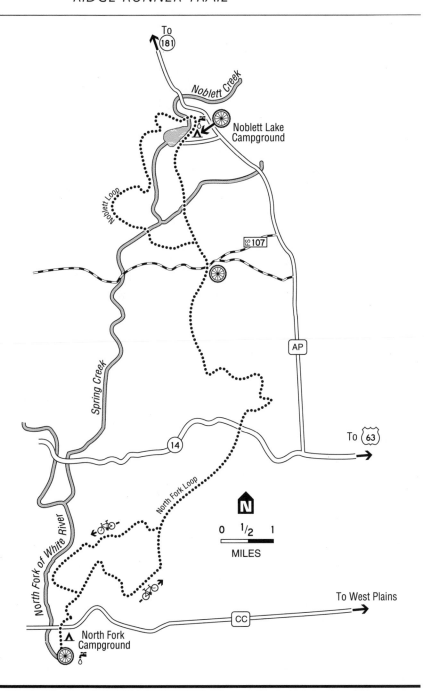

Single-track through the forest along the connector trail between the North Fork Loop and the Noblett Loop of the Ridge Runner Trail.

The North Fork Loop of the Ridge Runner, named for the nearby North Fork of the White River, is a little easier. Still, it has several challenging sections, and can't be considered an easy ride. If you ride the North Fork counter-clockwise you will face the most difficult hill, the steep grade from the ridge above the White River down to stream level, as a long, scenic descent. You'll find that riding in that direction will enable you to stay on your bike for almost the entire ride if you are in good physical condition.

If you have the luxury of a support driver, try pedaling the Ridge Runner from Noblett Lake to North Fork Recreation Area. The trail connecting the two loops has some very scenic sections, passing through a forest burn and a huge, deep hollow. The hollow is known as the Blue Hole because of its appearance on misty mornings. If you stay on the easier eastern portion of the Noblett Loop and the scenic western portion of the North Fork Loop on either end of the connector, you will have a great point-to-point ride that you can cap with a splash in the White River at North Fork Recreation Area.

These loops sound tough, but don't let that scare you away from this beautiful spot in the southern Missouri Ozarks. This near-wilderness area is one of the more remote mountain biking experiences in Missouri. Though you face long and difficult climbs, the views from the ridge-tops and descents back to the hollows more than make up for the effort. For the easiest ride, ride the North Fork Loop by itself, pedaling the loop counter-clockwise to take advantage of the grade next to the North Fork as described above.

North Fork Recreation Area is also a great place to camp. Nestled in a bend of the North Fork of the White River, the area lies just across the water from Devil's Backbone Wilderness Area to the west. You can camp at North Fork, ride the trail one day, and hike in Devil's Backbone or take a relaxing canoe float on the White River the next. Outfitters are located in the nearby towns of Dora and Twin Bridges.

General location: 18 miles west of West Plains.
Elevation change: Elevation on the North Fork Loop ranges from 700′ along the White River to 1,050′ at several high points along the ridges. There are 6 major climbs ranging in length from a quarter to a half mile, with corresponding descents. The Noblett Loop elevations range from 800′ to 1,100′, with 7 challenging climbs of one-quarter to one-half mile.
Season: Spring and fall are best for riding the Ridge Runner Trail. Wildflower enthusiasts will especially love this trail in spring, when the woods and glades are covered with bird's foot violet, wild sweet William, wild blue phlox, spiderwort, spring beauties, flowering dogwood, and many other colorful blooms.

Because the trail often traverses south-facing slopes, summers can be sweltering. Swimming in the White River near the North Fork Loop and in Noblett Lake on the Noblett Loop can cool you off after a hot summer ride. The Noblett Loop also features 3 deep stream crossings on Noblett and Spring creeks. Those crossings make winter riding a chilling experience.

The North Fork Loop crosses few streams that flow all year, and is a better bet for winter riding.
Services: Drinking water and camping are available at both Noblett Lake and North Fork recreation areas. All other services except bike shops are available at Willow Springs, 15 miles east of Noblett Lake, and at West Plains, 18 miles east of North Fork. The nearest bike shops are in Springfield, 80 miles to the west.
Hazards: Many of the climbs and descents on the Noblett Loop are rocky, steep, and technical. Lack of caution could lead to oral soil sampling. Don't attempt to cross Spring and Noblett creeks during high water.

On the North Fork Loop the trail is a little easier, but is still difficult in places. You will need to be especially careful on the long grade from the White River to the ridge above Steam Mill Hollow. It is rocky, with steep drop-offs. You should take the loop counter-clockwise so that you can ride this as a descent rather than a climb.

Rescue index: While the Ridge Runner Trail is well marked and easy to follow, parts of it are only moderately used. On weekends you are likely to encounter other trail users. On weekdays, you will probably be on your own. The loop trails cross few roads, so you will have to make your own way back to the trailhead if you get in a jam.

The connector trail crosses MO 14. A half mile east of the crossing is Bill's Grocery, where you can get assistance. Another road crossed by the connector is Forest Service Road 107, near the Horton trailhead. There are farmhouses just east of Horton on FS 107, and County Road AP, 1 mile to the east.

Land status: National forest.

Maps: The Forest Service produces an excellent map of this trail. It is available at the Willow Springs office of the Mark Twain. The 7.5 minute topo covering the Noblett Loop is Dyestone Mountain. Those covering the North Fork Loop are Siloam Springs and Dora.

Finding the trail: There are 3 trailheads on the Ridge Runner. The northern one is in Noblett Lake Recreation Area. To reach it, drive 9 miles west of Willow Springs on MO 76 to MO 181. Turn south on 181, and go 1.5 miles to CR AP. Continue south (left) on CR AP an additional 3 miles to the entrance to Noblett Lake Recreation Area. The trailhead is just next to the campground.

The south trailhead is in North Fork Recreation Area on the White River. Drive 18 miles west of West Plains on CR CC to reach this campground. Park in the lot next to the Ridge Runner trailhead sign.

The third access point is Horton Cemetery, located in the northern section of the connector trail. Drive 3 miles south from Noblett Lake on CR AP to Forest Service Road 107. Go west 2 miles on FS 107 to the parking area for the Horton trailhead.

Sources of additional information:

Mark Twain National Forest
Post Office Box 99
Willow Springs, MO 65793
(417) 469-3155

The Alpine Shop
601 East Lockwood
Webster Groves, MO 63119
(314) 962-7715

Notes on the trail: The most difficult and technical grade on the North Fork Loop is near the White River, where the trail ascends to the ridge above Steam Mill Hollow. To avoid climbing this, ride this loop in a counter-clockwise direction.

On the Noblett Loop ascents are steep and rough, usually requiring technical bike skills. Beginners should not attempt the Noblett Loop.

The Ridge Runner Trail is marked by white plastic diamonds nailed to trees at intervals of 100–300 feet. A horse trail also passes through the northern portion of the Noblett Loop. It intersects the Noblett Loop at several points.

You will immediately notice your mistake if you accidentally get on the horse trail. It is marked by diamonds bearing a horse silhouette.

The distances marked on the Forest Service map are a bit off. They state the Noblett Loop as 8 miles, and the North Fork Loop as 12 miles. My bike computer pegged them at 12 and 14 miles respectively. If you ride from Noblett Lake to North Fork, you will cover around 22–25 miles, depending on which side of each loop you ride. The east portion of the Noblett Loop is better riding, while the west portion of the North Fork Loop gives you a beautiful descent to and ride along the White River. Total distance on that route is 22 miles.

About halfway between Noblett Lake and North Fork recreation areas, you will cross MO 14. If you ride east around a half mile, you will find Bill's Grocery, where you can get a cold drink and some trail food.

RIDE 28 *MARK TWAIN SOUTHWEST: KAINTUCK TRAIL*

The Kaintuck Trail is a good place for beginners, with its network of mostly easy-to-ride loop selections varying in length from 2 to 13 miles. The trail surfaces run the gamut, from gravel forest roads on the east side of the network, to double-track logging access roads along the west side, to narrow single-track and abandoned double-track roads on the rest of the system. Many side paths leading off the main route to old logging cuts offer additional miles of mountain biking. And, in the center of the network, a spectacular natural bridge awaits you.

Most of the trails here are easily handled by beginners, although a few rough and steep single-track sections will be more than most novices can take. The most difficult stretch is a steep and technical half mile in the northwest part of the main loop, where the trail climbs from Mill Creek to the top of the ridge dividing the Kaintuck and Mill Creek drainages.

The Kaintuck Trail encompasses Kaintuck Hollow, the ridge towering over Kaintuck to the west, several clear streams, springs, and the faint remains of old farmsteads.

One of the side loops leads to Wilkins Spring Pond, a beautiful little lake in the valley on the west side of the ridge. There is a picnic site at the spring, making it a perfect place for a mid-ride break. At the south end of the pond is the spring that feeds the lake. It puts out three million gallons of water a day.

Then you have the spectacular centerpiece of this trail system—the 175-foot-long natural bridge at the heart of the network. A spring bubbles out of the earth just north of the bridge, flows through the bridge, and joins a stream on the other side. The bridge is so large that you can hike through it with no trouble at all. A segment of the trail passes near this tunnel-like wonder, so it's easy to find.

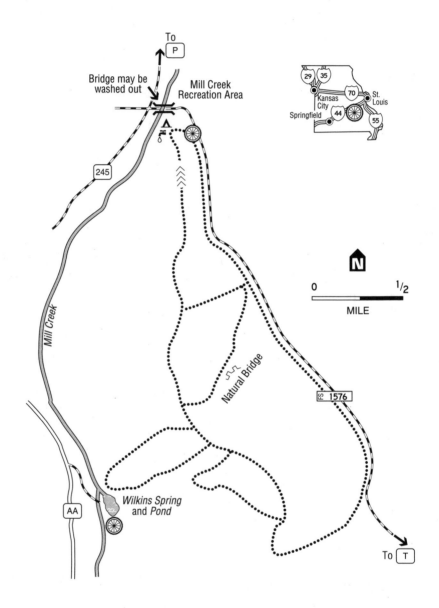

To
P

Bridge may be
washed out

Mill Creek
Recreation Area

245

Mill Creek

N

0   1/2
MILE

Natural Bridge

FS 1576

Wilkins Spring
and *Pond*

AA

To T

29 35
70
Kansas
City   St.
Louis
Springfield
44
55

General location: 15 miles southwest of Rolla.

Elevation change: Elevations range from 750′ at Mill Creek Recreation Area to 1,000′ in the southern reaches of the trail system.

Season: Spring and fall are the best seasons for riding this trail system. Summer can be good if you cool off in the streams flowing through the area. You can also hang out for a while in the cave created by the natural bridge. Winter riding can also be fun, but you should be prepared to deal with wet feet at creek crossings.

Services: Drinking water and camping are available at Mill Creek Recreation Area. Grocery stores and restaurants are in Newburg, 5 miles to the east of Mill Creek. All other services are available in Rolla, 15 miles to the east.

Hazards: Don't cross Kaintuck or Mill creeks during high water.

Rescue index: While sections of the trail in this network are seldom used, you are never far from a road. If you find yourself in trouble in the eastern portion of the loop, make your way to FS 1576 and await help. If you have problems along the loop's western edge, go to Wilkins Spring Pond; you will be likely to find help there.

Land status: National forest.

Maps: You can get a map of the Kaintuck Trail from the Forest Service office in Rolla. The USGS topo covering the area is the Kaintuck Hollow 7.5 minute map.

Finding the trail: Go 5 miles west from Rolla on Interstate 44 to the Doolittle exit. Drive 3 miles south on County Road T, passing through Doolittle and Newburg, to CR P. Go 3 miles west on CR P to CR 245, a dirt road leading south. There will be a sign pointing the way to Mill Creek Recreation Area, 2 miles down CR 245.

Following CR 245, turn left on FS 1576 just past Mill Creek Recreation Area's picnic site, and follow it one-half mile to a small parking area on the right side of the road. This is the trailhead. It is at the extreme north end of the trail system. The east side of the trail system follows FS 1576 to the south. Riding west from the trailhead on a double-track road will take you to the long, steep climb that ends at the ridge-top double-track which is the western edge of the trail system. (At the time of this writing, the bridge across Mill Creek on FS 1576 at the campground was washed out. If this is still the case, park your car at the picnic area, ford the creek with your bike, and ride the half mile to the trailhead.)

Sources of additional information:

Mark Twain National Forest
Houston-Rolla District
108 South Sam Houston Boulevard
Houston, MO 65483
(417) 967-4194

The Alpine Shop
601 East Lockwood
Webster Groves, MO 63119
(314) 962-7715

Notes on the trail: Forest Service Road 1576 to the east is an easy ride, taking you along the bottom of Kaintuck Hollow. The main trail at the west side of the system is fairly level riding along the ridge-top above the hollow. The rest of the trails climb and descend between these two paths. The most difficult climb occurs when you ride southbound from Mill Creek on the northwest side of the loop. To avoid a steep climb, ride this section of the trail northbound.

Because the trail markings in the Kaintuck are not very good, it can be easy to get lost. Adding to the confusion are several old logging roads branching off the official trail. Although they occasionally make things more confusing, these roads offer additional miles of trail riding. If you carry a map and consult it often to verify where you are, you will have little trouble finding your way.

Once you get to know this network, it will become one of your favorites. If you do become lost, work your way in any direction but south. To the east, you'll soon intersect FS 1576 or CR T. To the west, you'll reach either CR AA or CR 245, which you can follow back to Mill Creek. By working your way north, you will eventually reach either FS 1576 or Mill Creek Recreation Area.

Ozark Trail

In 1977, a group of land managers, land owners, and trail users met to discuss the possibility of a long-distance trail in the Missouri Ozarks. From this meeting grew the concept of the Ozark Trail. The Ozark Trail Council was formed to oversee the trail's development.

At the same time, a similar group was meeting in Arkansas to begin development of that state's Ozark Highlands Trail. The dream is to connect the two trails, resulting in a long-distance trekker's route reaching 700 miles from near Fayetteville, Arkansas, to the St. Louis area.

Two hundred miles of the Ozark Trail have now been completed. Those miles pass through a country of deep hollows, clear streams, breezy ridge-tops, and panoramic views. The trail follows single-track and abandoned logging roads common to the southern Missouri forests. Parts of this beautiful trail are rugged. Expect stream crossings, rocky stretches requiring portages, and some technical climbs and descents.

For the purposes of this book, the parts of the trail open to mountain biking have been divided into sections of 10–20 miles in length. Road return routes are described for those who don't wish to ride the trail both ways. Distances were chosen with an eye to difficulty and proximity to road crossings and trailheads. You should be able to cover any of these rides in one day. The trail is marked by white plastic diamonds and occasional plastic rectangles, both bearing the Ozark Trail symbol.

One of the best features of the Ozark Trail is its proximity to some of Missouri's best canoeing rivers. Leave your bike behind now and then, rent a canoe from one of the outfitters in the area, and do the Huck Finn thing. The Current and Jacks Fork rivers are easy to paddle and very accessible. The more remote Eleven Point River passes next to the Irish Wilderness Area. It has fewer access points, some mild rapids, and a secluded wilderness atmosphere.

The Ozark Trail is built and maintained by various land agencies and volunteer groups. If you would like to become involved in making the completion of the Ozark Trail a reality, write:

Missouri Department of Natural Resources
Ozark Trail Coordinator
Post Office Box 176
Jefferson City, MO 65102

RIDE 29 *MARBLE CREEK SECTION*

This is an eight-mile point-to-point ride between Marble Creek and Crane Lake on the Ozark Trail. There is an optional five-mile loop around the lake.

For most of its length the trail is single-track suitable for riders of all skill levels. The trail alternates between climbs to scenic ridge-tops and descents to cool, wooded hollows. There are a couple of very difficult sections that will require portages. The first of these is four miles west of Marble Creek. There the trail enters a set of small rocky glades, and then descends a steep, rugged slope. You will probably have to carry your bike for about a quarter mile.

There is also a very rough quarter-mile stretch on the loop around Crane Lake that will have to be portaged. The payoff for your trouble is the scenic beauty of the panoramic views from the glades, and a beautiful series of shut-ins, pools, and waterfalls in Reader Hollow near Crane Lake.

This ride is in the rugged St. Francis Mountains. Marble Creek is named for the deposits of colorful dolomite found along its course. These dolomites and sandstones in the valley were deposited as sediment on ancient sea floors 500 million years ago. Marble Creek is also the site of an old grist mill; the dam and building foundations are still in place.

General location: 20 miles west of Fredericktown.
Elevation change: Elevations vary from a minimum of 680′ at Marble Creek to a high of 1,100′ on the rough stretch of trail near the glade. On the trail between Marble Creek and Crane Lake there are 4 major climbs and descents. They vary in length from one-quarter to one-half mile. On the loop around Crane Lake, there is one major climb and long descent, each just under a half mile in length. If roads are used for the return to the trailhead, there will be another climb and descent.
Season: Spring and fall, with their more moderate temperatures, are the best times to ride this trail. While summer can be hot, the heat can be beaten by swimming in Crane Lake, splashing in the shut-ins along Crane Pond Creek below the lake's outlet, or in Marble Creek at the eastern trailhead.
Services: During the warm months, water is available at Marble Creek Recreation Area. It is turned off during the late fall and winter. No drinking water is available at Crane Lake. Camping is available at Marble Creek.

Gasoline, groceries, and restaurants are in Ironton, 15 miles west of Marble Creek on County Road E, or in Fredericktown, 20 miles to the east. Fredericktown also has hotels. The nearest bike shops are in St. Louis, 100 miles to the north.
Hazards: The few extremely rocky sections on the trail provide excellent opportunities to break some of those rocks with your teeth as you fly gracefully over your handlebars. Be careful! Portaging is encouraged.

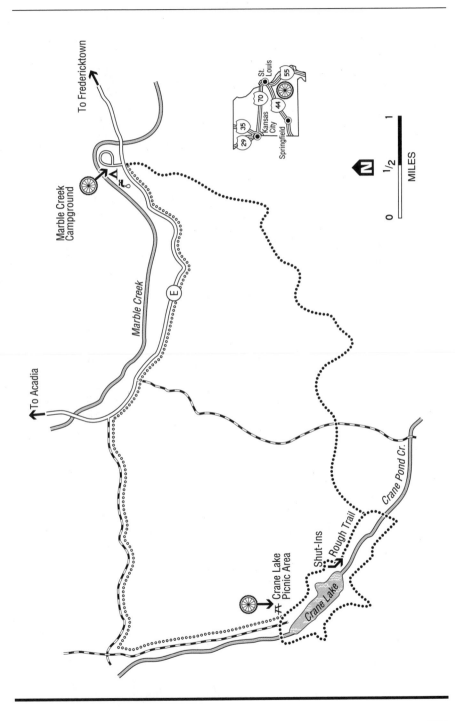

You should also be careful on the stretch of trail that passes the shut-ins on Crane Pond Creek, then climbs above them to the overlook. The view is great, but the fall is long.

Rescue index: The relatively short distance covered by this ride means you are never very far from help. Between Marble Creek and Crane Lake the trail crosses 2 gravel roads that offer escape points. The trail sees moderate use on weekends, so you should be discovered if you get into trouble. During the week you will probably be on your own, so you should make your way to one of the roads crossed by the trail. The nearest town is Ironton, 15 miles to the west.

Land status: National forest.

Maps: A map of the Fredericktown Ranger District of the Mark Twain National Forest will help you find the trail. The best map is that of the Marble Creek Section of the Ozark Trail. The Crane Lake Recreation Area brochure will show the trail around the lake. Should you wish to use a topo map, carry the 7.5 minute Des Arc NE.

Finding the trail: While starting at Marble Creek is recommended because water is available there, the ride can also begin at Crane Lake. To start from Marble Creek, drive 20 miles west of Fredericktown on CR E. You'll see the campground immediately after you cross the bridge over Marble Creek. Park at the trailhead parking lot for the Ozark Trail just inside the recreation area.

To start the ride from Crane Lake, drive 24 miles west of Fredericktown on CR E to a gravel road bearing south. There will be a sign indicating the way to Crane Lake. Follow this road 2.5 miles to an intersection, and turn left (south). Driving 2 miles down this road will take you to the lake. Park in the picnic area.

Sources of additional information:

Mark Twain National Forest
Route 2 Highways 72 and 0
Fredericktown, MO 63645
(314) 783-7225

The Alpine Shop
601 East Lockwood
Webster Groves, MO 63119
(314) 962-7715

Notes on the trail: The north side of the trail around Crane Lake follows Crane Pond Creek past a series of beautiful shut-ins, pools, and waterfalls in Reader Hollow. Then it climbs up a rocky hillside to ledges with great views of the lake and the rugged hollow containing the shut-ins. Though this stretch of the trail is rough and must be portaged, the scenic beauty is well worth the effort. If you don't feel like manhandling your bike over the rocks, stash it in the woods and hike to the overlook.

Note that parts of the loop around Crane Lake can be confusing. While the trail on the north side of the lake is a well-marked portion of the Ozark Trail, the southside markings were faint or nonexistent when this book was written. By carrying a map and studying it when in doubt, you should be able to avoid losing your way.

The south side of the lake is much easier riding than the northside trail, but it is much less scenic. Beginners riding from Marble Creek to Crane Lake are advised to avoid the unrideable portion by finishing the ride on the southside trail.

You can ride this trail three ways. If you want to stay in the woods and away from civilization, you can ride it as an out-and-back trail.

Second, if a support vehicle is available, you can ride the trail one way, with a pick-up at either end.

Third, if you don't want to cover the same ground twice and have no support option, you can make the ride into a loop by using gravel and asphalt roads to return to the starting point. To do this, start at Marble Creek and ride the trail to Crane Lake. Leave the lake northbound on the gravel road from the picnic area. Turn right at the first intersection about 2 miles north of the lake. Follow this second gravel road 2.5 miles to CR E. Turn right (east) on CR E and ride 4 miles to the trailhead at Marble Creek Recreation Area.

RIDE 30 OZARK TRAIL: *BLUE RIDGE TRAIL LOOP*

Scenic vistas, stream fords, caves, springs, wildflowers—this 21-mile loop is a wealth of wonders. That's why the Blue Ridge Trail Loop is my favorite ride on the Ozark Trail.

The north part of the loop follows the Blue Ridge Horse Trail, and the south leg follows the westernmost 11 miles of the Eleven Point River segment of the Ozark Trail. Six miles of the north leg along the horse trail are old washed-out double-track, 1.5 miles follow gravel roads, and three miles are on single-track. Short stretches of the single-track are technical, and may require portages.

The south half of the loop along the Ozark Trail follows nine miles of hilly single-track through the forest and two miles of double-track in open bottom-lands. The westernmost two miles of the south leg are rocky and moderately technical. These rough miles and the several other rocky stretches may force beginners to portage their bikes. Persevere, though, and you will find that the remaining single-track is less difficult. There will be long climbs and descents, but switchbacks make the grades manageable.

The Blue Ridge Trail Loop winds through low wooded mountains surrounding Spring Creek, a tributary of the nearby Eleven Point Scenic River. You'll climb to breezy ridge-tops, snake along through the highlands for a while, and then descend to shady, quiet hollows, where cool stream crossings await.

The many stream crossings are a blast for warm-weather riders. Depending on the amount of recent rainfall, the fords vary from brief splashes through shal-

RIDE 30   *OZARK TRAIL: BLUE RIDGE TRAIL LOOP*

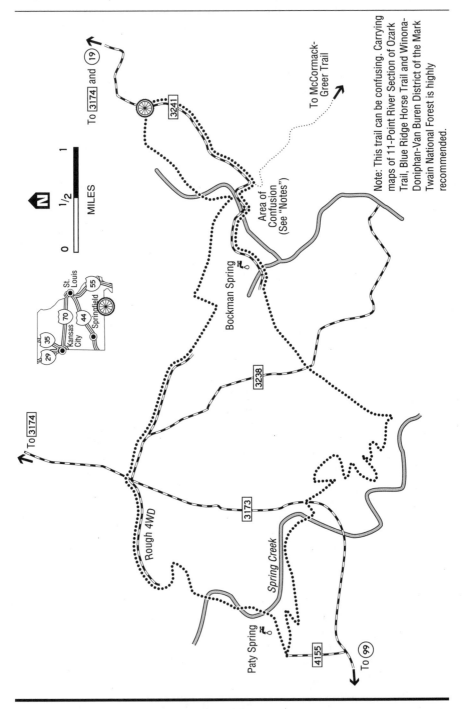

Note: This trail can be confusing. Carrying maps of 11-Point River Section of Ozark Trail, Blue Ridge Horse Trail and Winona-Doniphan–Van Buren District of the Mark Twain National Forest is highly recommended.

Ride the Blue Ridge Trail Loop in spring, and you'll splash through some great water crossings. Here, in the eastern part of the Blue Ridge Horse Trail, the water can be hub-deep.

low streams to 100-foot-long stretches where creeks flow down the double-track roads used by the trail. Paty Spring along the north side of the loop and Bockman Spring on the south bubble from the rocks and add their flows to the nearby creeks. Bockman Spring tumbles out of a shallow cave. The front of this cave was used for years as a natural refrigerator for early settlers in Bull Camp Hollow.

At the junction of Bull Camp and Wolf Pen hollows you'll cross large open meadows before climbing onto the Devil's Backbone, a narrow, rough, spine-like ridge dividing the two hollows. Along the south side of the loop, the trail follows a bluff for one-half mile, giving you a bird's-eye view of the lower Spring Creek drainage.

In spring on the Blue Ridge Trail Loop, swollen creeks often overflow and run down the trail for short distances, making your ride an enjoyable splash through streams.

General location: 15 miles southwest of Winona.

Elevation change: Elevation varies from a low of 650´ in the Spring Creek bottomlands to a high of 900´ at the trailhead. Cyclists riding the entire loop will face 5 climbs and descents varying in length from a quarter to a half mile, and one three-quarter-mile climb and descent. All are rideable by cyclists in good condition, provided they ride the loop in the recommended counter-clockwise direction.

Season: Spring and fall are the best seasons to ride the Blue Ridge Trail Loop. In addition to enjoying more stream fords, spring and early summer riders will be treated to awesome displays of wildflowers, including a large bed of honeysuckle, lilac, and multiflora rose near Paty Spring. Hummingbirds can often be spotted darting from blossom to blossom on this patch of blooms.

The numerous stream crossings possible in times of plentiful rainfall may make winter riding a chilly proposition. These creek fords will make the heat and humidity of summer rides easier to deal with, although if there's been a dry spell, the streams will probably be dry. Hot-weather cyclists should also be prepared to deal with ticks and mosquitoes in the Spring Creek bottomlands.

Services: No drinking water is available along the trail. Water from streams and springs should be purified before drinking. Water and camping are available at nearby McCormack Lake and Greer Crossing recreation areas.

Groceries, gas, and restaurants can be found in Winona, 15 miles to the northeast. Hotels are in Eminence, 35 miles to the north, or in Van Buren, 22 miles east of Winona. The nearest bike shops are in Springfield, 150 miles to the west.

Hazards: During heavy rains, flooding is a problem along Spring Creek. Do not risk your life by attempting to cross Spring Creek or other small streams during high water. If you meet horses on this loop, stand to the downhill side of the trail and wait quietly for them to pass.

Rescue index: The nearest town is Winona, 15 miles to the north. The Blue Ridge Horse Trail and the Ozark Trail are infrequently used. Should you get into a jam, try to make your way to one of the roads crossed by the loop and await a passing motorist.

Land status: National forest.

Maps: Maps of the Blue Ridge Horse Trail and the Eleven Point River Section of the Ozark Trail are excellent supplements to the accompanying map. Carrying both is highly recommended. A map of the national forest will also be a great help if you want to use forest roads to shorten your ride. The USGS topo for this loop is the 7.5 minute Piedmont Hollow map.

Finding the trail: Drive 10 miles south of Winona on MO 19 to Forest Service Road 3174 (known locally as Flat Pond Road). There will be a sign with a horse silhouette directing you to the trailhead. Drive west 1 mile on FS 3174 to FS 3241. Following another horse trail sign, turn south and follow FS 3241 2 miles to the trailhead for the Blue Ridge Horse Trail.

Sources of additional information:

Mark Twain National Forest
Route 1 Box 1908, Highway 19 North
Winona, MO 65588
(314) 325-4233

The Alpine Shop
601 East Lockwood
Webster Groves, MO 63119
(314) 962-7715

Notes on the trail: Although this superb trail has rocky and technical sections, it is rideable for most of its length by cyclists of all skill levels. If you are against walking your bike occasionally, don't ride this trail as a beginner. But with a positive attitude and good physical conditioning, you should have no problem. If you still find the trail to be too difficult, you can leave it at a road crossing and follow scenic forest roads back to your car.

The north part of the loop along the horse trail is marked by blue diamonds nailed to trees. The south side along the Ozark Trail is marked by white diamonds. I recommend that you ride the loop counter-clockwise. This lets you do the easier horse trail first, leaving the most technical sections as descents rather than climbs. At the end of the horse trail, stronger riders can then continue on with the loop, while those not wanting to continue the single-track riding can return to the trailhead via roads shown on the National Forest map.

The route gets a little confusing in the area of Bull Camp Hollow and Devil's Backbone, where the loop closes. Ride it counter-clockwise. You will be on double-track around a half mile east of Bockman Spring when you'll see a sign pointing to a connector trail back to the Blue Ridge Horse Trail. Following this connector will take you back to the trailhead, but you'll cover some trail you've already seen, and you will have to climb a steep, washed-out section of single-track through a clear-cut.

To take an easier and more scenic route back to the trailhead, follow the double-track connecting trail around a quarter mile. At that point, look for another double-track to your right. Take it. It will be marked by white Ozark Trail diamonds. You will cross a stream, climb up onto the Devil's Backbone, and find a fork in the road. Take the left fork, which is FS 3241 (unmarked), and follow it a mile and a half to the trailhead.

RIDE 31 *OZARK TRAIL: MCCORMACK-GREER AREA*

Long climbs and several rocky, technical sections make this stretch of the Ozark Trail somewhat difficult. It consists of 11 miles of single-track, with another 10 miles added on the road return route. It is recommended for experienced riders. However, since the trail is relatively short, with an opportunity to bail out three miles into the ride, more adventurous beginners may wish to give it a shot.

This first three miles is the easiest and most scenic. Novices should expect to portage their bikes several times. Nearly all the Ozark Trail on this section is single-track. The numerous rocks in the trail vary from beds of small loose stones to shelf-like rock outcroppings that are a fun challenge to cross. A few of the bottomland sections of the trail follow double-track hardpack roads. Windfall is common.

For its first four miles west of Greer Crossing the trail parallels the Eleven Point River. It alternates between flat bottomland and scenic overlooks high above this clear, spring-fed stream. One mile west of Greer, you will see Greer Spring Branch tumbling into the Eleven Point. This stream is fed by Greer Spring, the second largest spring in Missouri. Its output makes the river perceptibly larger below the branch. After your ride, cross the river and hike in to see this most beautiful spring.

Another mile west and one long climb later, you will be at the Boomhole View overlook, a bluff-top panorama of the Eleven Point. Around the turn of the century, the bluff across the river to the southwest held a wooden chute, down which large pine logs were plunged into the river below, splashing into the

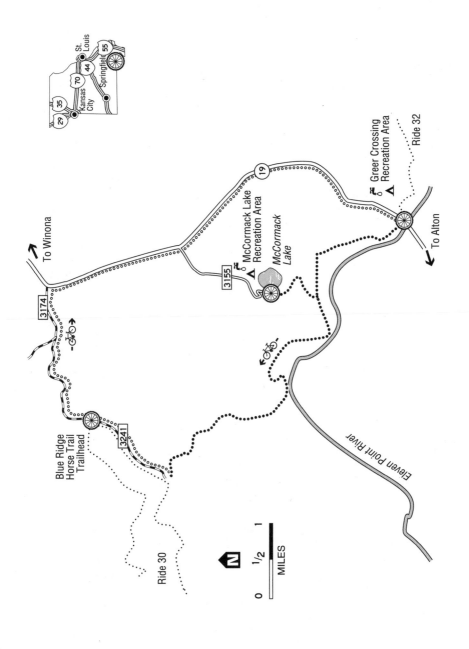

stream with a thunderous boom. Two miles past the Boomhole is a three-quarter-mile climb to the highest point on the trail, where rock outcroppings provide perfect seats for enjoying the view of the river below. Next, the trail descends for about a half mile back down to the Eleven Point, where it follows a shelf 100 feet above the river. The trail then leaves the river for good, climbing up to the head of Becky Hollow, and continuing west toward the junction with the Blue Ridge Horse Trail.

General location: 16 miles south of Winona.

Elevation change: The lowest points on this ride are along the Eleven Point River, which parallels the trail for several miles. From this low of 550′ you will climb three-quarters of a mile to a scenic overlook at 900′. There you will enjoy a fantastic view of the river below.

Following the climb is a descent back down to the Eleven Point. There are 3 other climbs and descents varying in length from one-quarter to one-half mile, and numerous smaller hills.

Season: Spring and fall are the best. Temperatures are moderate, fewer bugs are about, and spring wildflowers and fall colors decorate the landscape. Summer riding may be hot and humid, but a swim or canoe trip in the Eleven Point River will remedy those disadvantages. Views from ridge-tops are better in winter when the foliage is gone, but you should be prepared for chilly stream crossings.

Services: Drinking water and camping are available at Greer Crossing and McCormack Lake recreation areas. Groceries, gas, and restaurants are in Winona, 16 miles north of Greer Crossing.

Hotels may be found in Eminence, 35 miles to the north of Greer Crossing, or in Van Buren, 22 miles east of Winona. The nearest bike shops are in Springfield, 150 miles west of Winona.

Hazards: Do not ride in the Eleven Point River bottomlands or cross its tributaries during high water. Be cautious riding next to the cliffs near the Boomhole View overlook.

Rescue index: On nice weekends, the section of trail between McCormack Lake and Greer Crossing recreation areas sees lots of use. The remainder of the single-track trail is used only occasionally. If you have problems on this part of the trail, you should be prepared to take care of yourself.

Land status: National forest.

Maps: A map of the Eleven Point River Section of the Ozark Trail will show all the single-track covered by this ride. Also useful would be a map of the McCormack-Greer Trail, which shows the eastern end of this ride in greater detail. It would be especially useful for those who only want to ride this shorter and more scenic part of the trail.

A map of the Winona-Doniphan-Van Buren Ranger District of the Mark Twain will show you how to use roads to return to the trailhead, and will be useful for other rides in the area. The USGS topos for the area are the 7.5 minute Piedmont Hollow and Greer maps.

Finding the trail: Greer Crossing Recreation Area is the best starting point for this ride. It is 16 miles south of Winona on MO 19, where the highway crosses the Eleven Point. Park in the picnic area. The trail begins there, and goes under the highway bridge next to the river.

The trail can also be accessed from McCormack Lake, 14 miles south of Winona on MO 19 and then 2 miles southwest on Forest Service Road 3155. From McCormack Lake, a 1-mile spur trail leads south from the dam to the main trail.

Sources of additional information:

Mark Twain National Forest
Route 1 Box 1908, Highway 19 North
Winona, MO 65588
(314) 325-4233

The Alpine Shop
601 East Lockwood
Webster Groves, MO 63119
(314) 962-7715

Notes on the trail: As stated in the introduction, this trail is not recommended for beginners. Novices with a positive attitude may want to try it anyway. If you find it too difficult, it's easy enough to bail out at McCormack Lake after 3 miles. You will have seen some of the best scenery by this point, anyhow, and will have covered the easiest stretch of the trail.

The first time I rode this trail one of our riders was a beginner. Although the ride was difficult, she didn't find the trail too intimidating. She thought it was well worth the effort.

The trail is marked by white plastic diamonds. The only confusing point comes at mile 11, where you will need to leave the trail to return to Greer Crossing via roads. You will have just climbed out of Becky Hollow, crossed a gravel road, and descended into Three Mile Hollow. At the bottom of Three Mile Hollow, the trail strikes a rutted double-track road, then follows it to the west.

After about a half mile of level riding, the road and trail veer to the right and begin to climb up onto Devil's Backbone. One-quarter mile up the climb, the double-track turns hard right to the northeast, and the Ozark Trail leaves the double-track to the west. Veer to the right and stay on the double-track, still climbing, and a short distance later you will come to a fork. The left fork goes downhill to connect with the Blue Ridge Horse Trail Loop. You should take the right fork, continuing uphill. This is FS 3241, and following it for 1.5 miles will take you to the Blue Ridge Horse Trail parking area.

Continue north past the trailhead on FS 3241 approximately 2 miles to its intersection with FS 3174. Turn right on FS 3174, and ride 1 mile to MO 19.

Turning south (right) on MO 19 and riding 6 miles will take you back to the trailhead in Greer Crossing Recreation Area.

RIDE 32 OZARK TRAIL: SINKING CREEK LOOKOUT TO GREER CROSSING

This 18-mile, out-and-back section of the Ozark Trail can be made into a loop by returning to the starting point on gravel forest roads. Using the road return route results in a total distance of 30 miles.

While most of the all-single-track trail is not extremely difficult, it does include a deep stream crossing, several short technical sections that may require portages, and several long climbs. Deadfall is common along the trail.

This ride is recommended for riders with intermediate skills, but could be handled by novices with adventurous attitudes. Beginners should be prepared to portage when necessary. The option to leave the trail at its midpoint and return to the trailhead by road will make it less intimidating (see "Notes on the trail").

The Sinking Creek Lookout Tower, the eastern trailhead for this trail section, is on the divide between the Current and Eleven Point rivers. This part of the Ozark Trail undulates like a roller coaster over the ridges and hollows of the tributaries of the Eleven Point River. You will enjoy riding a narrow wilderness trail, working your way up long climbs to breezy ridge-tops, and descending into the next hollow.

Hurricane Creek, near the halfway point of the single-track, is a knee-deep splash through a clear Ozark stream. Just west of the creek is a half-mile climb to Letter Look, a scenic view of the junction of the valleys of Hurricane Creek and the Eleven Point.

Continuing west, you'll ride through Wilderness Hollow and Graveyard Hollow, and then end your trail ride at Greer Crossing Recreation Area on the Eleven Point River. A swim in this cool, spring-fed stream is a perfect way to cap a fun and challenging ride, so I recommend that you ride east to west.

If you have an extra day to kill, camp at Greer Crossing and float the Eleven Point in a canoe. It is one of Missouri's best float streams. Canoe rentals are available from several outfitters in the area. Check with the Forest Service for phone numbers of local outfitters.

General location: 20 miles southeast of Winona.

Elevation change: At 1,025´, Sinking Creek Lookout Tower is the highest point on this ride. From this peak, the trail drops to 525´ at Greer Crossing on the Eleven Point River. There are 8 climbs and descents. The longest is three-quarters of a mile, and the shortest is one-quarter mile. With the exception of a few short and rocky sections, all the climbs are rideable by cyclists in good physical condition.

RIDE 32 OZARK TRAIL:
SINKING CREEK LOOKOUT TO GREER CROSSING

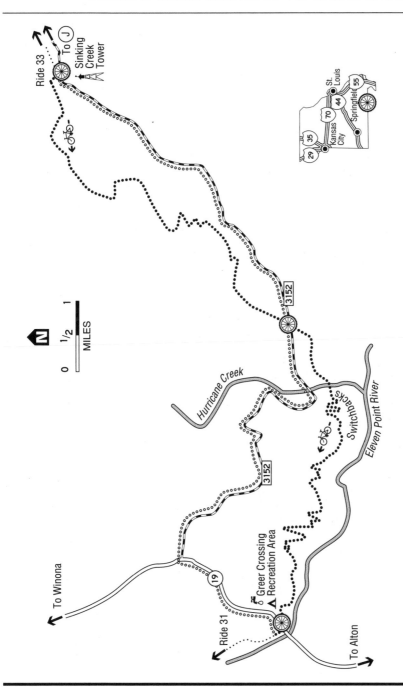

Season: Spring and fall are best for riding anywhere in the Ozarks, and this trail is no exception. Summer riding can be good here, since the ride can be combined with a canoe trip or swim in the Eleven Point. Good riding days occur in winter, but the knee-deep crossing of Hurricane Creek will mean wet and chilly feet.

Services: Water is available at Greer Crossing Recreation Area on the western end of this section of the Ozark Trail. Camping is also available at Greer. Another nearby campground is McCormack Lake Recreation Area, 8 miles to the northwest.

Gasoline, groceries, and restaurants are in Winona, 16 miles to the north. Hotels are in Eminence, 35 miles north, or in Van Buren, 22 miles east of Winona. The nearest bike shops are in Springfield, 150 miles west of Winona, or in Cape Girardeau, 120 miles to the east.

Hazards: Be careful on the descents from the ridge-tops. They occasionally have steep drop-offs, and a fall to the downhill side could mean a long slide over rocky slopes before you stop yourself. Don't attempt to cross Hurricane Creek during high water.

Rescue index: Because this trail is not heavily used, you should be prepared to take care of yourself. This is especially true on weekdays, when you are not likely to see anyone. There is only one road crossing. It is near the midpoint of the ride, and offers the only option to bail out of the trail (see "Notes on the trail").

Land status: National forest.

Maps: This trail uses portions of two sections of the Ozark Trail, the Between the Rivers Section and the Eleven Point River Section, so maps for both sections would be useful. The 7.5 minute topos covering the trail are Greer and Wilderness.

Finding the trail: There are 3 access points for this trail. The eastern trailhead is reached by driving 9 miles south from Fremont on County Road J to Forest Service Road 3152. Turn west (right) on FS 3152 and drive 1 mile to the Sinking Creek Lookout Tower, where there is a trailhead and parking area at the base of the tower. A spur trail across the road to the north leads to the trail, where you should turn west.

The western trailhead is at Greer Crossing Recreation Area, 16 miles south of Winona on MO 19, where the highway crosses the Eleven Point River. Park in the picnic area. The third access point is near the midpoint of the trail, where it crosses FS 3152. There is a parking area and trailhead for the Ozark Trail here. You can reach it by driving 14 miles south of Winona to FS 3152 and then turning east 6 miles to the trailhead, or by driving west 5 miles from Sinking Creek Lookout Tower.

Sources of additional information:

Mark Twain National Forest
Route 1 Box 1908, Highway 19 N
Winona, MO 65588
(314) 325-4233

The Alpine Shop
601 East Lockwood
Webster Groves, MO 63119
(314) 962-7715

Notes on the trail: I recommend that you ride this trail east to west. Riding westbound lets you finish at the river, where you can swim, camp, or picnic at Greer Crossing Recreation Area. You will also have 1 less climb if you travel east to west.

The trail is marked by white plastic diamonds. Riding west from Sinking Creek Tower, it passes over several ridges and hollows before crossing FS 3152 at mile 8, where there is a trailhead and small parking area. This is where the Between the Rivers and Eleven Point River sections of the Ozark Trail join. It's also the only opportunity you will have to bail out of the trail and return to the car at the Sinking Creek Tower, 5 miles to the east via FS 3152. Once you pass this trailhead westbound you are committed to pedaling all the way to Greer Crossing.

After reaching Greer, you may prefer to return to Sinking Creek Tower by road. To do this, ride 1.5 miles north of Greer on MO 19 to FS 3152. Turn right, and ride east. Six miles east is the trailhead where this ride crosses FS 3152, and 5 miles beyond that is the Sinking Creek Tower and trailhead.

RIDE 33 *OZARK TRAIL: NORTH PART, BETWEEN THE RIVERS SECTION*

This 23-mile out-and-back trail is a great ride through the land between two of Missouri's Wild and Scenic rivers. It can also be ridden as a loop by returning to the trailhead via forest roads and paved highways. The total distance would be 40 miles round trip. Shorter options are available by leaving the trail at road crossings and riding those roads back to the starting point (see "Notes on the trail").

From the north trailhead near Van Buren to the crossing of County Road C, a distance of around seven miles, the trail can easily be ridden by beginners. From CR C to Forest Service Road 3145, the trail is more difficult, but could be handled by inexperienced riders in good condition and with positive attitudes.

The trail continues in much the same condition from FS 3145 to CR J, except for the last two miles before reaching CR J. This two-mile stretch is not hilly,

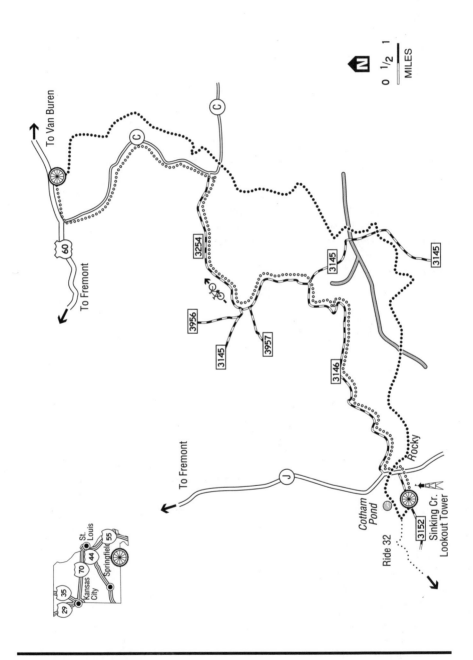

but it passes over a bed of large loose rocks, and will be difficult for even an expert to ride. The remaining 1.5 miles from CR J to Sinking Creek Lookout Tower are a piece of cake.

The entire trail is single-track, ranging in condition from hardpack to loose rocky descents and climbs. Windfall is common.

The ride begins near the Current River, a popular float trip destination. The trail meanders among the hollows and ridges of the river's tributaries and ends at the Sinking Creek Lookout Tower, which sits on the divide between the drainages of the Current and the Eleven Point rivers.

This is a land of clear streams, dry, open glades, rock outcroppings, and cool deep forests. Numerous stream crossings cool you on your ride through the deep woods. The deepest fords are the two crossings of Barren Creek and the ford of the North Prong of Cedar Creek. The water at these fords may come up to your hubs. If you want to take a real swim, dive into Cotham Pond, 1 mile east of the Sinking Creek Lookout Tower.

There are lots of climbs on this challenging trail, but the payoff for these is great vistas from the top and exhilarating downhill runs when the trail drops into the next valley. Five miles east of the trailhead at Sinking Creek Lookout you will pedal through an old clear-cut on a ridge-top. Here the views are especially spectacular.

You may want to consider making a weekend of it, riding the trail one day and canoeing the nearby Current and Eleven Point rivers the next. Canoe rentals are available from several outfitters in nearby Van Buren and Alton.

General location: The east trailhead is 4 miles west of Van Buren.

Elevation change: Elevations range from a low of 580′ at the crossing of Barren Creek to a high of 1,025′ at Sinking Creek Lookout Tower. There are 11 climbs and descents, varying in length from one-quarter to three-quarters of a mile each. Most of these climbs are rideable, but some have rough or steep sections that will have to be portaged.

Season: Spring and fall are great times to ride this trail. Summer can be good, but winter riding is a chilly proposition with the many stream crossings on the ride.

Services: No drinking water is available along the trail. Fresh water is available in Van Buren, as are all other services except bike shops. The nearest full-service bike shops are in Cape Girardeau, 100 miles to the east.

Hazards: Though this ride is remote, serious hazards are few. Just be careful on the rocky stretches, and don't attempt to cross the creeks during high water. This is the longest stretch of the Ozark Trail covered by one ride, and it will take a long time. Be aware of the time, making sure you will have enough daylight to make it back to your car. If necessary, bail out and ride one of the roads back to the trailhead.

Rescue index: This section of the Ozark Trail is infrequently used. If you run into problems, don't wait for help to come to you. Work your way to one of the roads crossed by the trail every 6–8 miles and wait for help there.

Land status: National forest.

Maps: A map of the Between the Rivers Section of the Ozark Trail is indispensable. A map of the Winona-Doniphan-Van Buren District of the Mark Twain National Forest will be helpful in finding alternate road return routes. USGS topos covering the trail are 7.5 minute Van Buren, Handy, and Wilderness maps.

Finding the trail: Access to the northeast end of the trail is 3.5 miles west of Van Buren on US 60. Look for a parking area on the south side of the road; this parking area is a designated trailhead for the Ozark Trail.

To reach the southwest end of this ride at Sinking Creek Lookout Tower, drive 9 miles south of Fremont on County Road J, and then 1 mile west on Forest Service Road 3152. There is a small parking area at the base of the tower. A short spur path across the road to the north leads to the trail.

Sources of additional information:

Mark Twain National Forest
Post Office Box 69, Watercress Road
Van Buren, MO 63965
(314) 323-4216

The Alpine Shop
601 East Lockwood
Webster Groves, MO 63119
(314) 962-7715

Notes on the trail: Though parts of the trail are difficult, this beautiful and secluded wilderness ride should not be missed. Except for several road crossings and an occasional power line cut, few signs of man exist along the ride. It is marked by the white diamonds found all along the Ozark Trail.

For those not wishing to ride this trail section's entire length, there are 2 chances to bail out and return to the trailhead by road. Pedaling southwest from the trailhead near Van Buren, the first option is at mile 7, where the trail crosses CR C. Leaving the trail and riding north on C for 5 miles will bring you to US 60. Turn east and ride 1 mile to the trailhead.

The second option is at mile 13.5, where the trail crosses FS 3145. This will be just after your first crossing of Barren Creek. Turn north (right) on FS 3145 and ride 4.5 miles to FS 3254. Turn east (right) on FS 3254 for 4 miles to CR C. Turn north on CR C and ride 4 miles to US 60, and follow that highway east 1 mile to the trailhead.

After you've ridden the entire trail to Sinking Creek Lookout the road return route is as follows: Ride 1 mile east from the tower on FS 3152 to CR J. Turn north on CR J a quarter mile to FS 3146. Ride east (right) 5.5 miles on FS 3146 to FS 3145. Turn north (left) on FS 3145 and ride 2 miles to FS 3254. Turn east (right) on FS 3254, follow it to CR C, go north on C to US 60, and east on US 60 to the trailhead. All the roads used by these return routes are marked.

RIDE 34 OZARK TRAIL: NORTH TRACE CREEK SECTION

The north half of the Trace Creek Section of the Ozark Trail is a 14-mile out-and-back ride. It can be made into a loop by returning to the starting point via county highways and dirt roads that add another 13 miles (see "Notes on the trail").

This moderately difficult trail is not excessively rocky or technical, but you will need to be in good physical condition to handle the long distance and numerous climbs between the ridges and creek bottoms. With a little perseverance and a good attitude, a beginner could enjoy this ride. It is almost all single-track, with a few short sections following abandoned forest roads. Most of the trail is sandy hardpack with a few stretches of rock and loose gravel.

The Trace Creek Trail passes through typical Missouri Ozark Mountain topography. You'll pedal through oak, hickory, and pine forest, climb to windy ridge-tops, and descend into quiet shaded hollows. If you enjoy stream crossings, you will love this ride. Immediately south of Hazel Creek Camp, you'll cross Hazel Creek, a major permanently flowing stream. It's usually knee-deep.

If there has been enough rainfall, you'll cross smaller creeks at the end of every long descent. The trail often parallels these rock-strewn stream beds for short distances before starting the climb to the next ridge. Spring riders will pedal through hollows dotted with wildflowers and flowering dogwoods, and those braving the cool temperatures of late October will ride through blazing fall foliage.

General location: 20 miles southwest of Potosi.
Elevation change: Beginning at 900′ at Hazel Creek Campground, the trail reaches its maximum elevation of 1,200′ at the crossing of County Road DD. There are 6 long climbs riding southbound, and 5 riding northbound.
Season: Spring and fall are the best seasons for riding this trail. Warm days sometimes occur during winter, but stream crossings can still chill you. Summer often offers good riding, and the Missouri heat and humidity could be offset with dips in creeks along the ride, or in nearby Council Bluff Lake.
Services: Drinking water is not available on the trail. During the warm months, fresh water is available at Council Bluff Lake. John's Bait and Tackle at the intersection of County Roads C and DD has gasoline, groceries, and the nearest phone.

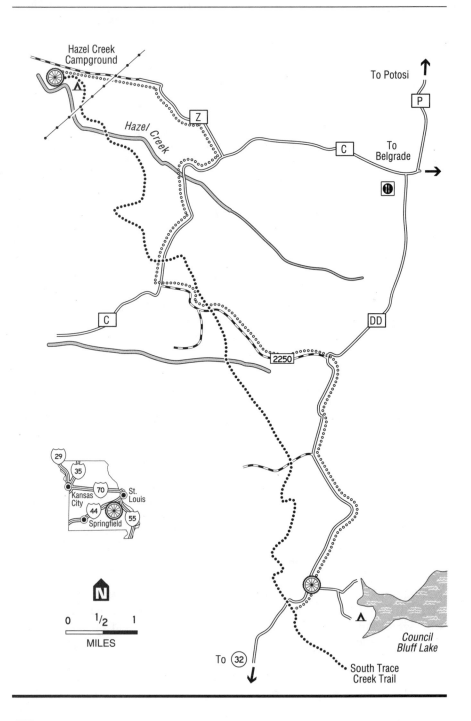

Hazel Creek
Campground

To Potosi

P

Z

C

To
Belgrade

Hazel Creek

C

DD

2250

29

35

Kansas
City

70

St.
Louis

44

Springfield

55

N

0   1/2   1

MILES

Council
Bluff Lake

To 32

South Trace
Creek Trail

Many of the small towns in the area have restaurants and grocery stores, but the best bet is Potosi, at the intersection of MO 21 and MO 8 around 20 miles northeast of the trail. The nearest bike shops are in St. Louis.

Hazards: Be cautious during stream crossings. Rocks in the stream bottoms can be very slick.

Rescue index: The trail crosses a road every 5 miles, so you are never very far from an escape point. It also sees moderate use by both equestrians and hikers, and passes through a heavily used motorcycle-trail network. So you have a good chance of being found in case of emergency.

Land status: National forest.

Maps: The best map available is that for the Trace Creek Section of the Ozark Trail. A map of the Salem-Potosi Ranger District of the Mark Twain National Forest may also be helpful for finding road routes back to your starting point. USGS topos for the trail are the Courtois, Palmer, and Johnson Mountain 7.5 minute maps.

Finding the trail: Access to the north end of the trail is at Hazel Creek Campground, a beautiful, primitive site in the forest. From Potosi, drive south on CR P to CR C. Go west on CR C to CR Z. Drive north on CR Z approximately 3 miles to Hazel Creek Camp (1 mile after the pavement ends). Park in the campground. The trail leaves the campground southbound.

Access to the south end of the ride is at Council Bluff Lake. To reach it, drive south from Potosi on CR P to CR C. Go west a quarter mile on CR C to CR DD. Go south 7 miles on CR DD to the entrance to the lake and recreation area. Park your car in the parking lot at the entrance, and ride your bike an additional three-quarters of a mile south on CR DD to where the trail crosses the road. Turn right (north) onto the trail to begin riding toward Hazel Creek Campground.

Sources of additional information:

Mark Twain National Forest
Post Office Box 188
Potosi, MO 63664
(314) 438-5427

The Alpine Shop
601 East Lockwood
Webster Groves, MO 63119
(314) 962-7715

Notes on the trail: This is a well-maintained trail with something for riders of all skill levels. Climbs are challenging, but rideable. The trail (which is marked by white diamonds nailed to trees) can be ridden one way, or as a loop using county roads to return to your starting point.

If you start at Hazel Creek and ride to CR DD, you may want to ride back to the trailhead on roads, rather than beating yourself up on the trail for another 14 miles. To do so, turn left (north) on DD, and ride around 5 miles north to FS 2250. It is unmarked, but will be the first wide, well-maintained gravel road to the left. Follow it west for 3 miles to CR C. Turn right (north) on C and ride 2.5 miles to CR Z. Turn left (north) onto Z and follow it 3 miles to Hazel Creek.

If you missed the turn off DD onto FS 2250, it's no big deal. Just continue until DD intersects CR C. Turn left on C and ride to CR Z, where you'll turn north to ride to Hazel Creek. It's only 3 miles longer than using FS 2250. There are other options for making shorter trail-road combinations, too. A map of the Salem-Potosi Ranger District of the Mark Twain will help you explore all the possible loops you can make on the Trace Creek Trail.

RIDE 35 *OZARK TRAIL: SOUTH TRACE CREEK SECTION*

The south portion of the Trace Creek Section of the Ozark Trail is more diffi-cult than the northern segment. It is 13 miles long, with the road return option adding an additional 16 miles (see "Notes on the trail"). This stretch of the Ozark Trail has several technical sections, several long climbs, and occasional areas of loose, fist-sized rocks. It is not recommended for beginners.

The trail is mostly single-track, mixed with short rides on old double-track roads. One of the toughest sections is a long uphill from the south trailhead to the top of the ridge above. If you ride the trail from north to south, you'll get to enjoy this as a descent.

The stream crossings along this trail add to the riding experience, especially the knee-deep ford of Ottery Creek at the south end of the ride. It can make a perfect ending for a tough ride on a hot summer day. Spring wildflowers dot the streamsides during April and May, and the dogwood and redbud blooms in early April are spectacular.

There are 2 caves just off the trail in Peter Cave Hollow. They can be found with a topo map and a little investigative hiking.

Across from the parking area at the south end of the trail is Bell Mountain Wilderness Area. A 1.5-mile hike into the wilderness will take you to the top of the western summit of Bell Mountain and treat you to a great view of the surrounding countryside. DO NOT RIDE YOUR BIKE INTO THE WILDER-NESS AREA.

General location: 16 miles southwest of Belleview.
Elevation change: Pedaling southbound on this trail, there will be 7 descents and 6 climbs ranging in length from one-quarter to three-quarters of a mile. The lowest point on the ride is at the Ottery Creek ford at the trail's southern end, where the elevation is 950′. The peak elevation is 1,350′ at the crossing of MO 32.
Season: Although good riding days occur during any season in Missouri, spring and fall offer the best riding experiences. Summer is a distant third. With several stream fords and the knee-deep crossing of Ottery Creek, winter riding is a cold prospect.

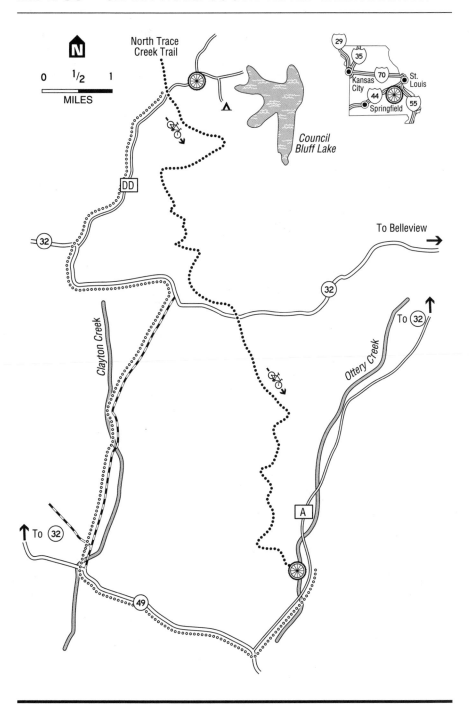

Services: No drinking water is available along the trail. Council Bluff Lake, the trail's northern terminus, has water during the peak camping months, but it is turned off in winter. You'll find restaurants in the nearby towns of Potosi, Belgrade, Caledonia, and Belleview. Groceries and gas may be found in Potosi.

The nearest hotels are in Flat River and Fredericktown, 30 miles to the east. Camping is available anywhere in the national forest, and developed sites can be found at Council Bluff Lake on County Road DD at the north end of the loop. The nearest bike shops are in St. Louis, 90 miles to the north.

Hazards: The trail is rocky and rough in several spots, especially on the descent to Ottery Creek at the southern end. In some areas, the trail markings are poor, so pay close attention to avoid getting lost. Avoid crossing Ottery Creek during high water.

Rescue index: Since this trail sees only light use, your chances of being found in case of emergency are fair at best. Plan to take care of yourself. If riding on your own, let someone know where you are going and when you expect to be back.

Land status: National forest.

Maps: The best guide to this trail is the Trace Creek Section map of the Ozark Trail. The 7.5 minute topo for this ride is Johnson Mountain. A map of the Salem-Potosi District of the Mark Twain National Forest would also be helpful.

Finding the trail: The recommended starting point is at Council Bluff Lake Recreation Area at the north end of this trail section. To reach it, drive south from Potosi on CR P. When you reach CR C, go west a quarter mile to CR DD. Go south 7 miles on CR DD to Council Bluff Lake. Park your car in the lot just inside the entrance and ride three-quarters of a mile farther south on DD, where you will intersect the trail as it crosses the highway. Ride south, or left.

If you want to start at the south end, drive 17 miles south from Potosi on MO 21 to MO 32. Go west 8 miles on MO 32 to CR A. Drive south 6 miles on CR A to the parking area next to Ottery Creek and the Bell Mountain Wilderness. The trail immediately crosses Ottery Creek and proceeds north up a long switchback climb, so you are better off starting in the north.

Sources of additional information:

Mark Twain National Forest
Post Office Box 188
Potosi, MO 63664
(314) 438-5427

The Alpine Shop
601 East Lockwood
Webster Groves, MO 63119
(314) 962-7715

Notes on the trail: This is a tough trail, and is not recommended for beginners. Its southern part is little used and poorly marked. The primary markings are white diamonds on trees. Where diamonds are missing, they are supplemented by streamers of brightly colored ribbon tied to trees. In spite of these difficulties, you'll be able to follow the trail fairly easily if you carry a map and pay attention to where you are.

Regardless of which end you choose to start from, you should ride the trail from north to south. There is a three-quarter-mile climb at the trail's southern end. While climbing this hill is nearly impossible, it can be negotiated as a descent if you ride cautiously.

The parking lot at the south end of the trail also serves as a trailhead for hikers entering the Bell Mountain Wilderness Area across the highway to the east. DO NOT RIDE YOUR BIKE INTO THE WILDERNESS AREA.

You can ride the trail as a loop by returning to your car via county roads. To do so after riding from Council Bluff Lake to the parking area on CR A, continue south on A 3 miles to MO 49. Go west 3 miles on MO 49 to a bridge across a creek. Turn right (north) on the gravel road just east of the bridge, and ride 6 miles north to MO 32. Turn west on MO 32 and go 2 miles to CR DD, where you will turn north 2.2 miles to Council Bluff Lake. A map of the Salem-Potosi Ranger District of the Mark Twain National Forest will help you explore all the loop options possible here.

RIDE 36   *OZARK TRAIL: VICTORY SECTION*

The Victory Section of the Ozark Trail is a 22-mile point-to-point ride with a six-mile loop on its eastern end. It can be handled by cyclists of all skill levels. While there are short and steep sections that will require portages, most grades are gentle enough to be ridden by beginners. The trail surface is single-track and old double-track roads. In the future, the Forest Service plans to connect the Victory Trail to the Lake Wappapello Trail in the east, and the main stem of the Ozark Trail in the west.

On the Victory Trail you will pedal through a typical Missouri hardwood forest with scattered stands of pines. Upalika Pond Recreation Area is near the midpoint of the trail. It is an excellent campsite if you're interested in riding the trail in two days, with a support vehicle meeting you at the campsite. If you don't feel like riding the trail back to your starting point, you can make it into a loop by returning to your car via forest roads (see map and "Notes on the trail").

General location: 8 miles northwest of Poplar Bluff.
Elevation change: Elevation along the Victory Trail varies from 500′ along the creek bottom southwest of the Wrangler Trailhead to 700′ near Upalika Pond. There will be many climbs and descents ranging in length from one-quarter to one-half mile. There will be a few short and steep sections requiring portages.
Season: Spring and fall offer spectacular riding. In those seasons, the trail is decorated with spring wildflowers and the blaze of autumn colors. It's hot and humid in summer. Carry plenty of water if you plan to ride then. Winter riding

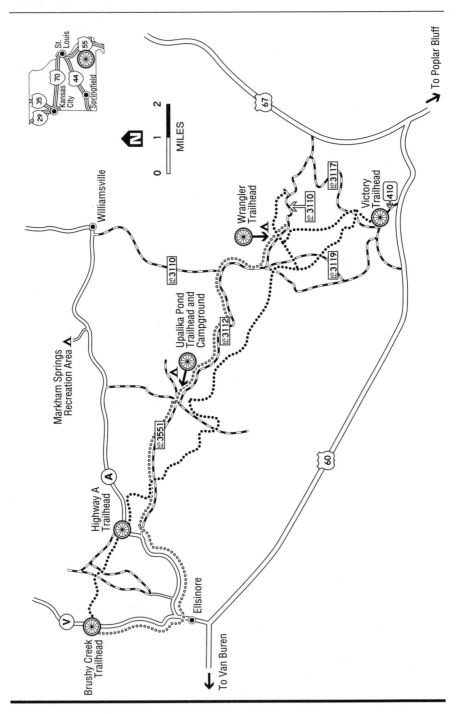

To Poplar Bluff

St. Louis

55

70 44 Springfield

Kansas City

35

29

MILES

N

0 1 2

67

Williamsville

Wrangler Trailhead

3117

Victory Trailhead

410

3110

3110

3119

Upalika Pond Trailhead and Campground

3112

Markham Springs Recreation Area

3551

60

Highway A Trailhead

A

Ellsinore

Brushy Creek Trailhead

V

To Van Buren

on the Victory Trail can be fun. There are no bugs, or deep stream crossings to get your feet wet, and the views are better.

Services: Drinking water is not available anywhere along the trail. Poplar Bluff, 8 miles from the eastern trailhead, has all services. The trail's western trailhead is 3 miles north of Ellsinore. In Ellsinore you can find food, water, and gasoline.

Camping is at Upalika Pond, a national forest campground just off the trail at the halfway point on Forest Service Road 3112. Markham Springs Recreation Area, 6 miles east of the trail on County Road A, has a huge campground near one of Missouri's many beautiful springs. Camping is also allowed anywhere in the national forest.

Hazards: There are short stretches of rocky, technical trail that can throw unsuspecting riders. This is a popular deer hunting area. Avoid riding during deer season, and don't wear anything white.

Rescue index: Since this ride crosses roads at 9 points, the rescue index is very good on the Victory Trail. In case of emergency, make your way to one of these road crossings and await a passing motorist.

Land status: National forest.

Maps: You'll find a map of the Victory Section of the Ozark Trail, which shows contour lines, very useful. You can get one by writing to the national forest at the address below. Topos for the Victory Trail are the 7.5 minute Williamsville and Ellsinore maps.

Finding the trail: To access the trail at its southeastern end, drive 3 miles west on US 60 from US 67. Go north 1 mile on County Road 410 to FS 3117. Turn north (right) on FS 3117 and drive 100 yards to the trailhead. This will put you at the bottom end of the 6-mile loop.

A second access point is at Wrangler Trailhead. It is 3 miles north of US 60 on US 67, then west 3 miles on gravel FS 3110. Finding FS 3110 may be a little tricky. It takes off from a short frontage road along US 67. You will probably overshoot it and have to backtrack.

At this trailhead you will be on the upper portion of the 6-mile loop, near the eastern end of the trail. To access the trail's western end, drive 3 miles north from Ellsinore on CR V. There will be an Ozark Trail trailhead on the west side of the road next to Brushy Creek.

Sources of additional information:

Mark Twain National Forest
1420 Maud, Post Office Box 988
Poplar Bluff, MO 63901
(314) 785-1475

The Alpine Shop
601 East Lockwood
Webster Groves, MO 63119
(314) 962-7715

Notes on the trail: The Victory Trail is marked by gray plastic diamonds placed at intervals on trailside trees. Carsonite posts labeled with horse silhouettes are found at all road crossings. The 6-mile section on the western end between CR A and CR V is marked by white Ozark Trail diamonds.

After riding this point-to-point trail, you might want to ride back to the starting point on roads. Carrying a map of the Poplar Bluff district of the Mark Twain will help you choose road return alternatives.

To return by road after riding from Brushy Creek to Wrangler Trailhead, begin riding west on FS 3110. Follow it around 2 miles to FS 3112. At this point, FS 3110 will veer north, and you will bear west on FS 3112. Follow FS 3112 along Cane Ridge for about 5 miles to a T intersection. Turn north (right) for a quarter mile to a 4-way intersection, then turn west (left) on FS 3551. Follow FS 3551 to CR A. Turn left on CR A and follow it to Ellsinore. Go north from Ellsinore on CR V to the Brushy Creek trailhead.

ARKANSAS RIDES

State Parks and Corps of Engineers Land Trails

RIDE 37 DEVIL'S DEN STATE PARK

Devil's Den State Park is mountain bike heaven. The park management enthusiastically supports the sport of mountain biking, and most trails in the park are open to cycling. Two mountain bike festivals are held there each year. Several of the park rangers ride mountain bikes, and they ask that you stop by the Visitor Center to go over the trail system with them before riding. Here they will show you which trails are open, and guide you to routes that match your skill level and time constraints.

The two loops most used by mountain bikers are the Fossil Flats Trail, an easy three-mile loop that is excellent for beginners, and the Holt Road Loop, a ten-mile ride that is a bit more challenging. The trail surface is a combination of single-track and double-track over rocky terrain.

Devil's Den is nestled in the steep-sided valley of Lee Creek. Trails in the park meander along the rock-lined creek, follow the ridges above the stream, and climb or descend the steep hills between the creek's tributaries and the ridges that rise above them. Several abandoned farmsteads can be seen from the trails. The designated mountain bike routes follow the rough, rocky roads that once served these farms in the early part of the century.

Riding the Holt Road Loop, you will be treated to several spectacular vistas reached via wide, rocky trails and challenging stretches of single-track. The side trails off the loop lead to a waterfall, a cave, and a deep swimming hole in Lee Creek. Check with rangers in the Visitor Center for guidance to all points of interest in Devil's Den State Park.

General location: 26 miles south of Fayetteville.
Elevation change: Elevations in the park range from 1,000′ at Lee Creek to 1,600′ at the trailhead for the Holt Road Loop. Holt Ridge features 1 long climb, 1 long descent, and many smaller hills. The Fossil Flats Trail is fairly

RIDE 37 *DEVIL'S DEN STATE PARK*

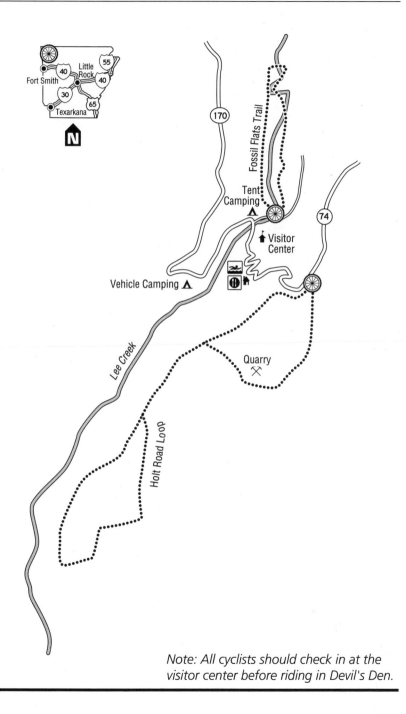

Note: All cyclists should check in at the
visitor center before riding in Devil's Den.

Upper crossing of Lee Creek on the Fossil Flats Trail, Devil's Den State Park.

level, making it best for beginners. Most other trail options are steeper, with more technical climbs and descents.

Season: Spring and fall are the best seasons to ride in Devil's Den State Park. Heat makes it tough in summer, but there is a swimming pool in the park for cooling off after your ride.

Services: Drinking water, camping, and cabin rentals are available in the park. The park restaurant, store, and swimming pool are open from Memorial Day to Labor Day. Mountain bike rentals are available at the Visitor Center. All other services are available in Fayetteville, 26 miles to the north.

Hazards: Do not attempt crossings of Lee Creek during high water. Ride cautiously on steep and rocky single-track in the park. Be especially careful at the several drop-offs along the park's trails.

Rescue index: Devil's Den is one of the safer places to mountain bike in Arkansas. It is staffed year-round, and is very popular during the warmer months. Should you get into trouble on the trail, there is a good chance you'll soon be found by another cyclist or hiker. The park rangers ask that you check in at the Visitor Center and let them know where you plan to ride.

Land status: State park and national forest.

Maps: A map of Devil's Den and Upper Lee Creek Valley, available at the Visitor Center, shows all the trails in the park and nearby national forest. Most of the trails in the Devil's Den area fall onto the Strickler and Winslow 7.5 minute topos. Approximately 25 percent of the southern portion of the area falls onto Rudy NE and Mountainburg.

Finding the trail: From Fayetteville, drive south on US 71 to West Fork. Turn west (right) on AR 170, and follow it 18 miles to the park. From Fort Smith, drive north on US 71 to Winslow. Turn west (left) on AR 74, and drive 13 miles to Devil's Den. Before riding, please check in with the rangers at the Visitor Center.

Sources of additional information:

Devil's Den State Park
Route 1 Box 118
West Fork, AR 72774
(501) 761-3325

The Pack Rat
2397 Green Acres Road
Fayetteville, AR 72703
(501) 521-6340

Notes on the trail: At the time of this writing, Devil's Den was developing a brochure and map specifically for mountain biking. Eventually, special mountain bike loops will be marked to lead cyclists through the park's trail system. For now the Devil's Den and Upper Lee Creek Valley map, coupled with advice from park rangers, will clearly guide you through this beautiful mountain biking area. There are other trails open to mountain biking in the park, and the rangers can point out the ones best suited to your skill level.

RIDE 38 *BENCH ROAD TRAIL*

The Bench Road Trail is a four-mile ride on an abandoned double-track road encircling Mt. Nebo 300 feet below its summit. Suitable for riders of all skill levels, the trail surface is mostly hardpack with a few rocky sections and rock slabs.

Rising over 1,800 feet above the surrounding countryside, Mt. Nebo overlooks the Arkansas River valley below. Summer visitors enjoy high-altitude breezes, temperatures 10 to 15 degrees below those on the valley floor, and spectacular views in all directions. To the north lie the Ozark Mountains and Lake Dardanelle. To the south rise the Ouachita Mountains. In the hazy distance to the west is Mt. Magazine, the highest point in Arkansas. The Arkansas River snakes away to the east.

RIDE 38 *BENCH ROAD TRAIL*

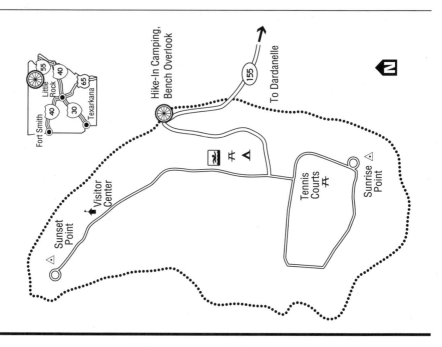

Mt. Nebo has been a favorite vacation spot since pre–Civil War times. During the 1890s, a resort hotel was built to house steamboat passengers traveling on the Arkansas River below. The area became a state park in 1933. Many of the park facilities, including the trails, were constructed by the Civilian Conservation Corps. Today, hang gliders soar with the hawks and vultures riding the updrafts off the peaks.

In addition to the normal Arkansas wildlife found on Mt. Nebo, birdwatchers may spot the rufous-crowned sparrow, a bird normally found only in the southwest. It makes its home in the high-altitude outcroppings on Mt. Nebo.

When the day is done, cap your ride on this high island in the Arkansas countryside by drawing straws—the unlucky person in your group gets to drive the car down off the mountain, while the rest of you enjoy the long and scenic switchback descent on AR 155 to the valley floor below.

General location: The Bench Road Trail is located in Mt. Nebo State Park, 8 miles southwest of Russellville.

Elevation change: Elevation changes are minimal on this trail. It stays around 1,400´. There is 1 gradual climb and 1 gradual descent with a few other short and steep pitches thrown in. Overall, this trail is a very easy ride.

Season: Since it is so short, the Bench Road Trail is a good ride any time of year.

Temperatures are most favorable from April to October. Winter riding, when views are unobstructed by foliage, can be spectacular.

Services: Drinking water is available in the park. There are also 10 rustic and 4 modern A-frame cabins for rent, along with campsites, picnic pavilions, tennis courts, and a swimming pool. All other services are available in Russellville, 10 miles to the north.

Hazards: Be careful at overlooks and drop-offs, particularly in winter when the trail may be icy. Rocks on the edges of cliffs and overhangs may be loose, and your weight could send them tumbling.

Rescue index: You are never more than 2 miles from the park headquarters when riding this trail. Several connector trails leading from the Bench Trail to the summit give you easy access to help.

Land status: State park.

Maps: The Mt. Nebo State Park Trail Map, available at the Visitor Center, covers the entire trail. The topos covering the area are the Chickalah Mountain East and Dardanelle 7.5 minute maps.

Finding the trail: Mt. Nebo State Park is 7 miles west of Dardanelle on AR 155. Park in the lot designated for hike-in camping, just east of the Bench Overlook on AR 155 (see map).

Sources of additional information:

Mt. Nebo State Park
Route 3 Box 374
Dardanelle, AR 72834
(501) 229-3655

Notes on the trail: The Bench Road Trail is blazed by yellow paint on trees and rocks along the ride. There are other trails in the park, but they are not open to mountain bikes. Note that there are also private residences on the summit of Mt. Nebo, and respect these private inholdings.

RIDE 39 *BEAR CREEK CYCLE TRAIL*

The Bear Creek Cycle Trail, a 31-mile point-to-point single-track trail designed for and used by motorcycles, follows the edge of Lake Greeson in southwest Arkansas.

The trail surface between Laurel Creek and Bear Creek recreation areas is extremely steep and rocky in many places, and should be ridden only by experts. Those riders more comfortable with easy terrain should limit themselves to the section between Bear Creek Recreation Area and Daisy State Park. Except for the last three miles, the trail surface there is hard-packed with few rocks, and

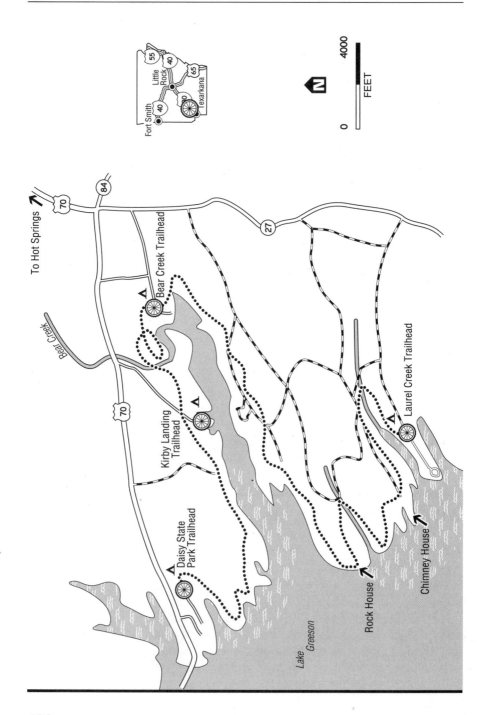

Single-track motorcycle trail through the forest east of Lake
Greeson, Bear Creek Cycle Trail.

the grades are gentle. The final three miles to Daisy State Park are rough, steep,
and rocky.

Wildlife is abundant in this riparian habitat. White-tailed deer and wild
turkey are common. While riding on the trail close to the lake you will spot large
turtles sunning themselves on driftwood, and startle ducks off the calm waters
of the coves. Spring wildflowers in this moist environment are spectacular. Large
beds of honeysuckle growing along the eastern part of the trail perfume the
warm spring air.

If you enjoy fishing, you may want to go after the striped bass, black bass,
crappie, walleye, and bream that inhabit the lake. If you are interested in
regional history, you won't want to miss the Rock House Loop, 5 miles north
of Laurel Creek. This short side trail takes you to the stone remains of a farm-
house and outbuildings dating from the early part of the century.

General location: The Bear Creek Cycle Trail is located on the north and east shores of Lake Greeson, immediately southwest of Kirby.

Elevation change: Elevation ranges from 560′ at the water's edge to a high of 700′.

Season: Spring and fall are best. Those braving summer heat, insects, and humidity will enjoy a swim in Lake Greeson.

Services: Drinking water and camping are available at any of the 4 recreation areas along the trail. Kirby Landing and Daisy State Park also have shower facilities. Gas, groceries, and restaurants can be found in several small towns along US 70 on the north side of the lake.

All services except bike shops can be found in Glenwood, 10 miles to the east. The nearest bike shops are in Hot Springs, 40 miles to the east.

Hazards: Be very careful if you choose to ride the steep and rocky section of the trail between Bear Creek and Laurel Creek. The rocks can easily cause you to lose control. Be ready to encounter motorcycles at any time.

Rescue index: On weekends the trail sees heavy use. You will be quickly found if you have trouble. On weekdays and during winter you may have to fend for yourself. In case of trouble, work your way to one of the several road crossings along the trail and await help.

Land status: Most of this trail is on US Army Corps of Engineers land. A short portion of the trail is located in Daisy State Park.

Maps: Maps of Lake Greeson, available at Kirby Landing and Daisy State Park, show the entire trail. If you want to use topos you will need the Narrows Dam 7.5 minute map.

Finding the trail: There are 4 access points for the trail. Laurel Creek, the southern terminus of the trail, is 4 miles south of Kirby on AR 27 and 4 miles west on marked gravel roads. Bear Creek Recreation Area, 18 trail miles north of Laurel Creek, is 1.5 miles east of Kirby on a marked paved road. Kirby Landing is 2 miles west of Kirby on US 70, and then 2 miles south on a marked paved road. Daisy State Park, the trail's western terminus, is 6 miles west of Kirby on US 70. All 4 sites have trailheads and parking facilities.

Sources of additional information:

US Army Corps of Engineers
Route 1
Murphreesboro, AR 71958
(501) 285-2151

Daisy State Park
Daisy Route, Box 66
Kirby, AR 71950
(501) 398-4487

Notes on the trail: This trail is marked by blue and yellow paint blazes. The blazes are supplemented by occasional metal plates with motorcycle silhouettes.

In some areas, particularly along the easy northern part of the ride, networks of side trails can add miles of riding. While these can be confusing, you should have little trouble staying on the main trail if you carry a map and pay attention to the markings. The lake bounds the area on the south, and US 70 keeps you from straying too far to the north.

As discussed in the introduction, the trail between Laurel Creek and Bear Creek is very difficult. It crosses roads every 3 to 5 miles, giving you the opportunity to bail out if the going is too difficult for you. A map will show these escape points. Find one of these roads, work your way east to AR 27, and follow it north to Bear Creek Recreation Area, where the gentle terrain begins.

Ozark National Forest Trails

Extensive logging in the 1800s destroyed this wild area in northwest Arkansas. Denuded slopes caused soil erosion, flooding, stream degradation, and wildlife decimation. To restore the land to productivity, the Ozark National Forest was established in 1908 by presidential proclamation. The forest was to be managed for water, timber, wildlife, forage, and recreation.

The recreational part of the plan has worked out well. Nineteen campgrounds await you, along with hundreds of miles of hiking trails. The longest of these is the Ozark Highlands Trail. It stretches 187 miles across the Ozark National Forest. In the future, trail groups hope to connect it with Missouri's Ozark Trail, giving hikers a total of 700 miles of continuous trail running from near Fayetteville to the St. Louis area.

Several lakes and five wilderness areas offer more hiking opportunities. On the Hurricane Creek Loop you will ride around the perimeter of one of the most spectacular of these, the Hurricane Creek Wilderness. Leave your bike behind and hike a few miles into the wilderness, where an impressive natural bridge will awe you. The Upper Buffalo Loop (see Buffalo National River section) circumnavigates the Upper Buffalo Wilderness of the Ozark National Forest. Leaving your bike and hiking 1.5 miles into this wilderness will take you to Hawksbill Crag, one of the most photographed sites in the Midwest.

On the White Rock Mountain Tour you'll huff and puff to the top of one of Arkansas's highest peaks, where you can enjoy the state's most expansive views. You can even rent a cabin or camp out on top of the mountain. The next day you can canoe the nearby Mulberry River or Big Piney Creek. The Buffalo National River just north of the Ozark National Forest offers still more riding, camping, and canoeing.

Hiking trails in the Ozark National Forest are not open to mountain biking. Most of the rides in the forest use forest roads. Luckily, many of these are remote, some are rough, and nearly all are scenic. If you are looking for the most challenging riding, go to the Moccasin Gap Horse Trail. While Moccasin Gap has loops that are suitable for beginners, its trails are all remote and parts of them will challenge even the most expert riders.

If you pass through gates, leave them open or closed as you found them. Don't ride on the hiking trails. Keep in mind that many tracts of private property are scattered throughout this forest. Respect the rights of property owners by obeying all No Trespassing signs.

RIDE 40 *HURRICANE CREEK WILDERNESS LOOP*

Except for a short segment on Forest Service Road 1209 on the east side of this 37-mile loop, little technical skill is needed for this ride. Eleven miles of the ride are on AR 123, a paved road with little traffic. The rest varies from a maintained gravel road along Parker Ridge to rough, rocky, hard-packed roads along Big Piney Creek on the western part of the loop, and on FS 1209 in the east. Beginners can easily handle this ride if they are in good physical condition for the long climbs and distances.

The Hurricane Creek Wilderness is a rugged scenic area at the eastern tip of the Boston Mountains. The Bostons were created when a high plateau eroded into a landscape of finger-like ridges, long narrow valleys, and clear streams. You are now the lucky beneficiary, able to enjoy a ride full of long climbs and descents, fantastic panoramic views from windswept ridges, dips into quiet, peaceful hollows, and refreshing fords of clear Ozark streams.

There is a great swimming hole in Big Piney Creek at the trailhead. It's a perfect spot to cool off after a hot summer ride. If you take the loop clockwise, you will ford Hurricane Creek just after beginning your ride. Just beyond the crossing, rock outcroppings jut over the road. After a rain, water trickles off these overhanging rocks and cools you as you pedal along the Big Piney.

When the ride leaves the creek, you will be treated to impressive views of the surrounding hollows as you climb up onto Parker Ridge. The rough southern portion of FS 1209 has a secluded wilderness atmosphere, and the end-of-the-ride downhill on AR 123 is a blast—particularly if you are there at sunset, when the hazy Boston Mountains are tinged with pink and crimson.

If you are interested in hiking, a six-mile trek into the Hurricane Creek Wilderness will take you to a natural bridge. Ask at the ranger district in Jasper for exact directions. DO NOT RIDE YOUR BIKE IN THE WILDERNESS AREA.

General location: 48 miles northwest of Russellville.
Elevation change: The elevation on the Hurricane Creek Wilderness Loop varies from 750′ along Big Piney Creek to 2,100′ at Millsap's Knob at the northern end of the loop.
Season: This ride is enjoyable year-round, although conditions are best in spring and fall. Warm riding days sometimes present themselves in winter, but you should be prepared for a chilly crossing of Hurricane Creek.
Services: No drinking water is available along the trail. The closest source of water and camping is Haw Creek Falls Campground, 1.5 miles west of the trailhead on AR 123. Food, water, and gasoline can be obtained in Pelsor at the intersection of AR 123 and AR 7.

RIDE 40 *HURRICANE CREEK WILDERNESS LOOP*

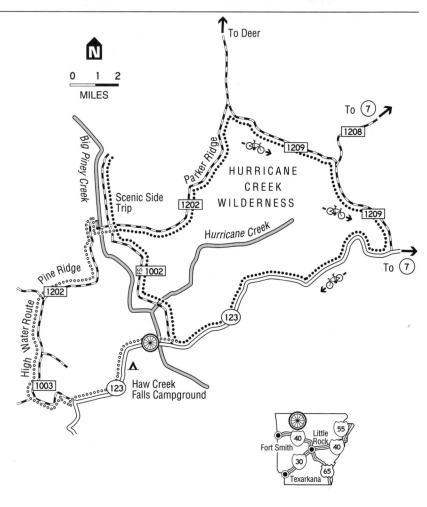

The nearest hotels, restaurants, and full-service grocery stores are in Jasper, 30 miles north of Pelsor on AR 7, and in Dover, 29 miles south on AR 7. The nearest bike shops are in Russellville, 40 miles south of Pelsor on AR 7.

Hazards: The biggest hazard you'll face on the Hurricane Creek Wilderness Loop is losing control of your bike on one of the long descents. Curves and switchbacks may come as a surprise while you are enjoying a fast, cooling descent after a long climb.

Rock outcroppings on FS 1002 along Big Piney Creek in the western edge of the Hurricane Creek Wilderness Loop.

Do not attempt to ford Hurricane Creek immediately after heavy rains when the flow is deep and fast. Instead, take the optional longer high-water route (see map and "Notes on the trail").

Rescue index: Though traffic is nearly nonexistent on this ride, most of the roads used by this loop see several cars per day. The exception is the southernmost 4-mile stretch of FS 1209. This section is too rugged for most vehicles. There are farms at either end of the rough stuff, though. If you get into a jam, go to one of these for help.

Land status: Most of the ride is through national forest land. You will occasionally cross private inholdings. Respect the rights of the owners by heeding all No Trespassing signs.

Maps: The Ozark National Forest map shows all roads used by this loop. It is hard to get lost if you carry this map. Topos covering the bulk of the route are the Deer and Ft. Douglas 7.5 minute maps. The 7.5 minute Sand Gap and Rosetta maps cover the remainder of the loop.

Finding the trail: To reach the trailhead, go 12 miles west on AR 123 from AR 7 at Pelsor. Just west of the Big Piney Creek bridge is a parking area for users of the Ozark Highlands Trail. Park here, ride back to the east side of Big Piney Creek, and turn north on the road that follows the east side of the creek. This is FS 1002, the first part of the loop.

Sources of additional information:

Ozark National Forest
Buffalo Ranger District
Highway 7 North, Box 427
Jasper, AR 72641
(501) 446-5122

Notes on the trail: This ride is best when you take it clockwise. Your ride will then begin with a level 6-mile stretch along Big Piney Creek. Your muscles will be warm when you hit the first major climb, as you turn away from Big Piney Creek and begin the 2-mile ascent onto Parker Ridge. The road then levels for a half mile, before climbing an additional mile.

After turning south on Forest Service Road 1209, you will descend for 2.5 miles to Slusher Creek. After a 2-mile level stretch and several half-mile climbs and descents on FS 1209, the 2.5-mile climb to AR 123 begins. On AR 123, there is a three-quarter-mile climb and descent before the loop ends with a scenic 3-mile downhill blast to the trailhead on Big Piney Creek.

If recent rains have swollen Hurricane Creek to levels too dangerous to cross, this loop can be ridden via another route. From the trailhead, ride 5 miles west on AR 123 to FS 1003. Turn north, and follow FS 1003 6 miles to FS 1202. Turn right, and follow FS 1202 5 miles to a T intersection. Turn right, and a quarter-mile ride will bring you to the Big Piney and junction with the normal route. The high-water route adds 11 miles and 1 additional long climb, but also gives you a 2.5-mile downhill from Pine Ridge to Big Piney Creek.

RIDE 41 *MOCCASIN GAP HORSE TRAIL*

Moccasin Gap Horse Trail, a 28-mile network in the beautiful hills and hollows of the southern Ozark Mountains, has rides to please all riders—but if you're looking for real challenge, you'll be especially happy here. The landscape alone is worth a visit; trails follow clear Ozark streams, climb to breezy ridge-tops, and meander through forests of oak and hickory in the bottomlands and stands of pine on the ridges. Views from ridges are spectacular, and the streams tumble over numerous waterfalls and rock ledges.

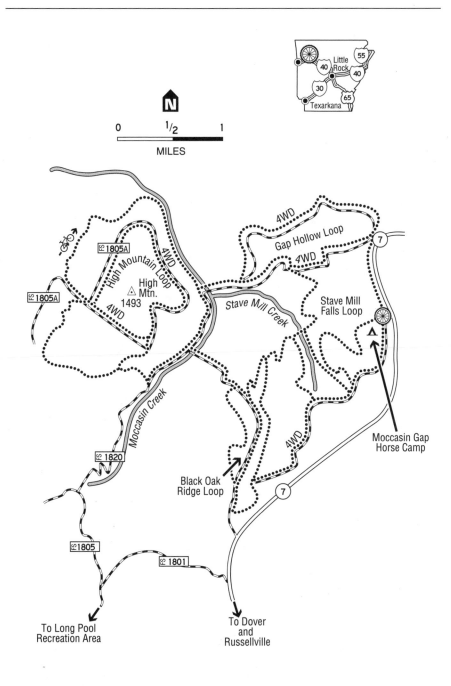

N

0   1/2   1

MILES

Little
Rock

Texarkana

4WD

Gap Hollow Loop

7

4WD

FS 1805A

High Mountain Loop

4WD

Stave Mill Creek

Stave Mill
Falls Loop

FS 1805A

High
Mtn.
1493

4WD

Moccasin Creek

Moccasin Gap
Horse Camp

FS 1820

4WD

Black Oak
Ridge Loop

7

FS 1805

FS 1801

To Long Pool
Recreation Area

To Dover
and
Russellville

Waterfall on Stave Mill Creek, Stave Mill Falls Loop, Moccasin Gap Horse Trail.

Especially beautiful is Stave Mill Falls on the Stave Mill Loop. Another impressive set of cascades is along Moccasin Creek on the High Mountain Loop, just north of the connector to the Gap Hollow Loop. This is on the section of trail considered too difficult for bikes. There is even a sign on the trail that recommends no bikes beyond that point, but it is worth the short hike required to reach the falls. The creek flows over a wide expanse of slickrock ledge, providing a perfect spot to play in the stream on a hot day or soak up some sun on a cooler afternoon.

The trails in Moccasin Gap are a combination of abandoned two-track road and newly cut single-track. They range from easy to very difficult. Beginners are advised to stay on the Stave Mill Hollow, Gap Hollow, and Black Oak Ridge loops. While parts of these loops are difficult, they can be ridden for most of their length. They are also relatively close to the trailhead if you decide to bail out.

The High Mountain Loop, while beautiful, is more remote. It takes a long ride and a long climb just to get there. All loops will have short stretches requiring portages, but the beauty of this trail system makes the trials and tribulations worth the effort.

General location: 23 miles north of Russellville on AR 7.
Elevation change: Elevation at the trailhead is 1,400′. From there, elevations range from a high of 1,500′ on the top of High Mountain to a low of 800′ along

Moccasin Creek. There are numerous climbs and descents of various lengths in this hilly part of the Ozarks. While the trails often follow ridge-tops and bottomlands, you can expect at least one climb of around one-half mile on any loop you choose to ride.

Season: Moccasin Gap is a pleasure to ride spring through fall. In spring, wildflowers dot the cool bottomlands traversed by the loops, and fall colors make autumn riding spectacular. Although summer riding can be extremely hot and humid, the crossings of Stave Mill Creek and Moccasin Creek will splash cooling relief on your misery. Breezes on the ridges reward you for the challenge of the climbs.

While winter riding can be pretty spectacular, relatively deep stream crossings on Moccasin Creek make it a chilly proposition.

Services: Camping is available at the trailhead. There is also water available at a hand pump there, but at the time of this writing it had not been tested for purity. Check with the Forest Service before using this for drinking water. Additional campsites are available at Long Pool Recreation Area 7 miles to the southwest.

Food, water, and showers are available at Mack's Pines, 1.5 miles south of the trailhead. All services, including hotels and bike shops, can be found in Russellville, 23 miles to the south on AR 7.

Hazards: Be careful when crossing streams, especially in spring, when Moccasin Creek can be deep and fast. Portions of the trail are very rocky. Use caution on these also. Because the northernmost segment of the High Mountain Loop is so rocky, you are advised to avoid it, unless you like the idea of pushing the bike for 2 miles. Be prepared to encounter equestrians at any time on all 4 loops. Dismount, stand quietly, and let the horses pass.

Rescue index: Gap Hollow, Black Oak Ridge, and Stave Mill loops are all fairly close to the highway. They are used regularly. If you run into problems here, you are likely to be helped by other trail users; or you can make your way to AR 7 and wait for help. If you ride the more remote High Mountain Loop, expect to be on your own.

Land status: National forest.

Maps: The Forest Service provides an excellent map of the network. It is color-coded to match markings on the ground, and shows contour lines for the area. This map is usually available at the trailhead. It is highly recommended that you carry this map when riding Moccasin Gap. With so many trails in the network, there are excellent opportunities to get lost.

To be sure you get a map, write the Forest Service at the address below. If you want to use a topo, you will find that the entire trail system falls onto the Simpson 7.5 minute map.

Finding the trail: The trailhead is just off AR 7, 23 miles north of Russellville. Look for a wooden Forest Service sign on the west side of the road indicating Moccasin Gap Horse Trail. A quarter-mile drive up a gravel forest road leads to the trailhead and parking area.

Sources of additional information:

Ozark National Forest
Bayou Ranger District
Route 1 Box 36
Hector, AR 72843
(501) 284-3150

Notes on the trail: This trail system is well marked, with color-coded horseshoe symbols differentiating each loop. Gap Hollow Loop is marked in blue. Most of it is easily rideable, but there are a few tough stretches on the northern leg.

Stave Mill Loop, closest to the trailhead and marked in orange, is almost all rideable. Black Oak Ridge Loop, marked in white, is all rideable except for one short stretch on its western side. It offers great views across Moccasin Hollow, though, so the tough part is well worth the effort.

The High Mountain Loop, marked in yellow, is the most remote and most difficult, but also the most scenic. Its inner loop is relatively easy, though a long ride is required to reach it. As mentioned previously, the northern segment of High Mountain is very rough. It's best to avoid it—although you should hike from the eastern end to the falls on Moccasin Creek. If you ride it anyway, follow it from west to east to take advantage of a fantastic (long but rough) descent. Expect to walk your bike between 1 and 2 miles along Moccasin Creek, but the scenery along the creek will be worth the effort.

Connector trails are marked with the color corresponding to the loop toward which you are riding. For example, the northern trail connecting Gap Hollow to High Mountain is marked in yellow for those headed toward High Mountain, and blue for those traveling toward Gap Hollow.

RIDE 42 *HUCKLEBERRY MOUNTAIN HORSE TRAILS*

This 40-mile trail system is a series of three loops around and near Huckleberry Mountain. The 11-mile White Loop is best for mountain biking, and beginners will enjoy it most. For most of its length it follows a combination of forest roads, unmaintained double-track, and abandoned logging roads. A bike club out of Fort Smith holds races on the White Loop each year.

The 29-mile Orange Loop is tougher, but has quite a bit of scenery to enjoy. It also uses forest roads and abandoned logging roads, with a little newly cut single-track for good measure. It can be divided into loops of 20 miles and 9 miles. If you start from Huckleberry Trail Camp, you could ride the nine-mile loop around Huckleberry Mountain. If you enjoyed that, you could then tackle the longer 20-mile loop. One place on the Orange that you may want to avoid is the stretch of trail along the power line cut (see "Hazards").

Mt. Magazine, 2,823 feet tall, is the highest point in Arkansas. It towers to the west and south of the Huckleberry Mountain Horse Trails. On the northwest part of the White Loop, there is a beautiful overlook from which you see the deep hollow of Shoal Creek in the foreground, with Mt. Magazine rising high above you in the distance.

The western leg of the Orange Loop parallels and crosses Shoal Creek many times. It follows a rough and unmaintained four-wheel-drive road. On the nine-mile loop around Huckleberry Mountain, there is a waterfall near one of the eastern stock ponds. This area is called Bell Springs, and has a really great swimming hole. It's worth stopping for, especially on hot summer days.

General location: 15 miles southeast of Paris.

Elevation change: The lowest elevation on both loops is 900′ along Shoal Creek. The White Loop reaches a peak of 1,700′ at the trailhead on the side of Mt. Magazine. The highest elevation on the Orange Loop is around 1,600′. The spur from the White Loop up to the trailhead is a steep 1-mile climb. There is 1 long climb and 1 long descent on the White Loop. Riding the White Loop clockwise results in your climb being smooth and your descent rough, technical, and fun.

The Orange Loop also has 1 long climb and descent. Both are fairly gradual, but stretch out over a couple of miles with many level breaks. Each loop has many shorter hills.

Season: Spring and fall are the best seasons to ride the Huckleberry Mountain Horse Trails.

Services: No drinking water is available along the trail. Water and camping are available at the nearby Cove Lake and Mt. Magazine recreation areas. Cove Lake also has swimming and showers. All services can be found in Ft. Smith, 35 miles to the west, and in Russellville, 35 miles to the east.

Hazards: Shoal Creek can be deep after a rainstorm. Don't try to cross it in flood stage. Watch yourself when riding the power line cut. It was cleared with a bush hog, leaving short, sharp stumps along the side of the trail. If you want to avoid the cut while riding the Orange Loop, ride Forest Service Road 1601. It parallels the trail section along the power line cut.

Rescue index: On weekends you will probably see other trail users. During the week is a different story. Even the roads that are open see little use. Be prepared to take care of yourself. Be ready to encounter horses at any time. Dismount, stand to the downhill side of the trail, and wait quietly for them to pass.

Land status: National forest.

Maps: The Forest Service has an excellent map of the trail system. It shows contour lines with 100′ intervals. Color coding shows the more difficult sections of the trail. All of the White Loop falls onto the Mt. Magazine NE 7.5 minute topo. Most of the Orange Loop falls onto the Mt. Magazine NE and Chickalah West 7.5 minute topos. A small section of the north part is on Scranton and New Blaine.

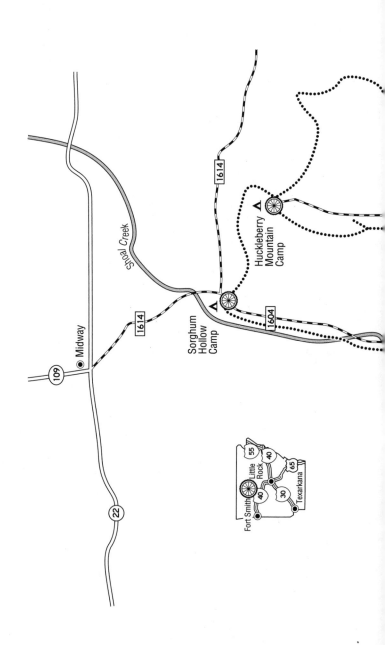

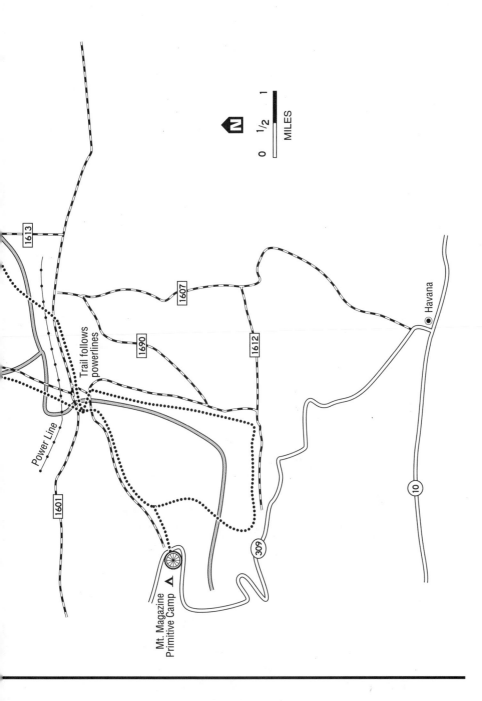

1613

1607

Havana

1690

1612

Power Line

Trail follows
powerlines

1601

10

Mt. Magazine
Primitive Camp

309

N

0   ½   1
MILES

Finding the trail: The trailhead for the White Loop is on the side of Mt. Magazine. From Paris, drive 16 miles southeast on AR 309. There is a primitive camp near the trailhead. Both the camp and the trailhead are just east of the facilities in Mt. Magazine Recreation Area.

The most accessible trailhead on the Orange Loop is at Sorghum Hollow Trail Camp. Drive 11 miles east from Paris on AR 22 to Forest Service Road 1614. Drive south on FS 1614 2.3 miles to FS 1604. Turn right on FS 1604 and drive a short distance to the camp.

Huckleberry Mountain Camp gives access to the short 8.6-mile loop on the Orange Loop. To reach it, drive south from Paris on AR 309. After 11 miles turn left on FS 1601 and follow it 8 miles to FR 1613. Turn left onto FS 1613, and follow it 3.5 miles to the camp.

Sources of additional information:

Ozark National Forest
Magazine Ranger District
Post Office Box 511
Highway 22 East and Kalamazoo Road
Paris, AR 72855
(501) 963-3076

Notes on the trail: This trail was finished just before press time. I was unable to go ride it myself, so please forgive any inaccuracies you find. The information presented here is based on phone conversations with the trail designer and a cyclist who had ridden the White Loop. The cyclist's club holds races on that loop. He had been told by equestrians that the Orange Loop may be too rough for bikers. On the other hand, the trail designer, an equestrian, thought most of it would be rideable. She said it was less rugged than the Moccasin Gap Horse Trails north of Russellville. Because most of the Moccasin Gap trails are rideable, I recommend checking out the Orange Loop.

From April to May, part of the Orange Loop is closed for turkey hunting, nesting, and hatching. Contact the Forest Service at the Magazine Ranger District for specific dates.

RIDE 43 *BUNCE GAP*

If some nice easy riding and beautiful views are the order for your day, you'll enjoy this 12-mile loop ride. For the most part, it follows beginner-suited gravel Forest Service roads. But experts don't be dismayed—one long section of Forest Service Road 1514 is narrow, washed-out, rocky, and perfect for mountain biking. There are also optional side trips on old logging roads that offer chal-

RIDE 43 *BUNCE GAP*

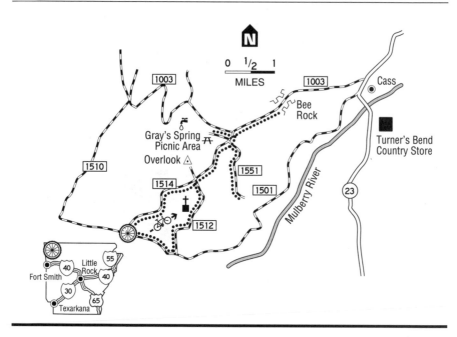

lenging trail riding. One good place for this bushwhacking is at the end of FS 1551, a dead-end road leading off the upper reaches of FS 1514. FS 1551 ends at a primitive campsite, and several four-wheeler trails radiate outward from there. Riding on these adds a little single-track experience to your outing.

Scenic vistas are the highlight of Bunce Gap. Just south of the junction of FS 1514 and 1512, a narrow road leads a short distance west to a small clearing. Ride to the west end of the clearing and look for a trail going off into the woods to the right. Follow this trail for around a quarter mile, and you'll arrive at a great view over Deep Hollow and Spirits Creek. There are flat, shaded rocks to sit on while you enjoy the scenery.

Another highlight is Bee Rock, 1.5 miles east of the junction at Bunce Gap. Here the road passes through a slot between two huge boulders. Then, one mile west of Bunce Gap Junction, you'll also find Gray's Spring Picnic Area, where you can have lunch with still another great view.

Traveling south on FS 1512 just past its junction with FS 1514, look for a faint road to the west. Following this a quarter mile will take you to a fascinating old cemetery, with graves from the mid-1800s to just after the turn of the century. The repeated appearance of the epitaph "Died At Birth" will make you reflect on how precarious life once was in the Boston Mountains.

Enjoying the view from the scenic overlook near the junction of Forest Service roads 1514 and 1512.

General location: 25 miles northwest of Ozark.

Elevation change: Elevation ranges from 900′ at the trailhead to 1,650′ at Bunce Gap. There is 1 major climb and 1 major descent.

Season: Spring and fall, with their cooler temperatures, are best for riding this trail. Since it's short, though, off-season riders can complete the ride before summer heat or winter chill have too much effect.

Services: Food, water, camping, and gasoline can be obtained at Turner's Bend Country Store just south of Cass. Look for it next to the Mulberry River Bridge on AR 23.

Water can be obtained during the ride by making the side trip to Gray's Spring Picnic Area. Water is also available at Shores Lake and White Rock Mountain campgrounds.

Hotels and restaurants are in Ozark, 17 miles south of Cass on AR 23. The nearest bike shops are in Fayetteville, 40 miles to the northwest.

Hazards: There are no real hazards on this loop. Be careful on the long descent down FS 1512. Some of the turns are sharp and the road surface is strewn with loose gravel.

Rescue index: With the exception of the upper part of FS 1514, this loop will see some automobile traffic. If you encounter trouble on FS 1514 or on the side trails, you will be on your own.

Land status: National forest.

Maps: A map of the Ozark National Forest is highly recommended as a supplement to the one in this book. The topo for the area is the Bidville 7.5 minute map.

Finding the trail: Start this ride from an undeveloped campsite at the intersection of Forest Roads 1501 and 1514. To reach it from Cass, drive west 8.5 miles on FS 1501 (known locally as Baptist Village Road). To reach the starting point from Mulberry, drive north from Interstate 40 on AR 215 until the pavement ends (about 17 miles). At that point, the road designation changes to FS 1501. Continue an additional 2 miles to the intersection with FS 1514.

Sources of additional information:

Ozark National Forest
Boston Mountain District
Highway 23 North, Post Office Box 302
Ozark, AR 72949
(501) 667-2191

Turner's Bend Country Store
HCR 63 Box 143
Ozark, AR 72949
(501) 667-3641

The Pack Rat
2397 Green Acres Road
Fayetteville, AR 72703
(501) 521-6340

Notes on the trail: It is best to ride this loop clockwise, going north on FS 1514 and returning south on FS 1512. FS 1512 is steep, gravelly, and winding. It is much more fun to descend on FS 1512 instead of fighting the gravel while climbing.

RIDE 44 *RAGTOWN ROAD RIDE*

This 18-mile loop is perfect for those of you who want to combine a mountain bike ride with a canoe trip on the nearby Mulberry River. At Turner's Bend, you can camp, rent your canoe and shuttle, and start your mountain tour on the Ragtown Road Ride. It's a great ride for beginners because it uses forest roads in good condition, letting inexperienced riders enjoy the Ozark Mountain scenery instead of watching the ground in front of the wheel. If you're lucky, you might spot one of the black bears found in this part of the national forest.

There are plenty of good vistas along this ride, but for one of the best, a side trip is in order. When you top out of the climb to Five Corners (so named

RIDE 44 *RAGTOWN ROAD RIDE*

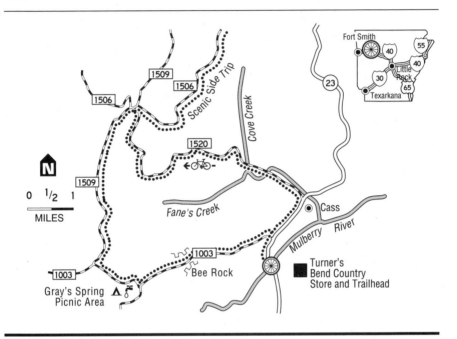

because of the five roads diverging from one point) deviate from the route shown on the map by riding east on Forest Service Road 1506. You will climb an additional mile to 2,200 feet, but your extra effort will be rewarded with views over the Mulberry River Valley that are surpassed only by those on White Rock Mountain.

After the one-mile climb, the trail winds for four relatively level miles along the ridge connecting Parker Mountain, Hoyle Mountain, and Fisher Gap. Upon reaching Fisher Gap, turn around and return to Five Corners, where you will ride southwest on FS 1509 to continue the loop.

Other highlights are two stream crossings on Fane's Creek, a side trip to Gray's Spring Picnic Area for its vistas, and a ride through Bee Rock, where the road passes through a slot between two huge boulders. Just past Bee Rock is the beginning of a fast 2.7-mile downhill back to AR 23 and Turner's Bend.

General location: 17 miles north of Ozark.
Elevation change: Starting at 800′ in Cass, you will ascend to 1,700′ at Five Corners. From this high point, the ride along FS 1509 (Ragtown Road) is level all the way to its junction with FS 1003. This level trend continues as you pedal east on FS 1003. The ride ends with a 2.7-mile descent back to Cass.

Season: Spring and fall are best for riding this loop. Summer riding can be good when combined with a swim or float on the nearby Mulberry River. Call Turner's Bend Country Store for boat rentals and information on river levels.

Services: Water, parking, food, camping, and gas can be obtained at Turner's Bend Country Store, the starting point for the ride. Water is also available at Gray's Spring Picnic Area, just off the route to the west on FS 1003.

Other campgrounds in the area are Forest Service campgrounds at Redding, Shores Lake, and White Rock Mountain. Hotels, restaurants, and grocery stores can be accessed in Ozark, 17 miles to the south on AR 23. The nearest bike shops are in Fayetteville, 40 miles to the northwest.

Hazards: You'll find no unusual hazards along the Ragtown Road Ride.

Rescue index: You are never more than 10 miles from Cass, and all roads used by this ride see some cars every day.

Land status: National forest.

Maps: The USGS topos for this ride are the 7.5 minute Bidville and Cass maps. A map of the Ozark National Forest may also be useful.

Finding the trail: The starting point for this ride is Turner's Bend Country Store, 17 miles north of Ozark on AR 23. Look for the store and campground just south of the bridge over the Mulberry. Check with the owners before leaving your car. They operate a busy canoe rental business and campground in the summer, and will appreciate your parking out of the way.

Sources of additional information:

Ozark National Forest
Boston Mountain District
Highway 23 North
Post Office Box 302
Ozark, AR 72949
(501) 667-2191

Turner's Bend Country Store
HCR 63 Box 143
Ozark, AR 72949
(501) 667-3641

The Pack Rat
2397 Green Acres Road
Fayetteville, AR 72704
(501) 521-6340

Notes on the trail: A map of the Ozark National Forest is highly recommended for this and other rides in the forest. In addition to helping you find your way on the rides, it will introduce you to other roads than can shorten, lengthen, or otherwise improve these loops. The map is $2, and can be obtained at Turner's Bend, or at any Forest Service office.

The only point of the Ragtown Road Ride that is confusing is at Five Corners, where Forest Roads 1520, 1509, and 1506 all come together. Adding to the confusion, FS 1520 is shown on the map as 1509-A, while it is marked on the ground as 1520. If you ride the trail counter-clockwise, you'll approach Five Corners on FS 1520, and be least likely to get confused.

RIDE 45 *SPY ROCK TRAIL*

Spy Rock Trail is the best ride in the White Rock Mountain area. If you're looking for a single-track experience, this 23-mile-long trail is moderately difficult, with some rocky and steep stretches requiring intermediate bike-handling skills. But these can easily be portaged by novices. All of the trail uses forest roads. The west side of the loop uses Forest Service Road 1504, a narrow, well-maintained gravel road. At mile 13, the trail makes a right turn onto FS 1533, an abandoned road used only by four-wheelers and mountain bikes. It is much rougher, and much more fun if you're looking for a more challenging ride.

All of FS 1533 is a narrow four-wheel-drive road that is as challenging as most single-track. There are also several interesting side trails leading off it. These make for great additional rough riding and exploration. Take a map of the Ozark National Forest with you, and have some fun exploring.

General location: 40 miles southeast of Fayetteville.
Elevation change: Elevation at the trailhead in Redding Campground is 800'. From there, the trail climbs over a 2.5-mile stretch to a peak of 1,800'. The middle part of the loop is relatively level, with short climbs and descents. The ride ends with a steep and rocky downhill back to FS 1003, and a level 3-mile cruise on FS 1003 back to Redding Campground.
Season: While spring and fall are best for riding this trail, year-round riding could be considered. Summer heat can be offset by a swim or canoe trip on the nearby Mulberry River. Because there are no stream crossings, those willing to deal with the cold could enjoy the ride in winter.
Services: Drinking water and camping are available at the trailhead in Redding Campground. Food, water, and additional camping are available at Turner's Bend Country Store just south of Cass.

Hotels, restaurants, and grocery stores are in Ozark, 17 miles south of Cass on AR 23. The nearest bike shops are in Fayetteville, 40 miles to the northeast.
Hazards: Parts of FS 1533 are rocky and washed out. On the fast descent near the end of 1533 the trail briefly parallels a barbed-wire fence. Don't lose control and get tattooed.
Rescue index: FS 1504 sees some traffic each day, so you will not have to wait long for help if you have a problem there. The much rougher four-wheel-drive

RIDE 45 *SPY ROCK TRAIL*

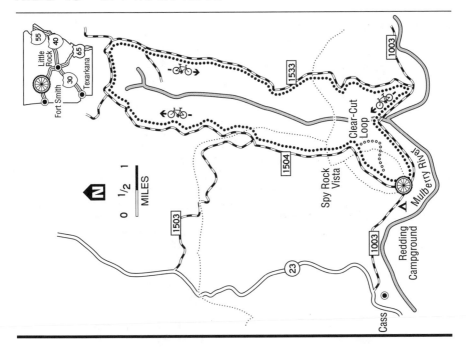

track of FR 1533 is a different story. If you get in trouble there, you will be on your own.

Land status: National forest.

Maps: 7.5 minute topos covering the area are Cass and Yale. A map of the Ozark National Forest is also helpful.

Finding the trail: The starting point for this ride is the Redding Campground. To reach it, go to Cass, 17 miles north of Ozark on AR 23. Just north of Cass, go east on FS 1003. Follow this gravel road 3 miles to Redding Campground.

Sources of additional information:

Ozark National Forest
Pleasant Hill Ranger District
Highway 21 North, Post Office Box 190
Clarksville, AR 72830
(501) 754-2864

On the climb northbound from Redding Campground on FS 1504, Spy Rock Trail.

The Pack Rat
2397 Green Acres Road
Fayetteville, AR 72704
(501) 521-6340

Turner's Bend Country Store
HCR 63 Box 143
Highway 23 North
Ozark, AR 72949
(501) 667-3641

Notes on the trail: This ride is best taken clockwise—you'll have a tough climb at the start, but at least it's on good road, saving the steep rocky part at the other end for a fast, fun descent.

After turning north on FS 1504 from Redding Campground, you will immediately begin the climb from the Mulberry River Valley to the top of Morgan Mountain. About 1 mile up the climb, you will see a narrow, unmaintained track into the woods to your right. This track is known to local riders as the clear-cut loop. By following it to the east and turning left at every fork, you will enjoy a 2-mile stretch of single-track that crosses a clear-cut with views of the Mulberry River Valley before curving back to the west to rejoin FS 1504.

Another highlight is near the top of the climb on FS 1504, where a spur of the Ozark Highlands Trail crosses the road. This trail is not open to bikes, but a quarter-mile hike to the west will take you to Spy Rock, a ledge overlooking the Mulberry River Valley.

Continuing north on FS 1504, you will follow a U-shaped ridge that surrounds the watershed of Herrod's Creek. Picking up FS 1533, the trail heads back south, passing small clear-cuts with sweeping views, a large glade, and the foundations and chimney of a farm dating from the early part of the century. If you've taken the ride clockwise, your ride finishes with a fast, rough 2.5-mile descent back to FS 1003, where you will ride west 3 miles back to Redding Campground.

RIDE 46   *WHITE ROCK MOUNTAIN TOUR*

Although the White Rock Mountain Tour is long, it is spectacularly beautiful, and fun for riders of all skill levels. Beginners will enjoy the lack of rough terrain, while more experienced riders can attack the long climbs along the way.

This 38-mile loop uses gravel or hard-packed roads for its entire length. All roads are in good condition and can be negotiated with little difficulty, leaving you free to enjoy the Boston Mountain scenery. Because of the long climbs on this tour, you should be in good physical condition before trying to ride the whole loop in one day.

The vistas on this ride are incredible. They make the long climbs well worth the effort. Another payback for the climbs is blowing down the long descents that follow. You'll cross several streams on Forest Service Road 1520, and go under overhanging rocks on FS 1505 and FS 1003. The most spectacular point on the ride is the summit of White Rock Mountain. A lookout on one corner of the mountaintop gives you a 270-degree panorama, and a preview of the road you'll take on your trip down the mountain.

General location: 35 miles southeast of Fayetteville.
Elevation change: From a low of 800′ near Cass, you will climb to 2,200′ at the summit of White Rock Mountain. Riding the loop counter-clockwise, there are

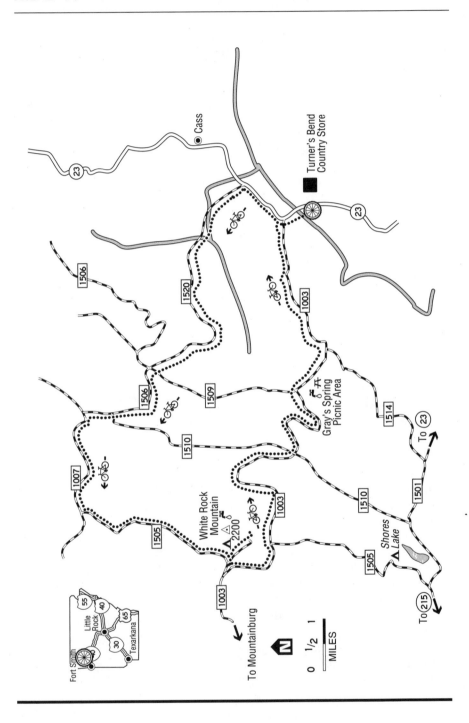

6 major climbs varying in length from 1 mile to 2.5 miles, with corresponding descents. The ride ends with a 2.7-mile descent.

Season: While you can count on a few good riding days any month of the year in Arkansas, spring and fall are the best times to ride the White Rock Mountain Tour. Winter riding can be chilly, but it offers better views from the many ridges traversed by the forest roads on the loop.

Services: Water is available at the campground on the summit of White Rock Mountain, at Gray's Spring Picnic Area on FS 1003, and at Turner's Bend Country Store, just south of Cass on AR 23. Turner's Bend also has gas, food, camping, showers, and canoe rental for floating the nearby Mulberry River. Riders are welcome to park at the store while they ride.

Other campgrounds in the area are Redding Campground, 3 miles east of Cass; Shores Lake Recreation Area, 5 miles south of the White Rock Mountain Summit; and on White Rock Mountain itself. There are also 3 rental cabins on the mountaintop. You'll find restaurants and hotels in Ozark, 17 miles south of Cass on AR 23. The nearest bike shops are in Fayetteville, 40 miles to the northwest.

Hazards: Because the White Rock Mountain Tour uses forest roads throughout its length, hazards are few. But don't get carried away on the downhills. Turns come up quickly and may be strewn with loose gravel. Be prepared to encounter an occasional car.

Rescue index: The White Rock Mountain area, with its cabins, spectacular views, and close proximity to Fayetteville and Fort Smith, is one of the more popular areas in the Ozark National Forest. If you run into trouble, you shouldn't have to wait long for a car or other rider.

Land status: National forest.

Maps: USGS topos covering this tour are the 7.5 minute Bidville, Cass, Delaney, and St. Paul maps. The guide best showing all roads used by this loop is the Ozark National Forest map.

Finding the trail: There are two starting points for this trail. One is Turner's Bend Country Store, 17 miles north of Ozark on AR 23, where the highway crosses the Mulberry River. Check with the owners when you arrive. They run a busy float trip business in the summer, and will appreciate it if you don't park in a critical area.

You could also start the ride from White Rock Mountain Summit. To reach it, go 14 miles north from Mulberry on AR 215 to FS 1505. Go left (north) on 1505 8 miles to FS 1003. Go northwest (left) on FS 1003 to FS 1505. Turn right on FS 1505 and follow it to the summit.

Rock outcroppings overhang FS 1505 near the top of the climb to the summit of White Rock Mountain.

Sources of additional information:

Ozark National Forest
Boston Mountain Ranger District
Highway 23 North
Post Office Box 302
Ozark, AR 72949
(501) 667-2191

The Pack Rat
2397 Green Acres Road
Fayetteville, AR 72704
(501) 521-6340

Turner's Bend Country Store
HCR 63 Box 143
Ozark, AR 72949
(501) 667-3641

Notes on the trail: The White Rock Mountain Tour is most enjoyable when you ride it counter-clockwise. Either direction out of Cass starts uphill almost immediately, but the climb on the north portion of the loop is less steep, and it's

Vista from the Summit of White Rock Mountain. It will be worth the climb!

easier on cold muscles. Riding the northern leg first also lets you end your ride with a fast 2.7-mile downhill.

This is a tough ride, but the scenery is worth every drop of sweat. If you don't feel up to the whole ride in one day, line up a support driver and make it a 2-day event. Stay in a cabin or campsite on top of White Rock Mountain, enjoying an evening at one of the highest summits in the Ozarks.

There is some confusion between markings on the Ozark National Forest map and road markings on the ground. To avoid confusion, here are the roads you should use on this loop. Leave Cass westbound on FR 1520 (shown on the map as 1509A). Follow 1520 8 miles to an intersection known locally as Five Corners, named for the five roads diverging radially from that point.

At Five Corners, take the second left, which is FS 1506. Follow 1506 3 miles to a T intersection, which is FS 1007. Turn left on FS 1007 and follow it 3 miles to FS 1505. Turn left on 1505, and ride 4 miles to a fork in the road. The fork

View from FS 1003 just east of White Rock Mountain.

to the left is the entrance to White Rock Mountain Campground and Recreation Area.

When you leave the mountain, take the other fork. It will take you west one-third mile to FS 1003. Turn left onto FS 1003, and follow it all the way back to AR 23 and Cass. Carrying the map in this book and a map of the Ozark National Forest and paying attention to the road signs will keep you from getting lost.

Buffalo National River Trails

Some think the Buffalo River was named for the small number of bison living in the river valley when the first settlers came. Others think it was named for the buffalo fish, a sucker that lived in the river in the old days. Another theory says that because the valley's earliest settlers were from Tennessee, they named the stream for the Buffalo River in their home state. No one knows the answer for sure. But it's certain that a lot of people care about this beautiful Ozark stream.

In the 1960s, a proposal for a dam and reservoir in the Tyler Bend reach of the Buffalo led to the formation of the Ozark Society. The society took action to preserve this wild river area. Their efforts bore fruit in 1972, when Congress designated the Buffalo a national river. Most of the land along the river was then purchased by the park service, and is being allowed to revert to its natural state.

The result is a unique combination of wild land and history. Hiking or riding in the area, you'll pass through hollows used as hideouts for guerrilla bands during the Civil War. Abandoned homesteads dot Buffalo River country. Several of these, like the Parker-Hickman Homestead on the Erbie Loop, have been stabilized, and look much as they did in the late 1800s. Others leave only old foundations, or tangled piles of lumber or logs to tell where the buildings once stood.

Especially interesting is the small town of Gilbert. The Gilbert Ferry operated there until around 1930, when a bridge was built nearby. A railroad spur once ran to Gilbert, where it picked up timber logged upstream on the Buffalo and floated down to the railhead. The Gilbert Store is still open. In addition to food and other supplies for river runners, this old general store has a collection of antiques and artifacts from past times on the Buffalo.

The scenery along the river is fantastic. Bluffs tower over 500 feet above the river. Peter Cave Bluff on the Snowball Loop has several overlooks where you can relax and watch the river snake through the valleys below. On the Woolum Ford and Richland Creek Tour, you'll ride next to The Nars, a razor-thin bluff separating the Buffalo from the Richland Creek Valley on the other side. Scramble to the top of The Nars and enjoy the view. Skull Rock, also known as Bat Cave, is a set of holes in a bluff you could paddle a canoe into when the river is at the right level. It's so beautiful here you shouldn't limit yourself to biking—take time out and float part of this beautiful Ozark river.

While the many miles of hiking trails in the park are not open to bikes, don't let that keep you from enjoying them, either. Leave your bike behind one day and put on your hiking boots. The trail to Hemmed In Hollow takes you to a beautiful waterfall. It's the tallest between the Rockies and the Appalachians. On the way you can hike the goat trail, a ledge 300 feet above the river, partway up the side of Big Bluff. From Cave Mountain Road above Boxley, a 1.5-mile spur trail leads to Hawk's Bill Crag in the Upper Buffalo Wilderness. The Crag offers one of the most dramatic vistas in Arkansas.

When you're through exploring the Buffalo National River's hiking trails, go get your bike and head for the many miles of old double-track that fan out over the hills on each side of the river. Once used to reach the homesteads along the Buffalo, they now bless mountain bikers with some first-class fun.

When combined with surrounding county roads and forest roads, these tracks make scenic loops that can be ridden by cyclists of all skill levels. It is easiest to find your way when you supplement the trail maps in this book with maps of Searcy and Newton counties.

There are 14 campgrounds in the Buffalo National River. Buffalo Point campground has cabins for rent, and canoe rentals are available from outfitters up and down the river. The Buffalo Outdoor Center in Silver Hill rents mountain bikes. The Buffalo is a great place to spend an entire week, enjoying a myriad of activities.

Just be careful of a couple of things. Never dive into the river from the bluffs or trees above. Every year there are injuries or deaths from people diving into the river, not aware of rocks just below the surface. If you plan to float on or camp next to the river, don't bring any glass containers. The park service wants future river users to be able to wade in the Buffalo without worrying about deep cuts on their feet. No glass containers are allowed on the river, on trails, in caves, or within 50 feet of any shoreline.

RIDE 47 *UPPER BUFFALO WILDERNESS LOOP*

While this 37-mile loop ride contains some steep climbs and a few rough, rocky sections, it is not technically difficult. It can be easily handled by beginners in good physical condition for the climbing. Eighteen miles of the loop take you along the paved surfaces of AR 21 and AR 16. The rest is on dirt and gravel roads that range in condition from good to poor. One four-mile stretch on Forest Service Road 1410 is in very poor condition. In other words, it is perfect for mountain biking. Several double-track roads split off FS 1410, making interesting and challenging side trips when you have the time to explore.

Located on the northern edge of the Boston Mountains, the Buffalo River descends steeply in its upper reaches, carving bluffs that reach as high as 500 feet above the river. These bluffs are cut from the sediment of ancient seabeds from which the Bostons arose. Caves are common in this remnant sea floor.

One of the better-known ones lies along the trail one-half mile south of the Buffalo River bridge on AR 21. Once called Dead Man's Cave because of a body discovered at its entrance, it is large enough to have served for years as a community gathering site. It hosted weddings, dances, revivals, and town meet-

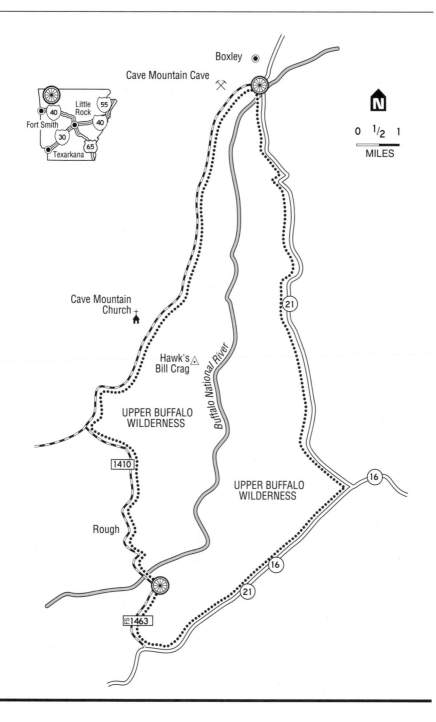

Boxley

Cave Mountain Cave

N

0 1/2 1
MILES

Little
Rock

40
55

Fort Smith
40

30
65

Texarkana

Cave Mountain
Church

Hawk's
Bill Crag

UPPER BUFFALO
WILDERNESS

Buffalo National River

21

1410

Rough

UPPER BUFFALO
WILDERNESS

16

16

21

1463

ings. During the Civil War, the Confederacy used it as a gunpowder factory until it was captured by Union forces. It's open from mid-May to mid-August on a self-guided basis, and closed for the rest of the year to protect a colony of endangered gray bats that hibernates there.

Seven miles farther south on Cave Mountain Road, just past the Cave Mountain Cemetery, you'll see a small parking area for wilderness access. A short hike east into the wilderness will take you to Hawk's Bill Crag, one of the most spectacular overlooks in all Arkansas. The crag is the subject of many postcards sold in the area, and once made the cover of *National Geographic*. HIKE, DON'T RIDE, IN TO THE CRAG. IT IS IN THE WILDERNESS AREA, WHERE BIKES ARE NOT ALLOWED.

At the southern end of FS 1410, the trail crosses the upper Buffalo. Here the stream flows over a set of rock ledges. It's a perfect place to admire the scenery, catch a few rays, and dangle your feet in the water.

General location: Near Boxley, just south of the junction of AR 21 and AR 74.
Elevation change: Elevations range from 1,100′ at the Buffalo River bridge on AR 21 to 2,400′ on the southern part of FS 1410, just before you begin the long descent to the upper Buffalo ford. There are 2 major climbs, 2 major descents, and many hills throughout the ride.
Season: Spring and fall are best for riding the Upper Buffalo Wilderness Loop. Summer is also good, but can be very hot and humid. A ford of the upper Buffalo can help offset the summer swelter, unless it has been so dry that there is no water in the upper river.
Services: No drinking water is available along this ride. Water and camping are available at Lost Valley Campground in the Buffalo National River, 4 miles north of Boxley on AR 74. Cabins and a small grocery store are in Ponca, 2 miles past Lost Valley on AR 74.

Hotels, restaurants, groceries, and gas can be found in Jasper, 20 miles to the east on AR 74. The nearest bike shop is The Bicycle Outfitter in Harrison, 35 miles to the northeast.
Hazards: Hazards are few on this ride. Don't cross the upper Buffalo ford during high water. Watch for cars on AR 16 and AR 21.
Rescue index: The rescue index is excellent along all sections of the ride except the rough part of FS 1410. It is seldom used. If you get in a jam here, you are on your own.
Land status: The Upper Buffalo Wilderness Loop passes through a combination of private property, national park land, and national forest. Respect the rights of private landowners by obeying No Trespassing signs.
Maps: Helpful maps are those of the Buffalo National River, the Ozark National Forest, and the 7.5 minute topos for Boxley and Fallsville.
Finding the trail: This ride may be accessed from 2 points. One is at the northern extremity of the loop, next to the Buffalo River bridge on AR 21. Park your

Crossing of the headwaters of the Buffalo River along the southern edge of the Upper Buffalo Wilderness Loop.

car on the shoulder of the dirt road next to the river. This road is Cave Mountain Road, which takes you past the cave, near Hawk's Bill Crag, and to FS 1410.

The access point at the southern end of the loop may be reached by driving northeast 1.5 miles from Fallsville on AR 16/21 to FS 1463. Turn north on FS 1463 and drive 1 mile to a wilderness access parking area.

Sources of additional information:

Ozark National Forest
Buffalo Ranger District
Post Office Box 427
Highway 7 North
Jasper, AR 72641
(501) 446-5122

Buffalo National River
Post Office Box 1173
Harrison, AR 72602-1173
(501) 741-5443

Notes on the trail: Much of what makes this ride enjoyable is off the trail. Cave Mountain Cave, Hawk's Bill Crag, and the upper Buffalo crossing are all interesting sites. Starting the loop at its northern end puts you closer to the cave and the crag, so that if you spend more time than you intended at either of these attractions, you can easily bail out and ride back to your car.

On the other hand, starting the loop at its southern end gives you a real parking lot and trailhead, as opposed to parking on the shoulder of a dirt road at the northern end. Parking in the south also puts you very near the upper Buffalo crossing, the roughest and most fun part of the ride with its many side trails to explore.

Base your decision on your interest, and have fun.

RIDE 48 *BUFFALO NATIONAL RIVER: ERBIE LOOP*

This 20-mile loop is a good introduction to the Buffalo River country. It can be ridden by cyclists of all skill levels. Two and a half miles of the loop use the paved surface of AR 7. There is a small shoulder that makes this portion of the ride safe, in spite of the highway traffic. Five miles of the loop on the north river road follow seldom-used four-wheel-drive tracks that are rough, rocky, washed-out, and fun. These old roads served homesteads in the days before the area became a national park. The rest of the loop is on maintained dirt and gravel roads.

If the river is up, you'll get a cool splash as you pedal across the slab at Erbie Ford. Depending on recent rainfall, there may be other stream crossings along the north river road.

Swimming in the Buffalo is a great way to cool off after a hot summer ride. Better still, spend a weekend on the Buffalo, combining mountain biking with a canoe trip on this scenic river.

You should take time to explore some of the abandoned side roads leading off the loop. Many lead to old homesteads. One of these, the Parker-Hickman Homestead, is located one mile west of the Erbie Campground. It has been stabilized and opened to the public. There is an interpretive sign there, but the site is otherwise unimproved—it looks as it must have in the old days. You are free to wander through the buildings, enjoying the atmosphere of days gone by on the Buffalo.

General location: 5 miles north of Jasper on AR 7.
Elevation change: Elevations range from 800′ along the river to 1,350′ at the high points along the north river road. This is a hilly ride. In addition to numerous small climbs and descents, there is a 1-mile ascent and a 1.5-mile descent on the north side of the river, and a 1-mile climb and matching descent while riding on AR 7 on the south side of the river.
Season: While there may be good riding days throughout the year in Arkansas,

RIDE 48 *BUFFALO NATIONAL RIVER: ERBIE LOOP*

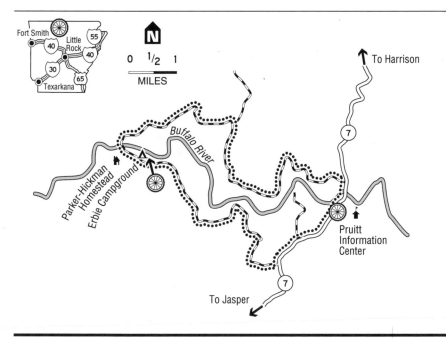

spring and fall are the best. These two seasons feature cooler temperatures, spring wildflower blooms, and blazing fall foliage outlined against the bluffs along the Buffalo.

Summer riding can be great, especially when combined with a swim or canoe trip on the Buffalo. Winter rides are good, too, but you may get your feet wet crossing the river at Erbie Ford.

Services: Drinking water is available along the ride at both Pruitt Information Station and Erbie Campground. The nearest camping is at Erbie Campground. Other sites, both public and private, can be found along the Buffalo. Pick up a map of the Buffalo National River at Pruitt, to see where the public campsites are.

Hotels, grocery stores, and restaurants are in Jasper, 5 miles to the south, and in Harrison, 21 miles to the north. The nearest bike shop is The Bicycle Outfitter in Harrison.

Hazards: Ride cautiously on the short stretch of the loop on AR 7. It can be busy on weekends and during rush hour. There is a 3-foot shoulder that will keep you out of harm's way.

Do not try to cross the Buffalo at Erbie Ford during high water. Flooding is most likely in early spring and during summer thunderstorms.

Rescue index: While most of this loop follows roads that see several cars per day, the rough 5-mile section of the north river road sees little use. If you have trouble on this stretch you will probably be on your own.

Land status: This ride passes through a combination of national park and private land. Respect the rights of property owners by heeding the No Trespassing signs on land along the way.

Maps: A Park Service map of the Buffalo National River will show where the various facilities are located, but will only show part of the ride. A map of Newton County will show most of the roads used by the Erbie Loop. The Jasper 7.5 minute topo shows all roads on this ride.

Finding the trail: There are 2 access points for this ride. The most convenient is Pruitt Information Center, where AR 7 crosses the Buffalo. It is 5 miles north of Jasper or 21 miles south of Harrison. If you want to camp before or after your ride, consider starting the ride at Erbie Campground. To reach it, go 2.5 miles south from Pruitt on AR 7. Turn north where a sign points the way to Erbie. Follow a gravel road (part of the loop ride) 6 miles to the campground.

Sources of additional information:

Buffalo National River
Post Office Box 1173
Harrison, AR 72602-1173
(501) 741-5443

The Bicycle Outfitter
110–112 North Walnut
Harrison, AR 72601
(501) 741-6833

Notes on the trail: The north side of the loop can be confusing. Keep the river to the south and maintain an east-west direction of travel, and you'll stay on the right path. Because there are no markings, you may be confused by several faint side roads leading south toward the river. If in doubt, check them out. You won't be able to stray too far off the route before you hit the river or the road disappears. You may find an interesting old homestead or scenic spot along the Buffalo.

One turn is fairly easy to miss. When riding the loop clockwise, you'll come to an intersection 4 miles east of the Erbie ford. The well-maintained road you will have been following will curve north not far after cresting a hill. To the right (south) goes a narrower road that immediately begins to descend. Take it. It is the rough and scenic north river road. There will be many side roads going off it. Just stick to the more obvious road and maintain an easterly direction and you'll reach Pruitt, about 8 miles later.

RIDE 49 *BUFFALO NATIONAL RIVER: MT. HERSEY LOOP*

This 20-mile loop is an excellent ride for beginners. It uses dirt and gravel roads, a portion of pavement on AR 123, and a fun stretch of narrow double-track on the descent from the south river road to Mt. Hersey ford. The only rough riding is on that descent, where this double-track through the forest bounces over rock ledges, through mudholes, and across gravel bars next to the river.

Riders looking for more challenging riding can check out the many double-track side roads leading off the main route. One of the more interesting side trips leaves the main loop approximately 1.5 miles east of Carver Access on the south side of the river. Turning left (north) off the main road and riding this narrow track for one mile will lead you to a crumbling log cabin and the remains of a farmstead next to the river.

The Buffalo River has carved its way deep into the surrounding Boston Mountains, leaving bluffs towering up to 500 feet above its meanders. A 250-foot example of these bluffs overlooks the river just south of Mt. Hersey Ford. The river crossing at Mt. Hersey is an exhilarating splash through the clear, gravel-bottomed Buffalo. It feels great on a hot summer day.

This ford will challenge those who don't like to get wet. Expect the water to be at least knee-deep and flowing strongly. It may be deeper during spring or in the few days after local rainfall.

General location: 25 miles southeast of Harrison.

Elevation change: From a low of 680′ at Mt. Hersey Ford, the trail reaches several high points of 1,250′ along the loop. There are 4 or 5 major ascents and descents, depending on your chosen direction of travel.

While this ride doesn't require high-level biking skills, many shorter ups and downs are interspersed among the longer ones, making the loop a challenge.

Season: Spring, summer, and fall are all excellent times to ride this loop. Temperatures are warm enough for crossing the Buffalo at Mt. Hersey during these seasons. The river crossing precludes winter riding for all but the most determined cyclists.

Services: Drinking water is available at Carver Access, the recommended starting point for the ride. Camping is available at both Carver and Mt. Hersey. All other services can be found in Harrison, 25 miles to the north.

Hazards: Crossing the Buffalo can be hazardous. Cross while walking at an angle downstream, holding your bike out of the water so it won't get swept away. Keep the bike downstream of you. If the current catches it while you hold it on your upstream side, you could be knocked over.

Don't cross at all during floods, or when the water is above mid-thigh in the current. If the current feels too strong, move up or downstream to a slow pool,

RIDE 49 *BUFFALO NATIONAL RIVER: MT. HERSEY LOOP*

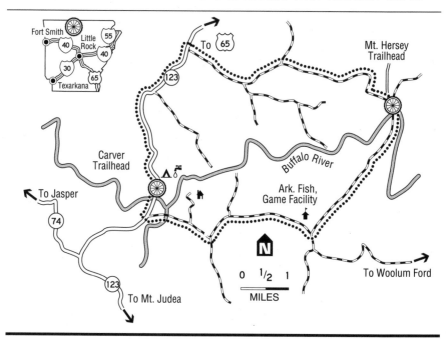

where the river, while deeper, can be crossed safely without the current sweeping you downstream.

Rescue index: With the exception of the rough double-track descending from the south side of the loop to Mt. Hersey ford, all roads used on this ride see several cars per day. You will probably be found quickly if you get into trouble. If you have problems on the double-track to Mt. Hersey, you will be on your own.

Land status: The Mt. Hersey Loop passes through land belonging to the Buffalo National River, through the Gene Rush Wildlife Management Area, and through private property on county roads.

Maps: A map of Newton County is best for riders pedaling the Mt. Hersey Loop. Topos covering the area are the 7.5 minute Mt. Judea, Hasty, Eula, and Western Grove.

Finding the trail: The best starting point for this loop is Carver, a river access site on the Buffalo. To reach Carver from Harrison, drive 12 miles southeast on US 65 to AR 123. Go south on AR 123, 13 miles to Carver. To reach Carver from Jasper, go east 10 miles from Jasper on AR 74 to AR 123. Turn north on AR 123 and drive 2 miles to Carver. Park in the lot next to the camp area.

Tumbledown log cabins, like this one on a side trail off the Mt. Hersey Loop, are from days gone by on the Buffalo National River.

Sources of additional information:

Buffalo National River
Post Office Box 1173
Harrison, AR 72602-1173
(501) 741-5443

Notes on the trail: As mentioned in the introduction, there are miles of old roads on Buffalo National River land, all open to mountain bikes. The south side of the loop, where the ride passes through the Gene Rush Wildlife Management Area, contains many of these. Most are rough four-wheel-drive tracks, and are a blast to ride. Just keep track of where you are. In this tangle of old trails in the woods, it's possible to get lost. Even on the main route it's fairly easy to take a wrong turn at several forks in the road. Be sure you bring a map with you while riding.

Start your ride from Carver Access and proceed around the loop counter-clockwise. Turn left (south) out of Carver Access onto AR 123. Take the first left after crossing the river and ride across Big Creek on a low-water bridge. About 2 miles down this gravel road there will be an old double-track heading north. Following this will take you to the tumbledown log cabin mentioned earlier.

About 5 miles into the ride, you'll see a fork in the wide gravel road on which you are traveling. Bear left here, staying closer to the Buffalo. Shortly past that fork, you'll pass an Arkansas Fish and Game Commission facility. Turn left on the road just past it, and ride north toward the Mt. Hersey ford.

You'll follow this road along a ridge-top for quite a while until it becomes rougher and begins to descend. Just past the beginning of the descent, next to a sign for the Gene Rush Wildlife Management Area, there will be another fork. Take the left one, and follow it to Mt. Hersey ford.

Shortly after fording the Buffalo at Mt. Hersey there will be another fork. Bear left here and pass an abandoned farmstead. Follow this gravel road west to AR 123, ignoring any side roads leading north and south. Turn left (south) on AR 123 and ride back to Carver Access.

RIDE 50　　BUFFALO NATIONAL RIVER: WOOLUM FORD/RICHLAND CREEK TOUR

This stunning and varied mountain bike tour can be ridden as either a 19-mile point-to-point trip between Richland Creek Campground in the Ozark National Forest and Woolum Ford on the Buffalo National River, or as a 40-mile loop. It shows you a little of everything that is attractive about northwest Arkansas. Your ride will traverse high mountains, drop down into farm valleys, and cross the Buffalo National River, one of the most scenic streams in the Ozarks.

Because the entire ride is on roads, it requires no technical bike-handling skills. It does require you to be in good physical condition, though. Passing through the mountainous terrain of the Boston Escarpment, you'll find yourself in a land of long climbs and exhilarating descents.

The payoff for the climbs is the scenery. This ride has everything. Stream crossings cool you on hot summer days—both Woolum Ford and Richland Creek have deep natural swimming holes for cooling off after a long ride. The pool at Richland Creek usually has a swinging rope above it, waiting for the more adventurous swimmers to drop in. A short hike up the creek into the Richland Creek Wilderness will take you to a secluded waterfall. And riding between Dickey Junction and Richland Creek, you'll be treated to breathtaking views into the rugged Richland Creek Wilderness Area.

On the longer loop ride you'll enjoy the panoramic views of the Bass Valley from the highlands above. After descending into the valley, you will be caught by the contrast between the pastoral lowlands and the rugged mountain highlands.

On the north side of the long loop, you'll coast down to Cave Creek and cross the stream on an old concrete ford. Farther on you'll bounce over one of the few stretches of slickrock in Arkansas—a phenomenon which caused locals to name this stretch Flat Rocks Road.

RIDE 50 *BUFFALO NATIONAL RIVER: WOOLUM FORD / RICHLAND CREEK TOUR*

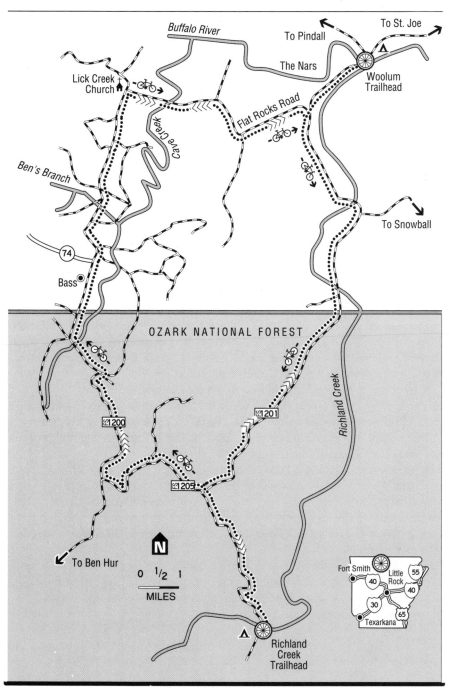

Buffalo River

To Pindall

To St. Joe

The Nars

Woolum Trailhead

Lick Creek Church

Flat Rocks Road

Cave Creek

Ben's Branch

To Snowball

74

Bass

OZARK NATIONAL FOREST

Richland Creek

1200

1201

1205

To Ben Hur

N

0   1/2   1
MILES

Richland Creek Trailhead

Fort Smith

Little Rock

55

40

40

30

Texarkana

65

This ride is more difficult to reach and more complicated to follow than many in this book, but don't let these hurdles keep you from enjoying this beautiful loop in northwestern Arkansas.

General location: 30 miles southeast of Harrison.
Elevation change: Elevation ranges from 660′ at Woolum Ford on the Buffalo River to 2,197′ at the summit of Round Hill on Forest Service Road 1201. Riders doing the point-to-point option will face a 3.5-mile climb, but will enjoy a descent of approximately the same distance.

Those riding the longer loop route will face 5 climbs and descents, most falling between one-half to three-quarters of a mile. The long loop also includes the previously mentioned 3.5-mile climb, but will have a descent of the same length.
Season: While this is a good ride year-round, spring and fall are the best seasons. Summer can be hot and humid, but 3 crossings of Richland Creek and a possible crossing of the Buffalo will cool you off.

The many ridge-top vistas on the loop are more spectacular during winter when the foliage is gone, but off-season riders should be prepared to deal with cold stream crossings.
Services: During warmer months, water may be obtained at Richland Creek Campground. No fresh water is available anywhere else on the ride.

The nearest campsites are at Richland Creek Campground in the Ozark National Forest and at Woolum Ford and Tyler Bend on the Buffalo National River. Canoe rentals, restaurants, and groceries can be found at any of several small towns along US 65, 10–15 miles east of the tour.

All services are available in Harrison, 30 miles to the northwest.
Hazards: The short 1-way option fords Richland Creek twice. The long loop has an additional stream crossing of Cave Creek. Those starting the ride from Woolum Ford will also cross the Buffalo River. While these are highlights of the ride, they can be very dangerous during high water.
Rescue index: Since most of this tour uses roads that see limited car traffic, you can usually wait for help to come to you. The exception is the northeast portion of the loop option between Lick Creek Church to the Richland Creek Valley, and south down the Richland Creek Valley to the junction with FS 1201 (Searcy County Road 12). The roads here are rougher and little used, so be prepared to take care of yourself.
Land status: Both options pass through a combination of national park land, national forest land, and private property on county roads. Respect the rights of landowners along the route by heeding all No Trespassing signs.
Maps: The map included in this book is the only single map covering the full loop. If you want to supplement it with topos, you'll need the 7.5 minute Moore and Eula maps. These cover all of both options except a 1-mile portion of the long loop falling onto Mt. Judea.

Wading across the Buffalo at Woolum Ford.

Other maps showing portions of the loop are the Searcy and Newton county maps and the map of the Ozark National Forest.

Finding the trail: You may start this loop from either Woolum Ford on the Buffalo River or at Richland Creek Campground in the Ozark National Forest. Woolum Ford is easier to reach. From St. Joe on US 65, drive southwest on a road with a sign pointing the way to Woolum Ford, and follow it 8 miles to Woolum. Cross the river and start the ride. The ford is usually too deep for cars.

To reach Richland Creek Campground, drive west from US 65 on AR 74. At Snowball, turn south on AR 377. It will take you through the small town of Witt's Spring. One-half mile past Witt's Spring, turn west (right) on a gravel road. This will become FS 1219. Follow it 3.5 miles to FS 1205. Go north 3.5 miles on FS 1205 to Richland Creek Campground.

During high water, Richland Creek is the recommended starting point, even though it is more difficult to reach and results in one additional long climb for those riding the longer loop option. High water on the Buffalo could prevent you from crossing the river and beginning the loop.

Sources of additional information:

Buffalo National River
Post Office Box 1173
Harrison, AR 72602-1173
(501) 741-5443

Ozark National Forest
Buffalo Ranger District
Post Office Box 427, Highway 7 North
Jasper, AR 72641
(501) 446-5122

Notes on the trail: This is a beautiful riding area. The climbs are long and challenging, but don't let that keep you from enjoying this tour. Your effort is more than repaid with beautiful and varied scenery. If you can, bring along a support vehicle. If the water in the fords is low, all but the rough portion of the loop between Cave Creek and the Richland Creek Valley can be negotiated by most vehicles. Or make it a 2-day ride, with an overnight at Woolum Ford or Richland Creek Campground.

Do carry maps. The short point-to-point route is not difficult to follow, but the long route passes many side roads. Carrying the Eula topo will do more than help you find your way. It will show you many interesting side trips, including a road to Hurricane Lake. It will also show you several ways to cut the loop short.

Riding the loop clockwise is recommended. If you don't, you'll face a long, washed-out, rocky climb westbound on Flat Rocks Road. This grade is better enjoyed while descending eastbound. To help you find your way around the long loop, here is a route description, starting from Woolum Ford and riding the loop clockwise.

When you leave Woolum Ford, you'll head south on a double-track following the base of a bluff called The Nars. At around 2 miles, there will be a road coming in from the right. This is Flat Rocks Road, which you will use to return to Woolum if you ride the loop.

About 5 miles from Woolum, you'll ford Richland Creek. Shortly after that, you'll hit a T intersection with Searcy County Road 12. Turn right, stick to the main road, and you will come to another ford of Richland Creek.

Shortly after the second ford, there will be a sign marking the boundary of the Ozark National Forest. The road is now designated FS 1201. In less than a half mile, you begin a serious climb. Except for a couple of breaks, it continues uphill for almost 4 miles. Stay on FS 1201 until you reach a T intersection with FS 1205 about a mile past the summit.

The decision point is at this intersection. Turning left and riding predominantly downhill for 5 miles takes you to Richland Creek Campground. To ride the 40-mile loop and return to Woolum Ford, turn right on FS 1205, and follow it to FS 1200. Turn north (right) on FS 1200, make a short climb, enjoy the view of the Bass Valley, and then begin the long descent down to the valley floor. At the end of the descent, you'll cross Cave Creek and hit another T intersection. Turn north (right) and, after a flat mile, you'll leave the Ozark National Forest.

Just past the forest boundary, you'll pass through Bass, or what used to be Bass. An abandoned store next to a house is your only hint that it used to be a town. Just past Bass, AR 74 comes in from the left. Continue north on the gravel road. You'll soon hit yet another T intersection, next to an abandoned gas station. There will be a stream crossing on the road to the right. Follow the fork to the left and continue riding north.

After a little more than a mile, you'll come to a confusing 5-road intersection next to the crossing of Ben's Branch. Cross the branch, then take the road that continues north. Follow the signs to Lick Creek Church. Continue riding north, climb a hill, and find a road going to the right across the road from Lick Creek Church. Turn right here, and begin descending immediately.

Near the bottom of the descent, you'll pass through an open farm valley, and then cross Cave Creek on an old concrete ford. Next comes a 1.5-mile climb. Near the top of the climb is a fork. Bear right.

One mile later is another fork, where you should bear left, and begin descending. You'll pass over the Flat Rocks, re-enter Buffalo National River land, and intersect the road to Woolum at the bottom of a long, washed-out, fun descent. Turn left, and ride north 2 miles back to Woolum Ford.

RIDE 51 BUFFALO NATIONAL RIVER: SNOWBALL LOOP

This 19-mile loop is a perfect ride for beginners. The trail surface covers 3 miles of pavement, 12 miles of gravel road, and 4 miles of rough and scenic four-wheel-drive road.

The gravel roads along the southern edge of the loop pass through open farm country, with the cleared countryside exposing views of the Boston Escarpment. The long, narrow profile of Point Peter Mountain extends like a ship's prow across the western skyline. This mountain is a local landmark, visible from the north, east, and west for miles.

The northern part of the loop enters national park land and parallels the Buffalo River. This section of the Buffalo is known as the middle river. It features serpentine meanders that have cut deeply into the bluffs on the outside of the river's curves, leaving prairie-like areas inside.

The bend that carves into Peter Cave Bluff is the high point of this ride. For a half mile, the trail follows the edge of the bluff, with spectacular views of a horseshoe bend in the Buffalo. All along Peter Cave Bluff are rock outcroppings that make perfect viewpoints for resting, snacking, and admiring the river meandering below.

RIDE 51 *BUFFALO NATIONAL RIVER: SNOWBALL LOOP*

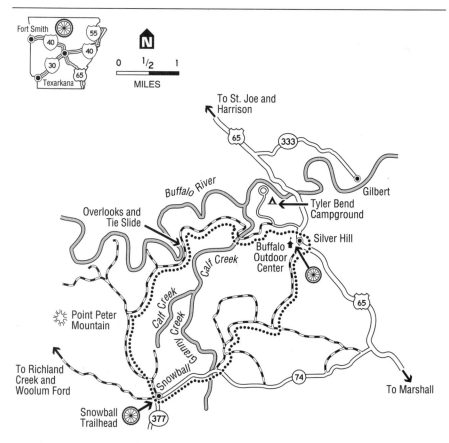

At the apex of this horseshoe bend, you may notice a curiously bare area running from the top of the bluff to the river below. This is the Tie Slide. Timbers for railroad ties were once cut in the forest along the bluff, slid off the bluff down to the deep pool in the river below, and floated downstream to the railroad near Gilbert. If you drive over to Gilbert after the ride, you will see portions of the old railroad. Gilbert also has an old general store, stocked with items of today and antique exhibits from yesterday.

General location: 12 miles northeast of Marshall.

Elevation change: Elevations range from 600′ at the Calf Creek ford to 1,000′ just south of Pate Mountain. There is a climb of 1 mile on the loop, and many rolling hills ranging in length from .1 to .5 mile.

Season: Spring, summer, and fall are the best seasons to ride this loop along the Buffalo River. Though summer is often very hot, a swim in the river after the ride makes any discomfort worthwhile.

Services: Drinking water is available at the store in Snowball, at the national park campground at Tyler Bend, and at the Buffalo Outdoor Center in Silver Hill. The campground also has showers. A limited supply of groceries is available at Silver Hill, and cabins can be rented at the Buffalo Outdoor Center.

Hotels, restaurants, and full-service grocery stores can be found in Marshall, 9 miles south of Silver Hill on US 65, and in Harrison, 30 miles to the north. The nearest bike shop is The Bicycle Outfitter in Harrison.

Hazards: Be careful while enjoying the scenery from Peter Cave Bluff and the Tie Slide. It's a long fall to the river.

Rescue index: The rescue index is very good, except on the 6-mile stretch of four-wheel-drive road from Peter Cave Bluff to the paved entrance road to Tyler Bend Recreation Area. Much of this stretch is too rough for cars. You will probably be on your own there.

Land status: The Snowball Loop passes through a combination of national park land and private land on county roads. Respect the rights of property owners by heeding all No Trespassing signs.

Maps: A map of Searcy County will show many of the roads used by this ride. The USGS topos covering the loop are the Snowball and Marshall 7.5 minute maps. The Snowball topo covers all the ride except the extreme eastern edge. It should be sufficient by itself.

The best guide can be picked up at the Buffalo Outdoor Center in Silver Hill. They pioneered this route, and have a good guide showing all the turns and mileages.

Finding the trail: The best starting point for this ride is Snowball, a small town at the intersection of AR 74 and AR 377. To reach it, drive 7 miles west from US 65 on AR 74. There is an old general store there with cold drinks and snacks to enjoy on your ride.

You can also start the ride from Tyler Bend Campground on the Buffalo National River. To reach it from US 65, drive 3 miles west from Silver Hill on a paved park road. If you start your ride from the campground, you will need to ride 2 miles back out on the park road to intersect the loop (see map).

You can also start the ride at the Buffalo Outdoor Center on the loop in Silver Hill. Get permission to park your car there before leaving it.

Take a break to enjoy the view of the Buffalo from one of the
overlooks along Peter Cave Bluff on the Snowball Loop.

Sources of additional information:

Buffalo National River
Post Office Box 1173
Harrison, AR 72602-1173
(501) 741-5443

Buffalo Outdoor Center
Route 1 Box 56
Highway 65 South
Silver Hill
St. Joe, AR 72675
(501) 439-2244

Notes on the trail: This ride was originally laid out by employees of the Buffalo Outdoor Center in Silver Hill. At that time, BOC was marking the trail with colored ribbons. If you have any questions about the ride, stop in the BOC and check it out. They have a map showing all the turns on the ride, and sometimes lead rides themselves. They also have cold drinks there, along with a limited number of cabins.

There are many turns and forks along the trail, so be sure you carry your map and consult it any time you're in doubt about the route.

Ouachita National Forest Trails

The Ouachita Mountains were first explored by the Hernando DeSoto expedition of 1541. After the Spaniards' brief forays into the area, the French explorers followed. Their influence shows in the many French place names scattered across the map of this forest. Ouachita is the French spelling of the Indian word *Washita*, which means "good hunting grounds."

Under the hands of pioneers and loggers, those good hunting grounds were decimated. A resident later referred to the Ouachitas as "that inaccessible, burned and bleeding wilderness of 1907." That year, President Roosevelt proclaimed the area the Arkansas National Forest. President Coolidge changed the forest's name in 1926, to reflect the surrounding Ouachita Mountains.

Under the management of the Forest Service, the Ouachitas renewed themselves. During the last 25 years, the Forest Service has managed the area with an emphasis on road building and logging. Because of public criticism of this developmental leaning on the part of the service, the forest plan has been amended to include the values of recreation, tourism, and wildlife. The Ouachita National Forest has now suspended clear-cutting in favor of selective cutting, and recreation is a priority.

Today, five wilderness areas totaling 49,300 acres are set aside in the Ouachita. Four hundred miles of trails lace the forest. Much of this is in the Ouachita National Recreation Trail, a 187-mile footpath running from the Oklahoma border to AR 9 near Little Rock. Lake Ouachita, administered by the Corps of Engineers, lies in the east-central part of the forest. It offers camping, swimming, boating, fishing, and other water sports. Over 30 recreation sites are scattered throughout the Ouachita.

Autumn colors paint the Ouachita Mountains yellow, red, orange, and brown. The peak colors usually fall in mid-October. Hundreds of wildflowers decorate the forest floor in spring. Over 100 species of birds live in the forest, including bald eagles, turkeys, and numerous songbirds. Black bears can be found in parts of the Ouachita, along with deer, squirrels, possum, raccoons, bobcats, fox, and many other mammals. In the evening, the 14 species of bats that inhabit the forest cruise the night sky.

The amended forest plan calls for 37 miles of new trail to be built each year between 1990 and 2000. Many of these trails will be open to mountain bikes. Most of the existing trails are open, too.

The Ouachita National Forest is very accommodating to our growing sport. When you head to the forest on a mountain bike foray, visit any of the Ouachita National Forest offices. You may find information on new trails not included here.

RIDE 52 *BEAR CREEK HORSE TRAILS*

The Bear Creek Trails are three scenic loops of 12 to 14 miles each in the northeastern Ouachita Mountains. The trails total 35 miles over gravel roads, abandoned logging roads, and single-track.

Though the east loop has some long climbs, it is suitable for riders of all skill levels. The western loop is a little more difficult, but can be handled by beginners with a positive attitude. The center loop offers some beautiful views, but because of steep and technical sections it is best left only to experts. See "Notes on the trail" at the end of the chapter for additional information on each loop.

Riders who like scenic vistas will love the Bear Creek Cycle Trails. From the trailhead, you will make your pre-ride preparations against a backdrop of the Ouachita Mountains marching away to the northern horizon. The trails follow quiet, forested bottomlands, climb to high ridges with spectacular views of the valleys below, and pass through the stands of pines that blanket the ridges with south- and west-facing slopes.

The east loop is in the Deckard Mountain Walk-In Turkey Hunting Area, from which all motor vehicles are prohibited. It's a quiet and wild place where you will be most likely to spot the abundant wildlife of the Ouachitas.

The western loop follows a ridge with superb views on the northern segment, and then descends to parallel Bear Creek on the opposite side. There is a waterfall on Bear Creek, only a half-mile side trip away from the trail (see "Notes on the trail").

Spring wildflowers blanket the bottomlands and sunny slopes early in the year, while autumn trips on Bear Creek will amaze you with the unbelievable fall colors that paint the mountainsides in late October.

General location: 7 miles northwest of Jessieville.
Elevation change: The low elevation of 800′ is found at Bear Creek along Forest Service Road 225 on the western loop. The highest elevations are 1,500′ at the trailhead and 1,550′ on parts of the center loop.
Season: Spring and fall are the best seasons to ride the Bear Creek Horse Trail system. With few stream crossings to deal with, winter riding can be safe and enjoyable. Just don't get caught by darkness on winter's short days. The long climbs on these loops could make hot and humid summer rides very difficult.
Services: There is no source of drinking water along the trail. Make plans to bring your own, or bring filters or tablets to purify stream water.

Camping is available anywhere in the national forest. The nearest developed campsites are at Iron Springs Recreation Area, 2 miles to the south on AR 7. Food, gasoline, and the local office for the Ouachita National Forest are located in Jessieville, 7 miles to the south on AR 7. Hot Springs, 25 miles to the south on AR 7, has all services, including bike shops.

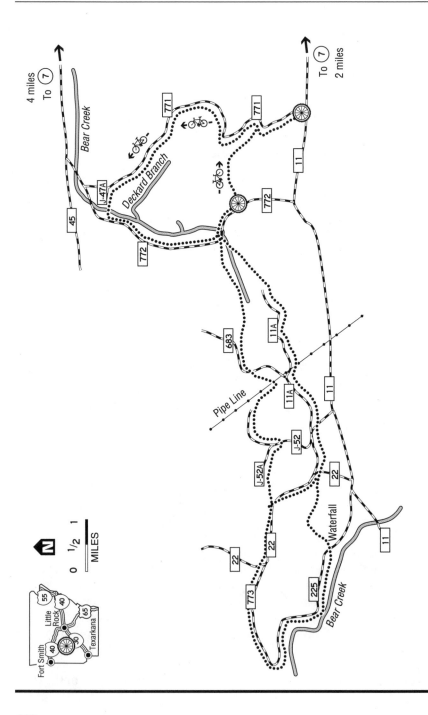

Hazards: Some stretches of the trail, particularly in the center section, are rocky. Be ready for equestrians at any time. Dismount, move to the downhill side of the trail, and stand quietly until they pass.

Rescue index: The eastern loop sees fairly regular use by both equestrians and mountain bikes. The center and western loops are less traveled. Be prepared to help yourself if you have trouble there. Roads cross or come near all 3 loops. Make your way to one of these and await help.

Land status: National forest.

Maps: The Ouachita National Forest provides excellent maps of the trail system. They are available at the address below. Those wishing to use topos will need the 7.5 minute Nimrod SW and Steve maps.

Finding the trail: Drive 5 miles north from Jessieville on AR 7 to Forest Service Road 11. Turn west on FS 11 and follow it 2 miles to FS 771. Turn north on FS 771 a short distance to one of the most scenic trailheads in this book.

Sources of additional information:

Ouachita National Forest
Jessieville Ranger District
8607 North Highway 7
Post Office Box 189
Jessieville, AR 71949
(501) 984-5313

Notes on the trail: The Bear Creek Horse Trail system is marked by yellow paint blazes and Carsonite posts with horse silhouettes. The east loop is best suited to mountain biking. It should be ridden counter-clockwise to avoid a steep climb on a bulldozed slope where the trail crosses a clear-cut. This rough trail section can be ridden when descending, but climbing will require a long portage.

The center loop is more difficult. Its northern side has a long but scenic climb westbound, a couple of rocky stretches, and a short unrideable stretch along a pipeline right-of-way. The south side of the center loop has a short section across a soft-surfaced, reseeded clear-cut. It also has several very steep climbs and descents. If you are going to skip a loop, make it the center one. You can use FS 22 and FS 11 to bypass it.

The western loop is a long way from the trailhead, but it is a great ride. Its northern leg follows the seldom-used double-track of FS 773, winding over rolling hills along the spine of a ridge. When FS 773 ends, the trail continues on single-track downhill to a dirt road. This is FS 225, which follows Bear Creek.

The trail parallels Bear Creek on FS 225 for several miles, leaving it just before a 100-foot-long concrete ford. Continuing along FS 225 another one-half mile past the ford will take you to the waterfall mentioned at the beginning of the chapter. It's worth the side trip.

For an easier ride nearby (suitable for any beginning bikers in your group) see the next ride description.

RIDE 53 *BUFFALO GAP MOUNTAIN BIKE RIDE*

The Buffalo Gap Mountain Bike Ride is named for a narrow gap that was the site of buffalo hunts in the early days of the Ouachitas. The loop ride is an easy seven-mile cruise for beginners on gravel forest roads. To make it more interesting, I've added an optional loop that will take you to the top of Ouachita Pinnacle. It adds 17 miles to the ride.

Forest Service roads 11 and 778 are very well maintained. FS 122 is a little narrower and rougher, as are most of the roads used by the Ouachita Pinnacle option. The difficulty lies in long climbs that will require you to be in good physical condition.

The climbs are worth the scenery. From the trailhead, you get a great vista of the Ouachitas stretching to the horizon in the north. Along FS 11 you see more great views, and again along FS 107 if you ride the long loop. That longer ride will take you to the peak of Ouachita Pinnacle, where you'll see Lake Ouachita spreading out over the lowlands below. If it rains, there will be many stream fords along FS 779. Although you'll face some long climbs on both loops on this tour, the downhills that follow will make it all worthwhile.

General location: 7 miles northwest of Jessieville.
Elevation change: Elevations range from 1,100′ to 1,500′ on the short loop. Those riding to the top of Ouachita Pinnacle will climb to just under 2,000′. There is 1 long climb and descent on the short loop, and an additional 1-mile climb and descent if you decide to ride the optional loop.
Season: Spring and fall, with their cooler temperatures, are always the best times to ride in Arkansas. Winter can be fun, too. Warm days are fairly common this far south in the state. Summer is usually hot and humid, and you'll have to deal with ticks and insects.
Services: No drinking water is available at the trailhead. You can camp anywhere in the national forest. The nearest developed campsites are at Iron Springs Recreation Area 2 miles south of FS 11 on AR 7. All services can be found in Hot Springs, 25 miles to the south.
Hazards: The only hazard you could run into on this trail is loose rock on turns during fast descents. Stay in control, and have fun.
Rescue index: You will be on roads throughout this loop. Chances are good you'll be found by a passing motorist if you get in a jam. An exception is FS 107 on the Ouachita Pinnacle Loop. It has a few rough spots that low-clearance vehicles avoid. You may be on your own on FS 107.
Land status: National forest.
Maps: The topos for this ride are the Jessieville, Hamilton, Nimrod SE, and Nimrod SW 7.5 minute maps. The Forest Service can provide you with a map

RIDE 53   *BUFFALO GAP MOUNTAIN BIKE RIDE*

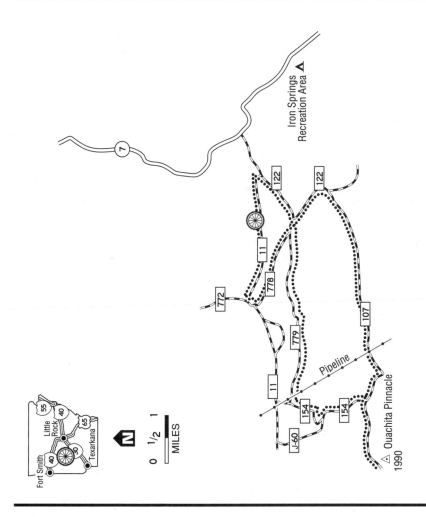

of the Buffalo Gap Mountain Bike Ride, but it does not show the Ouachita Pinnacle option.

Save a little money on topos, and just buy the Ouachita National Forest map. It shows all roads used by this ride.

Finding the trail: This ride uses the same trailhead as the Bear Creek Horse Trail. Drive 5 miles north from Jessieville on AR 7 to Forest Service Road 11. Turn west on FS 11 and follow it 2 miles to FS 771. Turn north on FS 771 and drive a short distance to the trailhead. It's not fancy, but the view is a highlight!

Vista from FS 107, just east of the Ouachita Pinnacle on the long loop of the Buffalo Gap Mountain Bike Ride.

Sources of additional information:

Ouachita National Forest
Jessieville Ranger District
Post Office Box 189
Jessieville, AR 71949
(501) 984-5313

Notes on the trail: Buffalo Gap offers a great option for those in your group who don't feel up to the more difficult Bear Creek Horse Trails. While the more experienced cyclists ride Bear Creek, those not up to any technical stuff could ride the gravel roads of the Buffalo Gap Ride.

To handle the gravel-covered grade on FS 122 more easily, ride the loop so that it is a descent southbound rather than an ascent northbound.

RIDE 54 *FLATSIDE WILDERNESS TOURS*

This set of rides centered around the Flatside Wilderness gives you a choice of 11-, 20-, 29-, and 41-mile loops. While none of the loop options require technical bike-handling skills, the long climbs and distances require that you be in good physical condition to enjoy these rides.

Because all options use forest roads, these tours are great for beginners. The roads used differ greatly. Forest Service Road 132 is part of the Winona Forest Drive, a scenic, well-maintained road that follows the ridge between White Oak Mountain and North Fork Pinnacle. FS 132-C is a rocky and level valley road that parallels the North Fork of the Saline River. FS 94 and FS 805 are narrow gravel roads. FS 86 in the northwest is a maintained logging access road. FS 124 along the western edge of the tour is steep, rough, rocky, and a blast on a mountain bike. Rarely will you meet a car on FS 124, since high clearance is needed to pass over rocks and washouts in the road. FS 212, roughest of all, is tough even on a four-wheel-drive vehicle.

The Flatside Wilderness offers you 10,105 acres of rugged terrain, small creeks, and panoramic views of the eastern Ouachita Mountains. Feast your eyes on the peaks of North Fork Pinnacle, Flatside Pinnacle, and Forked Mountain as they rise abruptly among the more rounded summits of the other mountains in the area. The barren rock faces of Flatside and Forked Mountain stand out in particularly sharp contrast with the lush green landscape of the surrounding national forest. It's a stunning sight.

As you may have guessed, the outstanding feature of this ride is its many spectacular views. A few others deserve special mention. North Fork Pinnacle offers a 360-degree view of the entire area. From Crystal Mountain, you can look south over Lake Winona. The best panorama of all is from the face of Flatside Pinnacle on FS 94. This view takes in the entire Flatside Wilderness. Look for Forked Mountain in the distance, at the western end of the wilderness. Another great view awaits you at the electronic tower along FS 212, where you have a view of Lake Winona.

If time permits, those of you riding the long loop around the wilderness should take a side trip up FS 793. It parallels Little Cedar Creek near the loop's western end. Closed to vehicles a short way up its length, FS 793 provides one of those peaceful, soul-soothing wilderness experiences we all seek. Along the way is a shallow cave, and not far beyond the cave is a beautiful waterfall and plunge pool on Little Cedar Creek. You'll find these falls about 3.5 miles up FS 793; they're a perfect place for a mid-ride swim. If you continue following FS 793, you will reach a road closure at the wilderness boundary. DO NOT RIDE INTO THE WILDERNESS AREA.

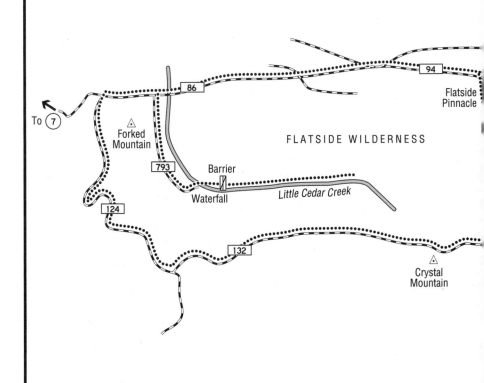

To ⑦

Forked
Mountain

86

793

Barrier

Waterfall

Little Cedar Creek

124

132

FLATSIDE WILDERNESS

94

Flatside
Pinnacle

Crystal
Mountain

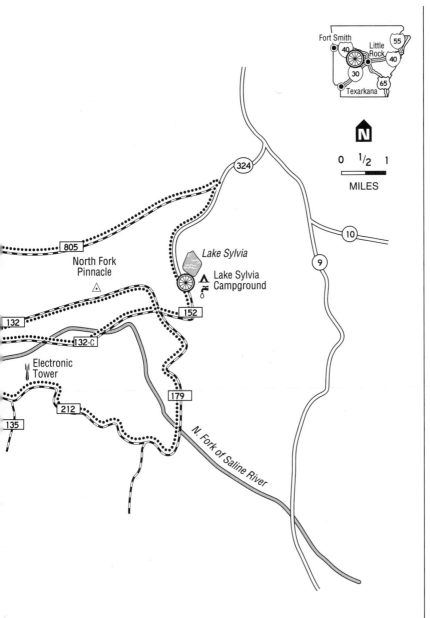

General location: 35 miles west of Little Rock.

Elevation change: From a low of 450′ along Cedar Creek, you will reach a high point of 1,724′ at the summit of Crystal Mountain. The most challenging climb is the rough and rocky 2.4-mile ascent southbound on FS 124 on the western edge of the loop. There is also a 1.6-mile ascent on FS 152 south from Lake Sylvia, a 1.3-mile ascent westbound on FS 805, and a 1.2-mile climb on FS 86 eastbound. There are lots of shorter hills, too.

Season: Spring, summer, and fall provide the best riding weather. Summer may be hot, but a swim in Lake Sylvia or a dip in the pool and cascade on Little Cedar Creek are good antidotes for the heat.

Services: Drinking water and camping are available at Lake Sylvia, the recommended starting point for these rides. Lake Sylvia Recreation Area is closed from mid-September to mid-May, though. Plan to bring your own water during these months.

The closest year-round camping is at Iron Springs Recreation Area, 4 miles north of Jessieville on AR 7. Other campsites are along AR 10 on the shores of Lake Maumelle and in Pinnacle Mountain State Park.

All other services are available in Little Rock, 35 miles to the east.

Hazards: While riding on FS 86, you will pass through Weyerhaeuser tree plantations. If cutting is going on in the area, logging trucks may occasionally blast past you. Keep an eye peeled for them.

Rescue index: Most roads used by the Flatside Wilderness Tours are used by cars, so help is normally not far away. FS 124 and FS 132-C are a little rougher, and don't see much traffic. If you have trouble on these roads, work your way a few miles to one of the more traveled routes. FS 212 is roughest of all. Don't wait for help to come to you on this one.

Land status: The Flatside Wilderness Tours travel through a combination of national forest, private land, and Weyerhaeuser tree farms.

Maps: Carrying a map of the Ouachita National Forest is highly recommended. It shows most roads and prominent landmarks in the area. If you want to use topos, you'll find that the Flatside Wilderness Tours fall onto six maps. Most of the loops fall onto the 7.5 minute Paron, Paron SW, and Nimrod SE. The rest fall onto Nimrod, Alpin, and Thornberg.

Finding the trail: From Little Rock, drive west on AR 10 to its junction with AR 9. Drive 1.5 miles north on AR 9 to AR 324. Go 4 miles west on AR 324 to Lake Sylvia Recreation Area. Leave your car in the parking lot for the beach and picnic area. If it is full, you may also park at the trailhead for the Ouachita National Recreation Trail, located just south of the campground entrance.

Cascades and pools along FS 793 in the Flatside Wilderness Tours are the perfect place for riders on the longer loop options to rest and take a cooling dip.

Sources of additional information:

Ouachita National Forest
Winona Ranger District
1039 Highway 10 North
Perryville, AR 72126
(501) 889-5176

Paul's Bike Shop
9807 West Markham
Little Rock, AR 72205
(501) 227-6700

Notes on the trail: The Flatside Wilderness Tours have something to offer everyone in your group. Non-riders can hang out at Lake Sylvia. Or they could tag along in the car, since all roads except FS 124, FS 212, and FS 132-C are passable for most vehicles.

Novices seeking a shorter ride could do the 10-mile loop on Forest Service roads 152, 132, and 132-C. A loop of 20 miles can be ridden via Forest Service roads 152, 132, 94, and 805. Another 20-mile loop leaves Lake Sylvia to the south, follows FS 132-C to FS 132, and loops around on FS 132, 135, 212, 179, 132, and back to Lake Sylvia on 152.

Those with plenty of energy and time can ride 41 miles via Forest Service roads 805, 94, 86, 124, and 152. If you take this option, don't leave out a side trip to the Flatside Pinnacle Overlook, only a half mile off the north side of the loop on FS 94. In the distance you can see Forked Mountain on the western end of the wilderness. It can serve as your landmark as you follow FS 86 along the northern part of the loop.

FS 86 passes through Weyerhaeuser land. This can be especially confusing. It is not well marked, and many side roads lead to tree plantations. Maintain an east-west direction along Cedar Creek while sticking to the main road. Use Forked Mountain as a benchmark to keep you headed in the right direction.

These loops sound pretty confusing. In reality, they are fairly easy to follow, especially if you carry a map of the Ouachita National Forest. It shows every road used by these tours. Pick up the map, and hit these beautiful trails.

RIDE 55 *LAKE WINONA LOOP*

This easy-to-ride road loop around Lake Winona gives you a choice of 21 or 25 miles. The 21-mile option is recommended for inexperienced riders; it uses gravel roads that are in fair to excellent condition.

Forest Service Road 114 is a level and wide gravel road that connects AR 9 and AR 7. FS 2 and FS 778 are narrower, less traveled, and have occasional steep or rough sections.

The longer option uses FS 212, a narrow, rough four-wheel-drive road across a mountainside above the lake. It is recommended for those who like a little challenge in their ride. All options involve climbing, so you should be in good physical condition for this loop.

Lake Winona is in the valley of the Saline River, surrounded by the summits of the eastern Ouachita Mountains. Crystal Mountain and Grindstone Mountain overlook the lake from the northwest, and Bread Creek Pinnacle, Angling Pinnacle, Muse Mountain, and Wolf Pinnacle rise above FS 778 to the southwest.

If you take on the challenge of FS 212, you'll be rewarded by a spectacular overlook along that road, next to an electronic transmission tower at its western end. FS 2 along the western side of the loop passes through several clearcuts, opening up expansive views of the surrounding mountains.

And just below the dam on FS 778 is a beautiful set of cascades on the Saline River. If the river is up, you'll finish your ride with a splash through the stream below the spillway.

General location: 35 miles west of Little Rock.
Elevation change: At the recommended starting point on Lake Winona, the elevation is 650′. From there you will climb to a high point of 1,350′ at the base of Muse Mountain on FS 778.

On the long route, there is a 1.1-mile climb from lake level to FS 212, several steep climbs on FS 212, and a long descent back to lake level. The rest of the ride

RIDE 55 *LAKE WINONA LOOP*

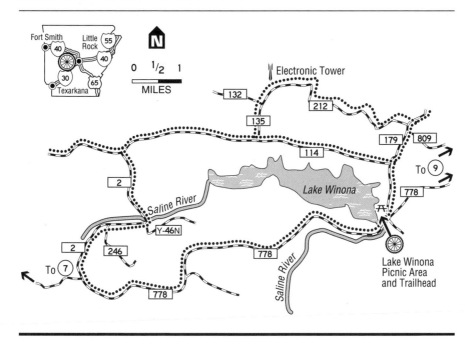

has 6 climbs and descents ranging in length from one-quarter mile to 1 mile.

Season: Spring and fall are the best times to ride this loop. Summer, while hot, can be fun if you combine your hot ride with a cool splash in the cascades on the Saline River below the outlet from the lake.

Services: Drinking water is available in the Lake Winona Picnic Area during summer months. Off-season you should plan to bring your own.

The nearest campground is at Lake Sylvia, 9 miles to the north on FS 179. A small grocery store is located 4 miles east of the lake at the junction of FS 778 and AR 9.

All other services may be obtained in Little Rock, 35 miles to the east.

Hazards: Do not cross the Saline River ford on the Lake Winona spillway when water levels are high. Check it out before you start, so you won't reach the end of your ride and find yourself stranded 100 yards from your car.

Rescue index: Except for FS 212, all roads used by this loop will see a few cars each day, so help won't be hard to find. If you get into trouble on FS 212, make your way to either end, where better-maintained roads will guarantee assistance.

Land status: National forest.

Maps: A map of the Ouachita National Forest would be very helpful on this

Playing in the Saline River below the Lake Winona outlet.

loop. The USGS topos for the area are the Paron and Paron SW 7.5 minute maps.

Finding the trail: From Little Rock, go west on AR 10 to AR 9. Go south 6 miles on AR 9 to FS 778. FS 778 is not marked here, but there is a small grocery store at the intersection. Turn west on this gravel road and drive 4 miles to Lake Winona. Park in the Lake Winona Picnic Area, or in the small parking lot next to the spillway.

Sources of additional information:

Ouachita National Forest
Winona Ranger District
1039 Highway 10 North
Perryville, AR 72126
(501) 889-5176

Paul's Bike Shop
9807 West Markham
Little Rock, AR 72205
(501) 227-6700

Notes on the trail: This trail is most enjoyable when ridden in a counter-clockwise direction. This lets you get the wide, more traveled FS 114 out of the way first, and saves the most enjoyable and most scenic roads for last.

Do carry a map when riding here. There are many side roads, and having this book or the map of the Ouachita National Forest with you will keep you from getting lost.

RIDE 56 *WILDCAT MOUNTAIN TRAIL*

This new trail system was under construction when this book went to press. There is no map, though one is being produced, and information about the trail is incomplete. Contact the Forest Service in Perryville for a copy of this newly developed trail map.

Here's what we know so far: In June 1993, a seven-mile loop had been completed. Work was in progress to expand the network to 11 miles by the end of the year. Plans call for the Forest Service and bike clubs out of Little Rock to expand the network further in the future.

In fact, to meet the demand for mountain bikers coming from Little Rock, the Winona Ranger District plans to develop several other bike trails over the next few years.

The Wildcat Mountain Trail follows logging roads abandoned years ago. Trails have been cut along these overgrown double-tracks. The trail starts out on top of the Jack Fork Shelf, a geologic formation running for miles through the Ouachitas. The nearby Winona Scenic Drive follows the shelf.

You'll drop off the shelf and ride through the hollows of tributaries of the nearby Saline River. Because it is designed specifically for mountain bikes, this trail should be a great ride.

General location: 30 miles west of Little Rock.
Elevation change: Elevations range between 600′ and 1,340′ as the trail drops off the Jack Fork Shelf and traverses the rough country below.
Season: Spring and fall are the best seasons to ride in the Ouachitas.
Services: No water is available along the trail. Water and camping are available at Lake Sylvia Recreation Area about 3 miles to the north. Lake Sylvia is closed during the winter. All services are available in Little Rock, 30 miles to the west.
Hazards: Be cautious in the woods during deer and turkey seasons. Wear hunter's-orange if you have it.
Rescue index: On weekends, you may be found by another biker. On weekdays, you will probably be on your own. Make your way to Forest Service Road 138 to the north, or FS 179 to the west, and await help.
Land status: National forest.
Maps: A brochure is in production as this book is going to press. It will be available from the Forest Service at the address shown below.
Finding the trail: Drive 3 miles south on AR 9 from its intersection with AR 10. Turn west off AR 9 onto FS 132. Follow FS 132 3 miles to FS 179. Turn south onto FS 179 and drive 100 yards to a parking area and trailhead on the east side of the road.

Sources of additional information:

Ouachita National Forest
Winona Ranger District
1039 Highway 10 North
Perryville, AR 72126
(501) 889-5176

Notes on the trail: This trail system is being developed by the Forest Service and bike clubs out of Little Rock. If you would like to volunteer time to improve the Wildcat Mountain Trail, contact the Forest Service at the address shown above.

RIDE 57 *WHITE OAK MOUNTAIN TRAIL*

Because the White Oak Mountain Trail was still in the conceptual stage when this trail guide went to press, information about this ride is only sketchy.

The trail will be developed through a unique partnership between the Forest Service, logging companies, turkey hunting organizations, and mountain bike groups. Timber companies will finish selectively logging the area in 1993. Except for roads and a few stumps, the forest will look as before. Roads developed for logging are usually torn out with a piece of equipment known as a "ripper." In this case, the Forest Service will leave out the middle tooth of the ripper, leaving a single-track trail perfect for mountain biking.

Mountain bike groups will then help blaze the trails. Clover, millet, and redtop, three plants that are like ice cream to deer, turkey, and quail, will be planted along the trail. You should see plenty of wildlife on the White Oak Mountain Trail.

Unless this project is derailed somehow, it should be finished by the end of 1994. When completed, the White Oak Mountain area will have an 11-mile trail on these old roads that should be easy for beginners. The area will also be managed for turkey hunting. It sounds like it will be really good for riders of all skill levels. Check with the Winona Ranger District of the Ouachita National Forest in Perryville.

General location: 40 miles west of Little Rock.
Elevation change: Unknown.
Season: Spring and fall are the best times to ride anywhere in the Ouachita National Forest.
Services: Drinking water will not be available along this trail. The nearest water and camping will be at Iron Springs Recreation Area on AR 7 to the west, and at Lake Sylvia Recreation Area to the east. All services are available in Little Rock, 40 miles to the east.

Hazards: Unknown.

Rescue index: This trail will be off the well-maintained Forest Service Road 114. If you get into trouble, make your way to this road and await help.

Land status: National forest.

Maps: When the trail is complete, the Forest Service will produce a map and brochure for White Oak Mountain. The topos covering the area should be Paron SW and Nimrod SE 7.5 minute maps. Verify this with the Forest Service.

Finding the trail: Plans call for the trailhead to be located at the intersection of FS 114 and FS 114B, about 7 miles west of Lake Winona on FS 114.

Sources of additional information:

Ouachita National Forest
Winona Ranger District
1039 Highway 10 North
Perryville, AR 72126
(501) 889-5176

Notes on the trail: Sorry there isn't more information available on this trail. It sounds like it will be great. It should be finished within a year after this book shows up on the shelves, so call the Forest Service and find out more about it.

Also, the Forest Service is always looking for volunteers to maintain trails in the Ouachitas. If you feel like contributing something to your sport, contact the Ouachita National Forest office in Winona and offer some of your time.

RIDE 58 *LITTLE BLAKELY TRAIL*

This challenging and scenic ten-mile trail was developed in the early 1990s by the Forest Service and the Ouachita Mountain Bikers. The three loops in this network are the six-mile South Loop, the four-mile Big Tree Loop, and the two-mile Glades Loop. Future plans call for adding more loops to the system.

The Little Blakely Trail uses a combination of single-track and double-track on abandoned roads. Parts of the trail are rough, so the route is recommended for experienced riders. Only beginners with positive attitudes should consider this ride. There is a two-mile stretch on the Big Tree Loop that only experts should ride.

There are many spectacular views of Lake Ouachita on both loops. The South Loop follows the edge of a small bay, then climbs up onto the ridge of the peninsula on which the trail system is located.

The Big Tree Loop is named for a grove of huge pines and oaks through which the trail passes—and so does a refreshing breeze, sighing as it goes. After your

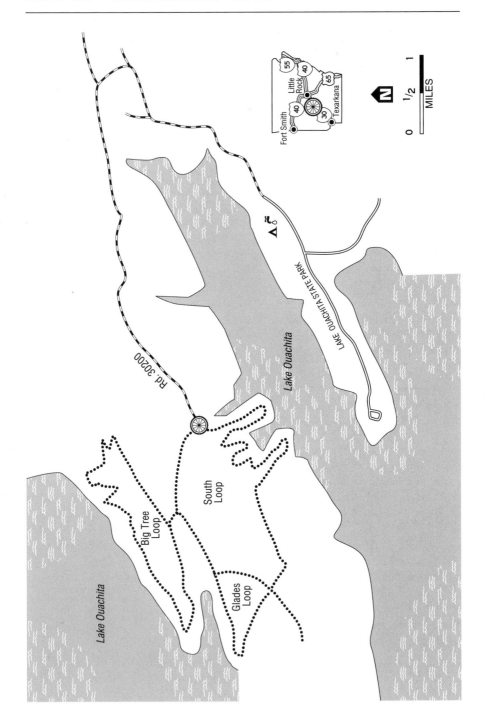

Lake Ouachita State Park

Lake Ouachita

Rd. 30200

Big Tree Loop

South Loop

Glades Loop

Lake Ouachita

ride, you can camp at Lake Ouachita State Park, take a shower or a swim, and watch the sun set over the lake.

General location: 20 miles northwest of Hot Springs.

Elevation change: Elevations on the Little Blakely Trail vary from 580′ along the shores of Lake Ouachita to nearly 1,000′ on the back loop. There are many short ups and downs along the lake on the South Loop. The same applies to the Big Tree Loop, which has 1 very difficult climb along its northwest reaches. Beginners should probably avoid that part of the Big Tree Loop.

Season: Spring and fall are best. Summer is not too bad, since you can cool off in the lake after your ride. Winter in south-central Arkansas often surprises you with warm riding days, too.

Services: No drinking water is available along the trail. Water, camping, showers, and swimming are all available at Lake Ouachita State Park, just across the bay from the Little Blakely Trail.

Hazards: The north 2 miles of the Big Tree Loop have some very rocky sections. It is too rough for anybody but an expert.

Rescue index: On weekends, there will probably be other trail users to help you if you get into a jam. On weekdays, you'll probably be on your own.

Situated on a peninsula jutting into the lake, the forest through which the trail passes is fairly remote. If you can't get to the trailhead, try to make it to the water's edge, where you might be able to flag a fishing boat.

Land status: National forest.

Maps: The national forest has a map of the trail that shows all 3 loops and the entrance road. You can get it at the address shown below. The topo for the area is the Mountain Pine 7.5 minute map.

Finding the trail: From Lake Ouachita State Park, drive east out of the park on AR 227. The pavement ends, and at 1.5 miles you'll come to a fork. Turn left, and go a short distance to a 3-way fork. Take the middle road, and follow it to Weyerhaeuser road 30200. Turn left, and follow it until it ends at the trailhead.

Sources of additional information:

Ouachita National Forest
Jessieville Ranger District
8607 North Highway 7
Post Office Box 189
Jessieville, AR 71949
(501) 984-5313

Notes on the trail: The Little Blakely Trail is marked by white rectangles nailed to or painted onto trees along the path. You'll notice that the road to the trailhead is pretty rough, but it is passable by all cars.

It's also a little confusing finding the right forks along the way. In the future, the Forest Service plans to improve the road and put up signs guiding you to the trail. Persevere, though, and you'll find your way to the trail with little trouble.

RIDE 59 *POSSUM KINGDOM RIDE*

This 12-mile loop ride is the perfect choice for a beginner's first outing. It is also fine for riders of any skill level looking for a quick jaunt in the woods to get away from it all.

The trail surface is primarily gravel road, with one short stretch of low-use paved county road. The ride takes you through pine-hardwood forest and past one pine plantation. Additional miles can be added by using roads shown on the map provided by the Forest Service. Most primitive roads leading south of Forest Service Road 811 lead to Lake Ouachita.

General location: 13 miles west of Jessieville on AR 298.
Elevation change: Elevation ranges between 600′ and 800′.
Season: All seasons are good for riding this easy trail.
Services: No drinking water is available along the trail. The nearest campsite is at Iron Springs, 5 miles north of Jessieville on AR 7.

Food, fuel, and Forest Service information is available in Jessieville, 13 miles to the east. All services are available in Hot Springs, 30 miles to the southeast.
Hazards: There are no unusual hazards on this short and easy ride.
Rescue index: Since much of this ride uses Forest Service roads, cyclists on the Possum Kingdom Ride will never be far from help.
Land status: National forest.
Maps: The Forest Service has printed maps of this ride. They are available by writing to the address below. Those wishing to use a topo should pick up the Avant 7.5 minute map.
Finding the trail: Drive 18 miles north from Hot Springs on AR 7 to AR 298. Go 12.5 miles west on AR 298 to a county road with a sign marked "Rifle Range." Go south three-quarters of a mile to Forest Service Road J-47. Turn right on FS J-47, cross a cattle guard, and park in a small open area immediately the right.

Sources of additional information:

Ouachita National Forest
Jessieville Ranger District
8607 North Highway 7
Post Office Box 189
Jessieville, AR 71949
(501) 984-5313

RIDE 59 *POSSUM KINGDOM RIDE*

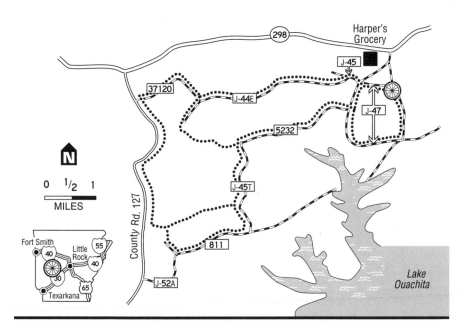

Notes on the trail: The Possum Kingdom Ride is marked by white paint blazes. Carsonite posts mark most intersections. Posts are numbered to correspond with points on the map. The map provided by the Forest Service includes a narrative to guide riders through the loop.

RIDE 60 *CHARLTON TRAIL*

The Charlton Trail is a four-mile point-to-point stretch of single-track trail suitable for riders of all skill levels. The trail surface is fairly uniform, posing no technical problems for beginners, but involves enough climbing to challenge more experienced cyclists. Beginners may have to walk their bikes for short stretches, but will be rewarded by panoramic views from the high points on the two ridges traversed by the trail.

In addition to the wildlife normally seen in the Ouachitas, you may also spot waterfowl attracted by the waters of Lake Ouachita. Eagles also make the lake their home during winter. Those riding this trail in summer will enjoy swimming in the lake, or in the pool along Walnut Creek at Charlton Recreation Area.

RIDE 60   *CHARLTON TRAIL*

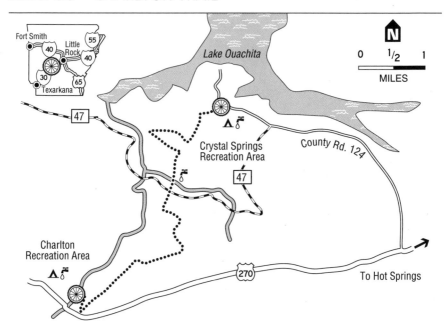

General location: 20 miles west of Hot Springs.

Elevation change: Elevations on the Charlton Trail range from 900′ on the ridge above Charlton Recreation Area to 600′ at the shore of Lake Ouachita at Crystal Recreation Area.

Season: Since this trail is relatively short, it makes a great ride any time of year. Only 1 small stream is crossed, reducing the risk of chilly feet during winter. For those riding in the heat of summer, there is swimming at either end of the trail at Lake Ouachita or Crystal recreation areas, and there is a spring and stream crossing at the midpoint of the ride.

Services: Camping, water, swimming, and showers are available at both Charlton and Crystal recreation areas. Crystal also has a marina, a restaurant, and fuel. All other services can be found at Hot Springs, 20 miles to the east.

Hazards: Be careful on the switchbacks during the descent to Charlton Recreation Area.

Rescue index: This trail is used regularly by both cyclists and hikers. At no time are you more than 1 trail mile from a trailhead or road crossing. Phones are located at both ends of the trail.

Land status: Most of the trail is on national forest land. The remainder is on Army Corps of Engineers property.

Maps: At the time of this writing, no official map of the trail existed. A hand-drawn map is available from the Forest Service by writing the address below. The trail falls onto the McGraw Mountain and Crystal Springs 7.5 minute topos.

Finding the trail: The Charlton Trail can be accessed from either end. To start riding from its southern end, drive 20 miles west from Hot Springs on US 270 to Charlton Recreation Area. The trail begins on the east side of Walnut Creek near the swimming area. The climb out of Charlton is very steep.

To start the ride from Crystal Springs on Lake Ouachita, drive 17 miles west of Hot Springs on US 270. Turn north on an asphalt road with a sign directing you to Crystal Springs Recreation Area. The recreation area is 2 miles down this road. The trailhead is next to the amphitheater.

Sources of additional information:

Ouachita National Forest
Womble Ranger District
Post Office Box 255
Mt. Ida, AR 71957
(501) 867-2101

Notes on the trail: To avoid the steep climb out of Charlton Recreation Area, you should start your ride at Crystal Springs. If you don't want to backtrack on the trail to the starting point, just ride 3 miles east on US 270 to the road leading to Crystal Springs. Be careful of the traffic.

The Charlton Trail is well marked by white paint blazes. It's tough to get lost on this ride.

The Forest Service has tentative plans to construct a 3-mile section of trail which will make this a loop ride, with connectors to trails on Hickory Nut Mountain to the west, and Bear Mountain to the east. Contact the Forest Service for additional information on this project.

RIDE 61 *WOMBLE TRAIL*

The Womble Trail, a 27-mile point-to-point ride with an optional 8-mile extension, is one of the best single-track trails in this book.

The designers did a superb job here. Switchbacks are used to keep grades manageable, and the trail surface is uniform hardpack with a few rocky stretches. Even beginners will seldom have to portage, unless they are not in good enough physical condition to make all the climbs.

This is a perfect trail for beginners to get their first taste of single-track. It crosses roads at regular intervals, giving new riders an opportunity to bail out if the trail proves to be too much for them.

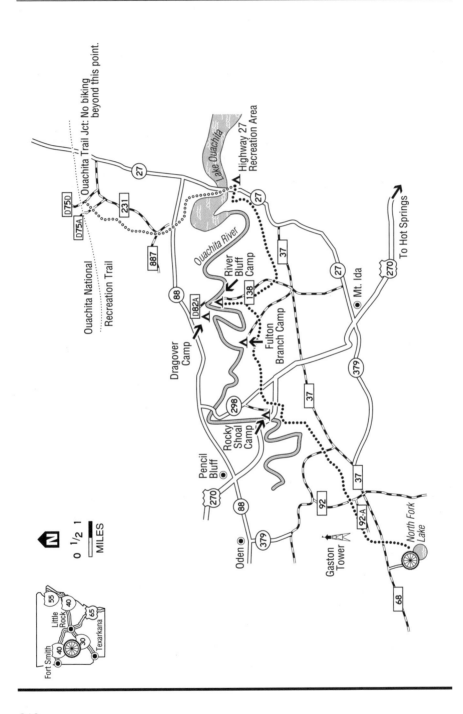

Rarely will you find a trail that traverses such rugged terrain and is still easy to ride. The Womble follows ridge-tops for miles, swooping you around the upper reaches of hollows containing tributaries of the Ouachita River. Fast, smooth descents are followed by long, gradual climbs to the top of the next ridge. Scenic views are everywhere. They are especially impressive in winter, when the thick Arkansas foliage is no longer obstructing the view.

One mile east of AR 27, the trail follows a bluff above the river. Here there is a stunning view of a horseshoe bend in the Ouachita River. The best vista, though, is 1.5 miles southwest of the US 270 crossing, where the trail follows a rocky bluff that towers straight above the Ouachita. Here you'll find several rock ledges where you can sit and watch the river roll by below. Bald eagles occasionally winter in this area, and can sometimes be seen roosting in the trees along the bluffs or fishing in the river.

General location: 7 miles northeast of Mt. Ida.

Elevation change: Elevation on the Womble Trail varies from 580′ on the shore of Lake Ouachita to a high of 1,200′ near the peaks of Reed Mountain, Gaston Mountain, and Mauldin Mountain.

The path follows the ridges above the Ouachita River for much of its length, resulting in surprisingly few climbs for the rugged terrain through which the trail passes. There are 4 major climbs and descents, ranging in length from one-half mile to 1 mile. Although some of the climbs are long, good use of switchbacks by the trail designers keeps the grades fairly easy.

Season: While spring and fall offer the best conditions, the Womble Trail is a good ride any time of year. Because it follows ridges and crosses only a few shallow streams, wet feet won't be a problem for winter riders. Summer riders will enjoy pedaling beneath the pine forests that shade the ride for most of its length.

Services: No drinking water is available along the trail. Spur trails lead off the Womble to River Bluff Float Camp (2-mile spur), Fulton Branch Float Camp (one-quarter-mile spur), Rocky Shoals Float Camp (one-quarter-mile spur), and at Highway 27 Recreation Area at the eastern end of the trail on AR 27. Water and camping are available at all these sites.

All other services except bike shops can be found in Mt. Ida. Bike shops are located in Hot Springs, 40 miles to the east.

Hazards: The Womble Trail follows bluffs above the Ouachita River in 2 places. These spots have precipitous drops to the river below. Especially dangerous is a stretch of trail 1.5 miles southwest of US 270. Walk your bike on this stretch and admire the scenery.

Rescue index: The Womble Trail is a popular ride for cyclists in west-central Arkansas. On a weekend it is likely that another cyclist or hiker will find you if you run into problems. On weekdays, you will probably be on your own. Make your way to one of the roads crossed by this point-to-point trail.

Land status: National forest.

Most of the Womble Trail is single-track in superb condition, like this stretch of the trail one mile west of Highway 27 Recreation Area on Lake Ouachita.

Maps: A map of the Ouachita National Forest will guide you to the several access points for the Womble Trail, and will be useful in finding forest road routes back to their starting points. The map of the Ouachita National Recreation Trail also covers the Womble. And the Forest Service produces a map of the Womble, showing access points and road crossings.

If you want to use USGS topos, you'll find that most of this trail falls onto the Mt. Ida and Reed Mountain 7.5 minute maps. The trail's western end falls onto the Oden 7.5 minute. Those riding the optional 9 miles north of Highway 27 Recreation Area (see "Notes on the trail") will also need the Story 7.5 minute.

Finding the trail: At its eastern end, the Womble can be reached from Highway 27 Recreation Area on Lake Ouachita, 7 miles northeast of Mt. Ida on AR 27.

To reach the trail after parking in the recreation area, ride west a half mile on the gravel road paralleling the lake's south shore from the AR 27 bridge over the lake. There will be an open grassy area at the trailhead.

The western trailhead is at North Fork Lake. To reach it, drive 2 miles south of Oden on AR 379 to FS 92. Turn south (right) on FS 92 and go 3 miles to FS 68. Turn west on FS 68, and drive around 2.5 miles to FS W-74. Turn south on FS W-74, and follow it a short distance to the lake and trailhead.

You can also access the Womble from FS 92 and avoid the climb up from North Fork Lake. FS 92 crosses the trail 4 miles south of Oden, where FS 92A branches west to the site of the old Gaston Fire Tower. There is no parking area here, so you'll have to park off to the side of the road.

The trail may also be accessed from Rocky Shoals Float Camp, 6 miles northwest of Mt. Ida on US 270. Another access point is Fulton Branch Float Camp, 1 mile northeast of Mt. Ida on AR 27 and 5 miles northwest on a gravel road. Other access points are at the trail's various road crossings. Study the map of the Ouachita National Forest, and you'll get the big picture of all the possible access points along the Womble Trail.

Sources of additional information:

Ouachita National Forest
Womble Ranger District
Post Office Box 255
Mt. Ida, AR 71957
(501) 867-2101

Notes on the trail: This is a beautiful trail. Don't blow it off just because it is a point-to-point trail with few road return options. This single-track is such a pleasure to ride that you won't mind pedaling out quite a few miles, then turning around and retracing your way back to the starting point.

Better yet, bring along a non-riding friend who can meet you at the far end of your ride. There are plenty of beautiful places in the forest or along the river for your driver to hang out while you ride the trail. He or she could even meet you at one of the road crossings with food and drink.

The trail is marked by white blazes painted on trees, supplemented by some signposts bearing bicycle symbols.

Here are approximate trail distances westbound, starting from AR 27: 8 miles, spur trail to River Bluff Float Camp; 10 miles, spur trail to Fulton Branch Float Camp; 13 miles, spur trail to Rocky Shoals Float Camp; 21 miles, FS 92 crossing; 23 miles, Gaston Mountain Lookout Tower; 27 miles, North Fork Lake.

Not covered is an additional 9 miles of the Womble Trail that runs northeast from Highway 27 Recreation Area to a junction with the Ouachita National Recreation Trail. It is not included because it is flat, passes through marshy land for much of its length, and is difficult to access at its eastern end. It connects to the Ouachita National Recreation Trail, which is not open to bikes.

RIDE 62 *MILL CREEK EQUESTRIAN TRAIL*

The Mill Creek Equestrian Trail, a 26-mile network developed in 1992, represents the only part of the Ouachita National Recreation Trail on which mountain bikes are allowed. Mill Creek uses a combination of gravel roads, abandoned double-track, and newly cut single-track, 4.5 scenic single-track miles of which follow the Ouachita trail.

These loops are somewhat difficult, with many stretches suitable only for experienced riders. If you are a beginner, but want to try your luck anyway, follow the suggestions under "Notes on the trail."

This trail system is worth the effort it takes to ride it. The reward for working your way to the top of Buck Knob, an old firetower site, is a spectacular 360-degree view of the surrounding Ouachita Mountains.

There is also a beautiful set of rock walls towering over a secluded section of Rock Creek along the eastern perimeter of the trail system, and farther down the same stretch of trail are three creek crossings.

The most fascinating stream crossing of all is on the west side of the trail system, where two creeks come together to form the headwaters of Turner Creek. As you descend from the Ouachita National Recreation Trail, you will be following an abandoned two-track. You will splash through these creeks on a rock ledge. It's the perfect place to take a break and dangle your feet in the waterfall.

General location: 30 miles west of Mt. Ida on US 270.
Elevation change: Elevations range from 880′ along Mill Creek at the trailhead to 2,285′ at Buck Knob. See "Notes on the trail" for loop choices that avoid the most difficult climbs.
Season: As with most rides in this book, spring and fall are the best seasons to ride this trail. Summer can be hot, but stream crossings, a swim at Mill Creek, and cool breezes on the ridges along the back of the trail network make it bearable.

Winter views from the ridge and from Buck Knob are spectacular. Just carry some extra socks. Some of the streams can't be crossed without getting your feet wet.
Services: Drinking water, camping, swimming, and showers are available at Mill Creek Recreation Area during the warm months. The recreation area is closed in the off-season.

RIDE 62 *MILL CREEK EQUESTRIAN TRAIL*

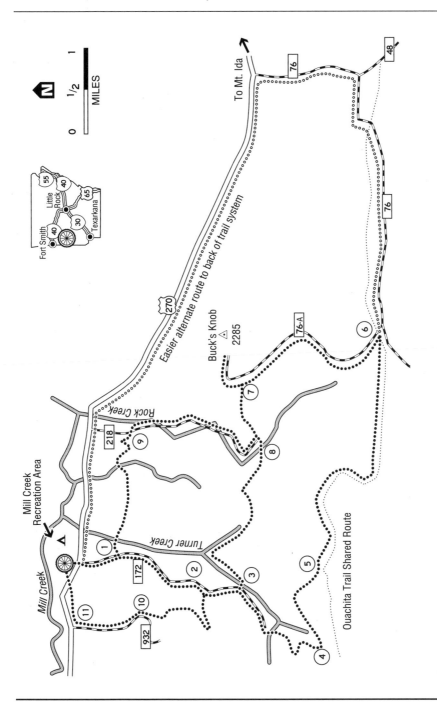

Big Brushy Recreation Area, about 11 miles to the east on US 270, is open year-round for camping. Additional camping, food, and fuel can be found in Y-City, 5 miles west of Mill Creek Recreation Area on US 270.

All other services except bike shops are available in Mt. Ida, 30 miles to the east. Full-service bike shops can be found in Hot Springs, 60 miles to the east.

Hazards: Riders opting for some of the really rugged stuff should exercise extreme caution. These sections of the trail are very rough in places. I highly recommend that you follow the suggestions in the trail notes.

Remember that this is also an equestrian trail. Be prepared to meet horses at any time. Move to the downhill side of the trail, stand quietly, and let them pass.

Rescue index: When you are riding in the southern reaches of the trail system, you'll be fairly remote. Be ready to take care of yourself in this area. In the north, near the highway, you won't be far from the road. You should be able to work your way to US 270 and await help.

Land status: National forest.

Maps: The Forest Service produces an excellent map of the trail system. It is usually available at the trailhead. If you want to use a topo map, you'll need the Buck Knob 7.5 minute. Carrying a map of the Ouachita National Forest will help you find your way along the alternate routes suggested under trail notes.

Finding the trail: The trailhead is located in Mill Creek Recreation Area, 5 miles east of Y-City or 30 miles west of Mt. Ida on US 270. If the recreation area is closed for the season, just park in the entrance. The trailhead is about a quarter mile down the entrance road.

Sources of additional information:

Ouachita National Forest
Poteau Ranger District
Post Office Box 2255
Waldron, AR 72958
(501) 637-4174

Notes on the trail: These trails are marked by yellow paint blazes. All trail intersections are numbered, both on the map and at each intersection. The sections between points 1 and 9 and between points 3 and 8 are very rough. Many portages will be required, and beginners should not use these sections of the trail. Experts might not like it much, either. Almost all the trail routes to the ridge are long and difficult climbs.

There is an easier option for those who don't feel up to the climb, but would still like to enjoy the fantastic scenery on the ridge in the southern reaches of the area. Ride east on US 270 about 7 miles to Forest Service Road 76. Turn right (south) on FS 76 and follow it as it curves south and west, then climbs more gently to intersect with the trail system near the junction of FS 76 and FS 76A.

From here, you can drop down the east side of the trail system, enjoy the fun descent to Rock Creek, then follow the impressive bluffs and splash through the 3 stream crossings on an easy 2-track road.

Those with a little more energy and riding talent can take the most scenic route of all. From the point near the junction of FS 76 and 76A, ride Ouachita National Recreation Trail an additional 4.5 miles west, then descend from point 5. There will be a few rough stretches requiring portages, but the panoramic views and the fun descent make the difficulties well worth the effort.

Just pay close attention as you approach point 5. The markings are a little confusing there, but with a little investigation you will be able to find the beginning of the fantastic descent back down to Mill Creek.

RIDE 63 *EARTHQUAKE RIDGE TRAIL*

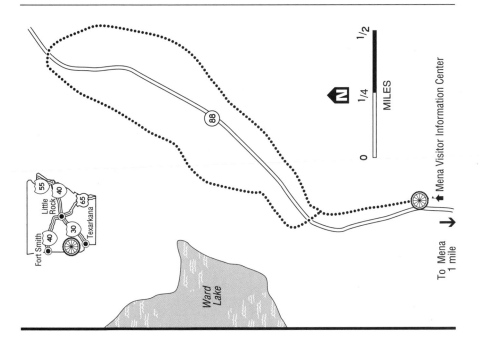

RIDE 63 *EARTHQUAKE RIDGE TRAIL*

This three-mile trail is all single-track with a few steep and rugged sections. Because it is short, it can be handled by riders of all skill levels. The trail surface is part rocky, part hard-packed dirt. It is well maintained, and makes good use of switchbacks to keep the grades manageable.

The ride traverses Earthquake Ridge, an escarpment towering above nearby Mena. On the western side of the loop, just past the crossing of AR 88, you will

Trailhead for the Earthquake Ridge Trail.

be treated to beautiful views of the Ouachita Mountains to the southwest. As you cross over the ridge and ride the loop's eastern side, you'll get a bird's-eye view of Mena.

General location: 1 mile west of Mena.
Elevation change: Elevations range from 1,038′ at the trailhead to 1,800′ at the upper crossing of AR 88. There is a half-mile climb to the top of the ridge, followed by a downhill of similar length.
Season: Since it is short, the Earthquake Ridge Trail can be ridden year-round.
Services: Drinking water is available at the trailhead. All other services can be found in Mena, 1 mile to the east.
Hazards: Other than a few rocky stretches, no hazards exist on the Earthquake Ridge Trail.
Rescue index: This is a short trail that sees much use. It also crosses AR 88 twice. Because of this, you are never far from help on this ride.

Land status: National forest.

Maps: The Forest Service produces a good map of the Earthquake Ridge Trail. It may be available at the Visitor Center at the trailhead. The topo for the area is the Mena 7.5 minute map.

Finding the trail: Drive 1 mile west of Mena on AR 88 to the Ouachita National Forest Visitor Information Station. The trail leaves the station from the north end of the parking lot.

Sources of additional information:

Ouachita National Forest
Route 3 Box 220
Highway 71 North
Mena, AR 71953
(501) 394-2382

Notes on the trail: This is the perfect short ride for those in search of their first single-track experience. It has a degree of difficulty that will challenge you, but is short enough to be ridden by anyone. Stronger riders could get a workout by riding the loop several times. The Earthquake Ridge Trail is also popular with local trail runners, so look out for them while riding the loop.

RIDE 64 *WOLF PEN GAP TRAIL*

The Wolf Pen Gap Trail is a 41-mile network of trails developed and maintained for mountain bikes and off-road vehicles. It is a mix of short sections of gravel road, abandoned two-tracks, and newly constructed single-track. Difficulty ranges from easy to extreme.

The map issued by the Forest Service is keyed to show the difficulty of each trail section here, so you can choose loops to match your abilities. You should expect occasional portages due to steep climbs, mud, stream fords, or to cross sections of rocky washouts due to ATV activity.

The trail network encompasses the drainages of Board Camp Creek and Gap Creek. Stream crossings add some excitement to this ride, especially along the northern perimeter of the area. Here the trail makes many crossings of Board Camp Creek.

The forest through which the trails run is predominantly oak and pine—most of it has been logged sometime in the past century. A two-foot-thick oak that somehow escaped the ax stands near the eastern trailhead.

Take some time to enjoy the panoramic views along the trail. The best ones are marked on the Forest Service map of the trail system. If you have the whole weekend to burn, you can camp at nearby Bard Springs or Shady Lake. Both are

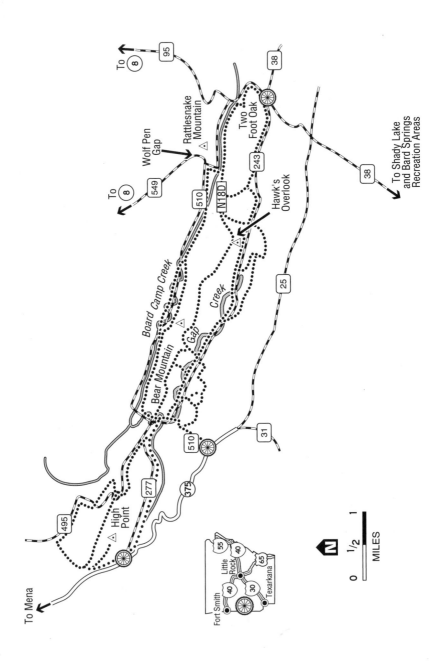

beautiful sites in the southern Ouachita Mountains, perfect for relaxing after a challenging day on the trail. They are also close to other rides in the Ouachita National Forest.

General location: About 12 miles southeast of Mena, just north of the Caney Creek Wilderness.

Elevation change: Elevation varies from 1,100′ at the crossings of Board Camp Creek and Gap Creek to 1,500′ along the shoulders of Bear Mountain and High Point. Those riding the spur trail to High Point will reach 1,900′.

Season: Late spring and fall, with their cooler temperatures, are the best times to ride this trail. The heat of summer can be offset by splashing through stream crossings. Cyclists braving the colder temperatures of winter will be rewarded by spectacular, foliage-free views. Fewer ATVs use the area during the heat of summer and dead of winter.

Services: No drinking water is available anywhere on the trail. Camping is allowed anywhere in the national forest. The nearest developed campsites are at Bard Springs, around 15 miles to the southeast, and at Shady Lake, 18 miles to the southeast. Bard Springs has a spring-fed swimming hole, camp shelters, and drinking water. Shady Lake offers swimming, water, and showers. All other services are available in Mena, 12 miles to the northwest.

Hazards: Wolf Pen Gap is designed for both mountain bikes and ATVs. Be prepared to encounter the latter at any time. If you meet one while you are descending, yield the trail. If you force them to stop while climbing, they may have a difficult time getting started again.

Rescue index: On weekends the complex sees relatively heavy use. Riders in trouble can get help from other cyclists and ATV operators. If you get into trouble on weekdays, you may be on your own. You should make your way to AR 375 or to Forest Service roads 25 and 38 on the southern and eastern edges of the trail complex.

Land status: National forest.

Maps: The Forest Service produces a good map of the trail, available at the address shown below. Those wishing to carry topos will need the 7.5 minute Eagle Mountain and Nichols Mountain maps.

Finding the trail: Drive east from Mena 1 mile on AR 8 to AR 375. Turn south on AR 375 and follow it approximately 9 miles to FS 277. Turn left on FS 277. The trailhead is 100 feet down this road.

There is a second trailhead 3 miles farther down AR 375, and a third on the far eastern edge of the trail system, near the junction of Forest Service roads 38 and 95.

Sources of additional information:

Ouachita National Forest
Mena Ranger District
Route 3 Box 220
Highway 71 North
Mena, AR 71953
(501) 394-2382

Notes on the trail: Since this is a large trail network, carrying a map is highly recommended. The map issued by the Forest Service is keyed to show difficult sections of the trail, so you can pick the loops best suited to your skills.

Routes are marked by Carsonite posts, reflective stickers, and paint blazes on the trees. Blazes are color-coded to help you stay on the chosen trail. Numerical trail symbols at each intersection correspond to trail numbers on the map.

RIDE 65 *COSSATOT MOUNTAINS LOOP*

This entire 25-five mile loop uses Forest Service roads. It is recommended for riders of all skill levels. Forest Service Road 38 on the west and FS 106 on the south side of the loop are medium-quality gravel roads. FS 512 on the east and north side of the loop is gravel for half its length, then degenerates to a rough four-wheel-drive road for its last five miles. Riders on this rough-but-fun section will enjoy the many crossings of Long and Sugar Creeks.

The Cossatot Mountains are a narrow band of peaks on the southern edge of the Ouachita National Forest. Clear streams parallel the ride for three-fourths of its length. On the south, the ride follows Blaylock Creek. The Little Missouri River, Long Creek, and Sugar Creek flow along the roads on the eastern portion of the ride.

On FS 38, on the west side of the loop, you will be treated to spectacular views into the Caney Creek Wilderness as you grind out the climb over the Cossatots and blast down the other side. In spring, when the streams and springs are flowing, the loop features more than 20 stream fords. Albert Pike and Bard Springs recreation areas are perfect spots for mid-ride swims.

The most spectacular view in the area is from the top of Tall Peak, a 2.8-mile side trip from Bard Springs. Although the entire distance is uphill, an old fire-tower at the summit treats those braving the climb to one of the most dramatic vistas in Arkansas. And after enjoying the view, you are rewarded by a 2.8-mile descent back to Bard Springs.

General location: 6 miles north of Langley on AR 369.
Elevation change: Elevations on this loop range from 900′ at Albert Pike

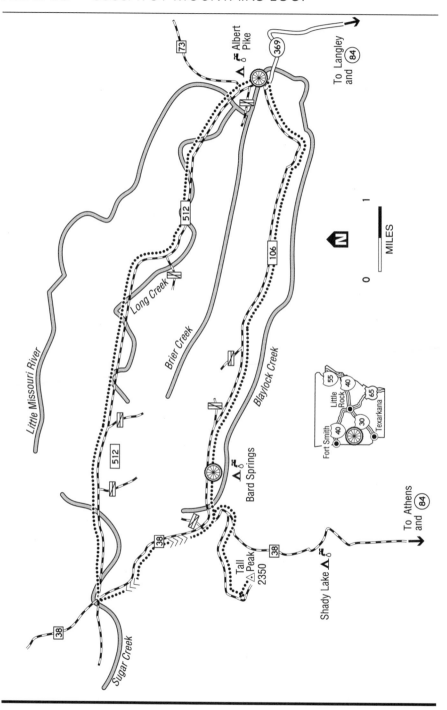

Recreation Area to 1,800′ at the Buckeye Mountain Trailhead on FS 38. Those taking the side trip to Tall Peak will top out at 2,350′. This side trip will require a 2.8-mile climb and corresponding descent. The main loop has a 1.2-mile climb and descent on FS 38, and 3 hills on FS 106 that result in climbs and descents between one-half mile and a mile.

Season: Weather is consistently warm from late March to late October. Some warm days will crop up during winter. Summer riding may be hot and humid, but numerous creek crossings and a swim in the Little Missouri River at Albert Pike Recreation Area will help you beat the heat.

Services: Drinking water is available on the loop at Albert Pike and Bard Springs recreation areas. Albert Pike has showers and a snack bar during the warmer months. There is a swimming hole in the creek at Bard Springs.

Most other services can be found in Glenwood, 25 miles to the east. All services, including bike shops, are available in Hot Springs, 60 miles to the northeast.

Hazards: There are roadside drop-offs along the climb and descent over the Cossatots on FS 38. Keep your bike under control on these, or you may end up soaring with the hawks and buzzards for a short while. Do not try to ford the Little Missouri River and other streams along the way during high water.

Rescue index: Except for the rough western section of FS 512, all roads on the loop see some cars. You will be quickly found if you run into trouble. If you have problems on the rough part of FS 512, you will have to take care of yourself.

Land status: National forest.

Maps: A map of the Ouachita National Forest will show the entire loop. The two USGS topos covering most of the Cossatot Mountains Loop are the 7.5 minute Big Fork and Nichols Mountain maps. A very small portion of the loop along FS 106 is on the Athens 7.5 minute.

Finding the trail: The best starting point for the ride is Albert Pike Recreation Area. To reach it, drive 6 miles north from Langley on AR 369 and FS 73.

The ride can also start from Bard Springs Recreation Area. It is 2 miles west of Athens on AR 246, 8 miles north on FS 38, and 1 mile east on FS 106.

Sources of additional information:

Ouachita National Forest
Caddo Ranger District
Post Office Box 369
Glenwood, AR 71943
(501) 356-4186

Notes on the trail: The Cossatot Mountain Loop will be fun for everyone in your group, including non-riders. While the bikers are out riding, those who aren't can hike the Little Missouri Trail, following the river 6 miles to Little Missouri Falls. Or they can act as sag drivers, tagging along with the other cyclists on the driveable parts of the loop. Then again, they could just hang out at Albert Pike, swimming, fishing, catching some sun, and taking it easy.

Splashing through Long Creek along FS 512 on the Cossatot Mountains Loop.

Riders of all skill levels will enjoy pedaling this loop. Beginners will like the non-technical ride. They will get a mild taste of off-road conditions on FS 512, where they will bounce over ruts and splash through the creek crossings.

Experienced riders will be challenged by this stretch, too, and by the rougher roads in the Leader Mountain Walk-In Turkey Hunting Area. Closed from February 1 to September 1 to protect nesting turkeys and their broods, Leader Mountain is open to bikes and ATVs during the winter. Located in the western end of the loop (see map), it offers rougher riding than the loop itself. Don't ride in Leader Mountain during its closed months.

KENTUCKY RIDES

Land Between the Lakes Trails

Kentucky Lake and Lake Barkley were formed by damming the Cumberland and Tennessee rivers, creating the largest manmade body of water in the world. Nearly 250,000 acres of lake surface were created when these two rivers, which flow parallel to each other for over 40 miles, were dammed. The Land Between the Lakes is the 170,000-acre peninsula between the two lakes.

Until the mid-twentieth century, this area was farmland. Historical cemeteries of Land Between the Lakes' original inhabitants dot the peninsula, and a living example of life on an 1850s farm can be viewed at The Homeplace. Here, park employees dressed in period clothing use nineteenth-century farming tools and methods to work the land as in old times in the land between the rivers.

Field crops weren't all that kept earlier residents of the area busy. Moonshine was a popular product around here, too. Golden Pond Moonshine was nationally known and asked for by name. In the Visitor Center in Golden Pond you can see an old still on exhibit, along with an explanation of how the moonshine producing process worked. Don't get excited—it's not detailed enough for you to copy at home.

If you're interested in wildlife, be sure to visit the Woodlands Nature Center. The center has live animals and birds, plant exhibits, and interpretive nature hikes. Wildlife common in the area include deer, turkeys, beavers, bobcats, coyotes, and, in a pasture near The Homeplace, buffalo. In spring and fall, the lakes are regular stops for thousands of migrating waterfowl. Eagles soar above the lakes, and songbirds flit through the peninsula's quiet forests.

There are plenty of activities besides biking here. Boating, skiing, windsurfing, fishing, and hunting are all popular pastimes for visitors. There are four campgrounds in the Land Between the Lakes, and around 200 miles of hiking trails.

Unfortunately, most of the trails are closed to mountain biking. Part of the North/South Trail near the Visitor Center is open, though, and is part of the Jenny Ridge Tour. All the roads in the area are open. Some of them are rough and fun. And the Tennessee Valley Authority, administering agency for the Land Between the Lakes, is studying the possibility of developing more trails specifically for bikes.

Check at park information centers when you arrive for additions and changes to the mountain biking situation in the area. Information stations are located at the north entrance, the south entrance, and at Golden Pond Visitor Center. Since it's hard to enter the Land Between the Lakes without passing one of these sites, you shouldn't have trouble finding one. They have all the maps and information you need to enjoy this wooded peninsula.

RIDE 66 *ENERGY LAKE LOOP*

The Energy Lake trails are a varied road network 19 miles long. The network is best ridden as a 12-mile loop (see map), exploring side roads for additional mileage as you ride the loop.

The side roads off Land Between the Lakes Road 327 all lead to secluded points at the edge of Lake Barkley. About three miles of the system follow paved roads. Another four miles use maintained gravel roads. The remaining 12 miles are on rougher dirt roads that are maintained little or not at all. You can judge the condition of each road by its number. Road numbers beginning with "1" are the easiest, while those beginning with "3" are roughest. All the Energy Lake roads can be handled by beginners.

Don't just ride the loop and be done with the riding. Check out the side roads, particularly those leading down to the lake off LBL 327. They lead to the water's edge. One of them leads to a nice beach when the water is at the right level. In fall, you'll see migratory waterfowl stopping on their flight south.

Nor should you disdain this ride because it follows roads. LBL 322, 324, and 333 are challenging double-tracks through the forest, and LBL 146 parallels a slough at the upper end of Energy Lake. After the ride, you can cool off with a dip in Energy Lake at the swimming beach near the campground.

General location: 8 miles northeast of Golden Pond.
Elevation change: The lowest point on this ride is 360′ on the shores of Lake Barkley. From there, you'll climb to a peak of 480′ along LBL Road 324. There are numerous climbs of various lengths, but all can be handled by riders in average physical condition.
Season: Spring and fall are the best seasons to ride here. The temperatures are more moderate and the summer crowds are gone. Winter can be fun, too. You will feel like you have the entire Land Between the Lakes to yourself, and since there are no stream fords, you won't have wet feet to chill you.
Services: Maps and information about Land Between the Lakes are available at both entrance stations and at the Visitor Center in Golden Pond. Water is available on the loop at Energy Lake Campground. Camping is also available there, and at several other campgrounds in the area.

Energy Lake also has swimming, showers, boat rentals, and a small store. Restaurants and hotels are in the nearby towns of Grand Rivers and Cadiz. The nearest bike shops are in Paducah to the north and Clarksville to the south.
Hazards: In late fall, Land Between the Lakes is full of deer and turkey hunters. If you must ride during hunting seasons, don't wear anything white, and don't sound like a turkey.
Rescue index: Most roads used by this network see several cars per day. The

RIDE 66 *ENERGY LAKE LOOP*

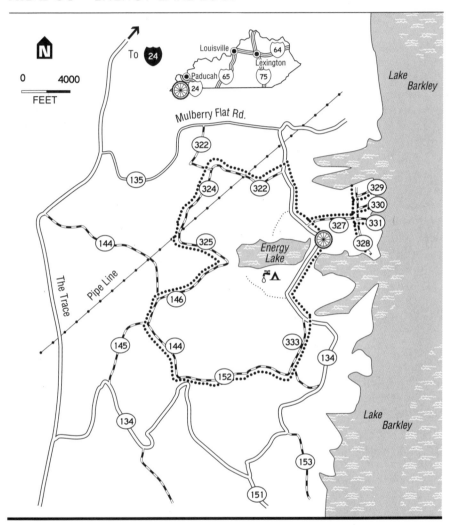

exceptions are the more rugged LBL Roads 322, 324, 325, and 333, where normal vehicles do not usually go. If you get into a jam on one of these, work your way to one of the roads beginning with the number 1, and await a passing motorist.

Land status: Tennessee Valley Authority.

Maps: An LBL Legal Road Map shows all the roads in Land Between the Lakes, including those in this network. If you want to use a topo, LBL also has one of the entire Land Between the Lakes which shows the whole recreation

Driftwood and natural sand beach on Lake Barkley at the end of dead-end LBL Road 331, Energy Lake Loop.

area. There is even a map of this trail system. All 3 maps are available at the entrance station and at the Visitor Center in Golden Pond.

If you want to use a USGS topo, you will find that most of the ride falls onto the Fenton 7.5 minute map. A small portion falls onto Mont.

Finding the trail: Turn east off The Trace onto Mulberry Flat Road (LBL Road 135). Follow it 4 miles to Energy Lake Road (LBL Road 134). Drive 3 miles east to Energy Lake. You can park in a lake access site next to the dam.

Sources of additional information:

Tennessee Valley Authority
Land Between the Lakes
Golden Pond, KY 42231
(502) 924-5602

Notes on the trail: Roads in Land Between the Lakes are well marked at each intersection, so you shouldn't get lost if you carry a map. These roads are designated mountain bike routes, and will be marked by arrows and bicycle symbols.

If you ever feel lost, don't get worried. You are never more than 2 miles from a paved road. Just keep riding. Unless the road on which you are lost is a dead end, you will soon hit one of the paved roads.

RIDE 67 *JENNY RIDGE TRAIL*

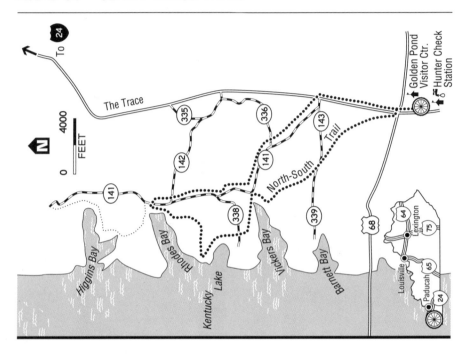

RIDE 67 *JENNY RIDGE TRAIL*

Eight miles of this 14-mile loop follow excellent single-track along the North/South Trail, a 65-mile path running the length of Land Between the Lakes. This is the only part of this great trail that is open to mountain bikes, and it is perfect for beginners who want a single-track experience. Four more miles follow gravel roads, and the remaining two miles follow the pavement of The Trace.

There are additional miles of riding on abandoned roads that lace the area, branching off the marked route at several points. Riding the loop clockwise will let you handle the worst grades as descents instead of climbs.

For a good side-road trip, take LBL Road 339. It's the first road you cross on the North/South Trail if you are riding northbound. Following 339 to the west, you'll parallel Barnett Creek on your way to Barnett Bay, where the road ends near Smith Cemetery.

Heading north on the single-track once more, you'll ride at the water's edge as you pedal around two small bays protruding into the Land Between the

Footbridge on the North/South Trail section used by the Jenny Ridge Trail.

Lakes. Sometimes you'll be so close that if you veer off the trail, you might take a dip. On a hot day, maybe you'll do it deliberately.

You may see quite a bit of wildlife as you ride this trail. When checking it out, I saw turkeys, deer, and lots of migrating waterfowl. As I reached the end of the single-track section, a bald eagle cruised past overhead at treetop level.

General location: This ride begins just south of the Golden Pond Visitor Center.
Elevation change: Elevations range from 360′ at the water's edge to 650′ at the Visitor Center. There are many climbs and descents along the way, but all are rideable by cyclists in good physical condition.
Season: Spring and fall are the best seasons for riding this trail. The only drawback may be high water in spring, which could cover parts of the single-track next to the lake. Summer can be fun since you can take a swim at several points along the way, but heat and ticks can be troublesome.
Services: Drinking water is available at the Visitor Center near the trailhead. There are 5 campgrounds in Land Between the Lakes, and hotels and restaurants in the nearby towns of Grand Rivers and Cadiz.
Hazards: The trail itself is pretty safe. Think twice about riding this trail in late fall, though, when deer and turkey season are in progress. Don't wear anything white during deer season. Wear hunter's-orange, if you have anything that color.
Rescue index: On the road portions of this trail, you can normally count on being found by a car. If you run into trouble on the North/South Trail, you may

be on your own. If it's a weekend, you may be found by another trail user.

Land status: Tennessee Valley Authority.

Maps: The LBL Legal Road Map shows all the roads in Land Between the Lakes, including the roads and trail used by this loop. There is also a topo of the entire LBL area which shows everything. The Legal Road Map is free, but you'll have to buy the topo. You can also get a flyer showing this mountain bike loop.

All 3 maps are available at the entrance stations and Visitor Center. If you want to use USGS topos, get the Fenton 7.5 minute map.

Finding the trail: Park your car at the Visitor Center or the hunter check station just to the south in Golden Pond. You can reach the trail where it crosses The Trace next to the hunter check station, or by a spur trail leading west from the Visitor Center.

Sources of additional information:

Tennessee Valley Authority
Land Between the Lakes
Golden Pond, KY 42231
(502) 924-5602

Notes on the trail: This is an official mountain bike trail, and is marked by arrows and mountain bike silhouettes. The stretch of the North/South Trail used by the Jenny Ridge Trail is the only hiking path open to mountain biking in Land Between the Lakes. Don't ride any of the others during your visit here.

RIDE 68   *TURKEY BAY OFF-ROAD-VEHICLE AREA*

The 2,350 acres of the Turkey Bay ORV Area represent a large network of challenging single-track trail. Nobody knows the exact number of miles available for riding here. It is recommended only for experienced riders.

The trails vary from wide, smooth hardpack in the bottoms and on the ridges to paths of loose, washed-out rock on some of the trails leading between the ridges and hollows. Choosing trails that follow ridges and bottomlands will result in the most enjoyable rides. The payoff for fighting your way to the tops of the ridges is in challenging technical descents back to the bottomlands.

You can choose loops of almost any length in Turkey Bay ORV Area. There are scenic views of Kentucky Lake on the western side of the area, and a spaghetti-like system of over 50 miles of challenging trails in the woods east of the lake. Because this relatively small geographic area is bounded by roads or the lake, it is hard to get lost. Important intersections in the trail system are marked both on the ground and on the map, giving you reference points that help you keep track of where you are in the system.

RIDE 68 *TURKEY BAY OFF-ROAD VEHICLE AREA*

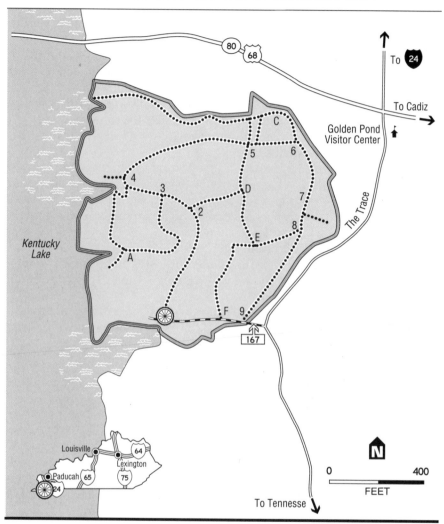

After you finish riding, you can pedal west on LBL Road 167 to Turkey Bay, where a cooling dip in the lake awaits.

General location: 2 miles southwest of Golden Pond Visitor Center in Land Between the Lakes.

Elevation change: Elevations range from about 350′ at the water's edge to 650′ at the high points in the trail system. Grades range from easy to impossible. The easiest riding is on the ridge-tops and along creek bottoms.

Season: Though spring and fall are great times to mountain bike in Kentucky because of their cooler temperatures, winter riding is great on this system. Fewer ORVs are out then, so you can have the trail system to yourself.

Services: No drinking water is available at the trailhead. Fill up at the Visitor Center. There are chemical toilets at the trailhead. Camping is available at 5 campgrounds in Land Between the Lakes.

Hotels and restaurants are in the nearby towns of Grand Rivers and Cadiz, and at Kenlake and Lake Barkley state resort parks. Bike shops and all other services are located in Paducah to the north and Clarksville to the south.

Hazards: Watch out for ORVs blasting down the trails in the area. If you go during the week and in the winter, you'll be less likely to encounter as many of these noisy contraptions. Be careful on the rocky slopes where ORV use has loosened the rocks in the trailbed.

Rescue index: You are never more than a mile from a road when riding in the Turkey Bay ORV Area. If you are in trouble, make your way east, north, or south until you hit one of the roads. Don't go west, since you'll hit Kentucky Lake. On weekends your chances of being found by another trail user are very good.

Land status: Tennessee Valley Authority.

Maps: You can pick up a map of Turkey Bay ORV Area at the entrance station to Land Between the Lakes. If you want to use a topo, you will need the Fenton and Rushing Creek 7.5 minute maps.

Finding the trail: Drive 2 miles south from Golden Pond on The Trace to LBL Road 167. Turn west and drive one-half mile on Turkey Creek Road (LBL Road 167) to a parking area. The trails spread out to the north from this parking area.

Sources of additional information:

Tennessee Valley Authority
Land Between the Lakes
Golden Pond, KY 42231
(502) 924-5602

Notes on the trail: From the parking area, this set of trails looks pretty rough and loose. Ride into the network, though, and you'll find some pretty good mountain biking. After a few passes through the area, you will have a good feel for what is there, and which parts of the area offer the best biking.

Other Kentucky Trails

RIDE 69 *MAMMOTH CAVE TOURS*

Mammoth Cave National Park protects the longest cave system in the world. Over 335 miles of known passages underlie this 52,700-acre scenic area in south-central Kentucky. While none of the hiking trails in the park are open to bikes, the scenic roads in and around the park offer excellent riding opportunities.

The 32-mile Ferry Loop crosses two ferries on its way around the western two-thirds of the park. It follows gravel roads for six miles of its length. The Flint Ridge Loop covers 12 miles of the eastern part of the park on paved roads. At nine miles, the Joppa Ridge Loop is shortest. It includes 2.3 miles of gravel on Joppa Ridge Road.

All rides are suitable for cyclists of all skill levels. You should be in good condition to handle the long climbs found on each loop.

Mammoth Cave is a great place for those who are tired of the rough stuff, but still want to enjoy riding in a scenic setting. When you get tired of riding, you can head to the park restaurant for a bite to eat. Camp at one of the park's campgrounds, or really rough it in the park hotel. Don't miss one of the many cave tours offered daily in the park. The tours often fill up, so make your reservation in advance, if possible. For information on cave tours call (502) 758-2328.

General location: 35 miles northeast of Bowling Green.
Elevation change: Elevations range from 450′ at the ferry crossings to around 850′ along Flint Ridge Road. On the Ferry Tour, there will be 2 climbs and descents of around a mile each, and many smaller hills. The Flint Ridge Loop has a 1-mile descent and climb, but is otherwise not too challenging. The Joppa Ridge Loop also has a 1-mile climb and descent.
Season: While spring and fall are the best seasons to ride in Mammoth Cave, all seasons offer enjoyable cycling. Warm days often occur during winter. On the cold days, you can hit the park's restaurant for a hot meal after a cold ride.
Services: All services except bike shops are available in the park. If you decide

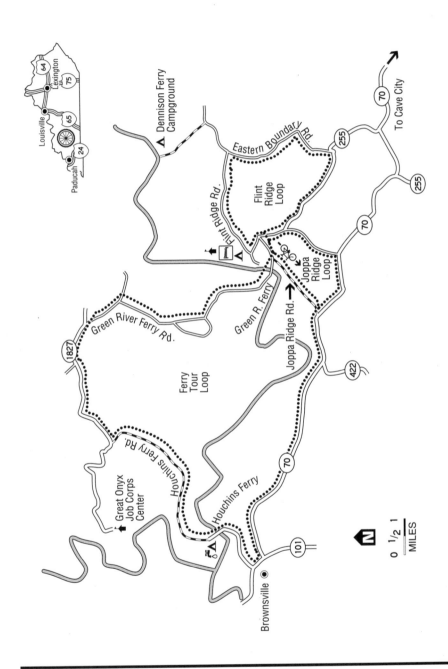

Joppa Ridge Road in Mammoth Cave National Park.

to do the Ferry Loop as a 2-day ride, camping and water are available at Houchins Ferry. There are also convenience stores about every 10 miles on the Ferry Loop. The nearest bike shops are in Bowling Green, 30 miles to the southwest.

Hazards: Watch out for cars on the 10-mile stretch of KY 70 when you're riding the Ferry Tour. Traffic is not usually heavy, but there is no shoulder for most of this distance.

Rescue index: Since you will always be on public roads when riding these loops, you should be found fairly quickly if you get into trouble.

Land status: Most of the roads used by these loops pass through national park land. Small portions cross private lands on public roads.

Maps: Maps of Mammoth Cave National Park are available at the Visitor Center. They show all the roads used by these rides. Topos covering most of the area are Mammoth Cave and Rhoda 7.5 minute maps. Small amounts of the northern part of the park fall onto Cub Run and Nolin Lake.

Finding the trail: All these rides start from the headquarters complex of the park. It has a campground, store, restaurant, gas station, and Visitor Center. To reach it, exit I-65 at the Park City exit. Turn west on KY 255, and follow the signs for about 7 miles to the Visitor Center.

Sources of additional information:

Mammoth Cave National Park
Mammoth Cave, Kentucky 42259
(502) 758-2251

Notes on the trail: These trails are all on public roads. While Mammoth Cave has over 60 miles of hiking trails, none of these trails are open to mountain bikes. Please respect the park rules and stay off the trails. You can be ticketed for riding on park foot trails.

RIDE 70 *OTTER CREEK TRAIL*

This eight-mile loop is perfect for cyclists of all skill levels. Except for a short stretch of the route that follows an abandoned double-track through the woods, the entire trail is hardpack single-track through the forest.

There are only two difficult parts that may require portages. See "Elevation change" for the best way to deal with these. With the exception of a few very short sections of trail along Otter Creek that will require portages, the loop is a great ride.

The natural beauty of this trail is its highlight. Riding north from the Nature Center, you'll pedal through woods and past the park campgrounds on your way to the bluffs along the Ohio River. For a quarter mile, you'll cycle along the bluffs, enjoying views of the river far below. Then you'll have to carry your bike for about one-tenth of a mile over the rock ledges on the descent to Otter Creek. It's worth the effort, though.

For the next four miles you'll pedal next to the creek, sometimes inches from the edge of the stream. Most of this stretch feels like untrammeled wilderness. When you finally leave Otter Creek and climb back onto the plateau where the bulk of the park is located, you'll ride through a large grove of pine trees that carpet the trail with their needles.

There is plenty to do in this park when your ride is over, too. You can take a dip in the pool, have dinner in the restaurant, or play a little Frisbee golf. There are guided tours of Morgan Cave, a cavern in the northwest corner of the park. You could rent one of the 23 rooms in the Otter Creek Lodge. Or stay in one of the park's rustic cabins, and spend a couple of days riding, hiking, and taking it easy in Otter Creek Park.

RIDE 70 *OTTER CREEK TRAIL*

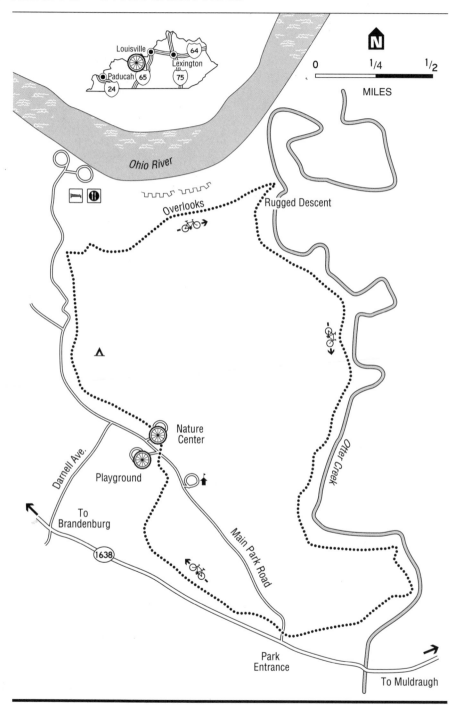

Secluded single-track along Otter Creek in the southeast part of the Otter Creek Trail.

General location: 25 miles southwest of Louisville.

Elevation change: Elevations vary from 650′ at the trailhead to 370′ along Otter Creek. Most of the park sits on a plateau above Otter Creek and the Ohio River. There is 1 long descent when you drop off the plateau down to Otter Creek, and an ascent when you climb back up to the plateau.

To deal with these grades most easily you should ride the trail clockwise. This lets you handle the unrideable grade near the Ohio River as a descent. You will have to carry your bike over 3-foot ledges, and hauling your bike down these is preferable to hoisting it over them.

Season: Spring and fall are the best seasons to ride this trail. Summer riding can be fun, since much of the trail is shaded. There are no stream crossings, so winter rides are possible for those who don't mind the cold.

Services: Drinking water is available at several points in the park. The nature center, one of the recommended starting points for the trail, has water and restrooms. Other facilities in the park include campgrounds, cabins, a hotel, a store, a restaurant, a pool, and a Frisbee golf course. The nearest bike shops are in Louisville, 25 miles to the northeast.

Hazards: The descent from the plateau down to Otter Creek near the Ohio River is very steep and rugged. Don't even think about trying to ride it. It's the most rugged one-tenth mile in this book. There are a few places along Otter Creek where the trail is inches from the creek. Be careful here, unless you want a surprise bath for you and your bike. If the creek is in flood stage, don't ride the part of the loop through the bottomlands.

Rescue index: About one-fourth of the Otter Creek Trail passes near developed campsites, picnic grounds, and cabins. You will easily find help if you have trouble there. Another fourth roughly parallels the entrance road and KY 1638.

The half of the trail following Otter Creek is more remote, but still sees quite a bit of use. If you don't want to wait around for help, bushwhack straight west. You'll soon find your way to the developed part of the park.

Land status: City park.

Maps: An excellent map of the park trail system can be picked up at the park administration office. It doesn't show contour lines, though. If you want to use a topo, get the Rock Haven quad.

Finding the trail: From Louisville, drive about 20 miles southwest on US 31W/60 to Muldraugh. From Muldraugh, drive 3 miles west to the park entrance. Turn north into the park. One mile down the park entrance road is the nature center. You can park your car and ride from there.

Closing times for the nature center are posted at the gate. If you don't plan to be back before the gate is closed, park at the recreation area 100 yards south on the park road.

Sources of additional information:

Otter Creek City Park
850 Otter Creek Park Road
Brandenburg, KY 40108
(502) 583-3577

Notes on the trail: The Otter Creek Trail is well marked by blue blazes. It's hard to get lost while riding this loop. If you do get lost, simply hike or carry your bike in a straight line in any direction. You will eventually hit a road, Otter Creek, or the Ohio River. There are several other trails in Otter Creek Park, but they are not open to mountain bikes. Cooperate with the park by not riding any trails other than Otter Creek.

Afterword

A few years ago I wrote a long piece on this issue for *Sierra Magazine*, and called literally dozens of government land managers, game wardens, mountain bikers, and local officials, to get a feeling for how ATBs were being welcomed on the trails. All that I've seen personally since, and heard from my authors, indicates there hasn't been much change. Which means we're still considered the new kid on the block, that we have less right to the trails than horses and hikers, and that we're excluded from many areas including:

a) wilderness areas
b) national parks (except on roads, and those paths specifically marked "bike path")
c) national monuments (except on roads open to the public)
d) most state parks and monuments (except on roads, and those paths specifically marked "bike path")
e) an increasing number of urban and county parks, especially in California (except on roads, and those paths specifically marked "bike path")

Frankly, I have little difficulty with these exclusions, and would in fact restrict our presence from some trails I've ridden (one time) due to the environmental damage and chance of blind-siding the many walkers and hikers I met up with along the way. But these are my personal views. They should not be interpreted as those of the authors, and are mentioned here only as a way to introduce the land-use problem and the varying positions on it which even mountain bikers hold.

You can do your part in keeping us from being excluded from even more trails by riding responsibly. Many local and national off-road bicycle organizations have been formed with exactly this in mind, and one of the largest—NORBA, the National Off-Road Bicycle Association—offers the following code of behavior for mountain bikers:

1. I will yield the right of way to other non-motorized recreationists. I realize that people judge all cyclists by my actions.

2. I will slow down and use caution when approaching or overtaking another and will make my presence known well in advance.

3. I will maintain control of my speed at all times and will approach turns in anticipation of someone around the bend.

4. I will stay on designated trails to avoid trampling native vegetation

and minimize potential erosion to trails by not using muddy trails or short-cutting switchbacks.

5. I will not disturb wildlife or livestock.

6. I will not litter. I will pack out what I pack in, and pack out more than my share whenever possible.

7. I will respect public and private property, including trail use signs and No Trespassing signs, and I will leave gates as I have found them.

8. I will always be self-sufficient and my destination and travel speed will be determined by my ability, my equipment, the terrain, the present and potential weather conditions.

9. I will not travel solo when bikepacking in remote areas. I will leave word of my destination, and when I plan to return.

10. I will observe the practice of minimum impact bicycling by "taking only pictures and memories and leaving only waffle prints."

11. I will always wear a helmet whenever I ride.

Now, I have a problem with some of these—number nine, for instance. The most enjoyable mountain biking I've ever done has been solo. And as to leaving word of destination and time of return, I've enjoyed living in such a way as to say, "I'm off to pedal Colorado. See you in the fall." Of course it's senseless to take needless risks, and I plan a ride and pack my gear with this in mind. But for me number nine smacks too much of the "never-out-of-touch" mentality. And getting away from civilization, deep into the wilds, is for many people what mountain biking's all about.

All in all, however, theirs is a good list, and surely we mountain bikers would be liked more, and excluded less, if we followed the suggestions. But let me offer a "code of ethics" I much prefer, one given cyclists by Utah's Wasatch-Cache National Forest office.

Study a Forest Map Before You Ride
Currently, bicycles are permitted on roads and developed trails within the Wasatch-Cache National Forest except in designated Wilderness. If your route crosses private land, it is your responsibility to obtain right-of-way permission from the landowner.

Keep Groups Small
Riding in large groups degrades the outdoor experience for others, can disturb wildlife and usually leads to greater resource damage.

Avoid Riding on Wet Trails
Bicycle tires leave ruts in wet trails. These ruts concentrate runoff and accelerate erosion. Postponing a ride when the trails are wet will preserve the trails for future use.

Stay on Roads and Trails
Riding cross-country destroys vegetation and damages the soil.

Always Yield to Others
Trails are shared by hikers, horses and bicycles. Move off the trail to allow horses to pass and stop to allow hikers adequate room to share the trail. Simply yelling "Bicycle!" is not acceptable.

Control Your Speed
Excessive speed endangers yourself and other forest users.

Avoid Wheel Lock-up and Spin-out
Steep terrain is especially vulnerable to trail wear. Locking brakes on steep descents or when stopping needlessly damages trails. If a slope is steep enough to require locking wheels and skidding, dismount and walk your bicycle. Likewise, if an ascent is so steep your rear wheel slips and spins, dismount and walk your bicycle.

Protect Waterbars and Switchbacks
Waterbars, the rock and log drains built to direct water off trails, protect trails from erosion. When you encounter a waterbar, ride directly over the top or dismount and walk your bicycle. Riding around the ends of waterbars destroys them and speeds erosion. Skidding around switchback corners shortens trail life. Slow down for switchback corners and keep your wheels rolling.

If You Abuse It, You Lose It
Mountain bikes are relative newcomers to the forest and must prove themselves responsible trail users. By following the guidelines above, and by participating in trail maintenance service projects, bicyclists can help avoid closures which would prevent them from using trails.

I've never seen a better trail etiquette-list for mountain bikers. So have fun. Be careful. And don't screw things up for the next guy.

Glossary

This short list of terms does not contain all the words used by mountain bike enthusiasts when discussing their sport. But it should be sufficient as an introduction to the lingua franca you'll hear on the trails.

ATB	all-terrain bike; this, like "fat-tire bike," is another name for a mountain bike
ATV	all-terrain vehicle; this usually refers to the loud, fume-spewing three- or four-wheeled motorized vehicles you will not enjoy meeting on the trail—except of course if you crash and have to hitch a ride out on one
bladed	refers to a dirt road which has been smoothed out by the use of a wide blade on earth-moving equipment; "blading" gets rid of the teeth-chattering, much-cursed washboards found on so many dirt roads after heavy vehicle use
blaze	a mark on a tree made by chipping away a piece of the bark, usually done to designate a trail; such trails are sometimes described as "blazed"
BLM	Bureau of Land Management, an agency of the federal government
buffed	used to describe a very smooth trail
catching air	taking a jump in such a way that both wheels of the bike are off the ground at the same time
clean	while this can be used to describe what you and your bike won't be after following many trials, the term is most often used as a verb to denote the action of pedaling a tough section of trail successfully
deadfall	a tangled mass of fallen trees or branches
diversion ditch	a usually narrow, shallow ditch dug across or around a trail; funneling the water in this manner keeps it from destroying the trail
double-track	the dual tracks made by a jeep or other vehicle, with grass or weeds or rocks between; the mountain biker can therefore ride in either of the tracks, but will of course find that

whichever is chosen, and no matter how many times one changes back and forth, the other track will appear to offer smoother travel

dugway a steep, unpaved, switchbacked descent

feathering using a light touch on the brake lever, hitting it lightly many times rather than very hard or locking the brake

four-wheel-drive this refers to any vehicle with drive-wheel capability on all four wheels (a jeep, for instance, as compared with a two-wheel-drive passenger car), or to a rough road or trail which requires four-wheel-drive capability (or a *one*-wheel drive mountain bike!) to traverse it

game trail the usually narrow trail made by deer, elk, or other game

gated everyone knows what a gate is, and how many variations exist upon this theme; well, if a trail is described as "gated" it simply has a gate across it; don't forget that the rule is if you find a gate closed, close it behind you; if you find one open, leave it that way

Giardia shorthand for *Giardia lamblia*, and known as the "backpacker's bane" until we mountain bikers expropriated it; this is a waterborne parasite that begins its life cycle when swallowed, and one to four weeks later has its host (you) bloated, vomiting, shivering with chills and living in the bathroom; the disease can be avoided by "treating" (purifying) the water you acquire along the trail [see "Hitting the Trail"]

gnarly a term thankfully used less and less these days, it refers to tough trails

hammer to ride very hard

hardpack used to describe a trail in which the dirt surface is packed down hard; such trails make for good and fast riding, and very painful landings; bikers most often use "hardpack" as both a noun and adjective, and "hard-packed" as an adjective only (the grammar lesson will help you when diagramming sentences in camp)

jeep road, jeep trail a rough road or trail which requires four-wheel-drive capability (or a horse or mountain bike) to traverse it

kamikaze while this once referred primarily to those Japanese fliers who quaffed a glass of sake, then flew off as human bombs in suicide missions against US naval vessels, it more recently has been applied to the idiot mountain bikers who far less honorably scream down hiking trails, endangering the physical and mental safety of the walking, biking, and equestrian traffic they meet; deck guns were necessary to stop the Japanese kamikaze pilots, but a bike pump or walking staff in the spokes is sufficient for the current-day kamikazes who threaten to get us all kicked off the trails

multi-purpose   a BLM designation of land which is open to multi-purpose use; mountain biking is allowed

out-and-back   a ride in which you will return on the same trail you pedaled out; while this might sound far more boring than a loop route, many trails look very different when pedaled in the opposite direction

portage   to carry your bike on your person

quads   bikers use this term to refer both to the extensor muscle in the front of the thigh (which is separated into four parts), and to USGS maps; the expression "Nice quads!" refers always to the former, however, except in those instances when the speaker is an engineer

runoff   rainwater or snowmelt

signed   a signed trail is denoted by signs in place of blazes

single-track   a single track through grass or brush or over rocky terrain, often created by deer, elk, or backpackers; single-track riding is some of the best fun around

slickrock   the rock-hard, compacted sandstone which is *great* to ride and even prettier to look at; you'll appreciate it more if you think of it as a petrified sand dune or seabed, and if the rider before you hasn't left tire marks (through unnecessary skidding) or granola bar wrappers behind

snowmelt   runoff produced by the melting of snow

snowpack   unmelted snow accumulated over weeks or months of winter, or over years in high-mountain terrain

spur   a road or trail which intersects the main trail you're following

technical   terrain that is difficult to ride due not to its grade (steepness) but because of obstacles—rocks, logs, ledges, loose soil . . .

topo
short for topographical map, the kind that shows both linear distance and elevation gain and loss; "topo" is pronounced with both vowels long

trashed
a trail that has been destroyed (same term used no matter what has destroyed it . . . cattle, horses, or even mountain bikers riding when the ground was too wet)

two-wheel-drive
this refers to any vehicle with drive-wheel capability on only two wheels (a passenger car, for instance, compared to a jeep), or to an easy road or trail which a two-wheel-drive vehicle could traverse

waterbar
earth, rock, or wooden structure which funnels water off trails

washboarded
a road with many ridges spaced closely together, like the ripples on a washboard; these make for very rough riding, and even worse driving in a car or jeep

wilderness area
land that is officially set aside by the Federal Government to remain *natural*—pure, pristine, and untrammeled by any vehicle, including mountain bikes; though mountain bikes had not been born in 1964 (when the United States Congress passed the Wilderness Act, establishing the National Wilderness Preservation system) they are considered a "form of mechanical transport" and are thereby excluded; in short, stay out

wind chill
a reference to the wind's cooling effect upon exposed flesh; for example, if the temperature is 10 degrees Fahrenheit and the wind is blowing at 20 miles per hour, the wind-chill effect (that is, the actual temperature to which your skin reacts) is *minus* 32 degrees; if you are riding in wet conditions things are even worse, for the wind-chill effect would then be *minus* 74 degrees!

windfall
anything (trees, limbs, brush, fellow bikers) blown down by the wind

STEVE HENRY grew up on a farm in the rolling hills of central Kansas, spending much of his youth working under the blue skies of the plains. After earning Bachelor's degrees in Marketing and Agricultural Economics at Kansas State University, he served a sentence of seven years in the offices of an insurance company. Missing the outdoor life, he finally left the insurance company in 1985 to cycle across the continent twice, including one trek from Anchorage, AK to Key West, FL. Since then, he has organized triathlons, led bicycle and backpack tours, written articles for *Cycle St. Louis* (a local bicycling publication) and headed to the mountain and desert West whenever he can shake himself loose. "The best thing about writing this guide was discovering the beauty of the Ozarks," says Steve. "I knew Missouri was beautiful, but Arkansas was a pleasant surprise to me. It's one of the best-kept secrets in the country."

DENNIS COELLO'S AMERICA BY MOUNTAIN BIKE SERIES

Happy Trails

Hop on your mountain bike and let our guidebooks take you on America's classic trails and rides. These "where-to" books are published jointly by Falcon Press and Menasha Ridge Press and written by local biking experts. Twenty regional books will blanket the country when the series is complete.

Choose from an assortment of rides—easy rambles to all-day treks. Guides contain helpful trail and route descriptions, mountain bike shop listings, and interesting facts on area history. Each trail is described in terms of difficulty, scenery, condition, length, and elevation change. The guides also explain trail hazards, nearby services and ranger stations, how much water to bring, and what kind of gear to pack.

So before you hit the trail, grab one of our guidebooks to help make your outdoor adventures safe and memorable.

Call or write
Falcon Press or Menasha Ridge Press
Falcon Press
P.O. Box 1718, Helena, MT 59624
1-800-582-2665
Menasha Ridge Press
3169 Cahaba Heights Road, Birmingham, AL 35243
1-800-247-9437

FALCON PRESS

Menasha Ridge Press

FALCONGUIDES *Perfect for every outdoor adventure!*

FISHING
Angler's Guide to Alaska
Angler's Guide to Montana

FLOATING
Floater's Guide to Colorado
Floater's Guide to Missouri
Floater's Guide to Montana

HIKING
Hiker's Guide to Alaska
Hiker's Guide to Alberta
Hiker's Guide to Arizona
Hiker's Guide to California
Hiker's Guide to Colorado
Hiker's Guide to Florida
Hiker's Guide to Georgia
Hiker's Guide to Hot Springs
  in the Pacific Northwest
Hiker's Guide to Idaho
Hiker's Guide to Montana
Hiker's Guide to Montana's
  Continental Divide Trail
Hiker's Guide to Nevada
Hiker's Guide to New Mexico
Hiker's Guide to North Carolina
Hiker's Guide to Oregon
Hiker's Guide to Texas
Hiker's Guide to Utah
Hiker's Guide to Virginia
Hiker's Guide to Washington
Hiker's Guide to Wyoming
Trail Guide to Glacier/Waterton
  National Parks
Wild Country Companion

MOUNTAIN BIKING
Mountain Biker's Guide to Arizona
Mountain Biker's Guide to
  Central Appalachia
Mountain Biker's Guide to Colorado
Mountain Biker's Guide to New Mexico
Mountain Biker's Guide to Northern
  California/Nevada
Mountain Biker's Guide to Northern
  New England
Mountain Biker's Guide to the
  Northern Rockies
Mountain Biker's Guide to the Ozarks

Mountain Biker's Guide to
  the Southeast
Mountain Biker's Guide to
  Southern California
Mountain Biker's Guide to Southern
  New England

ROCKHOUNDING
Rockhound's Guide to Arizona
Rockhound's Guide to Montana

SCENIC DRIVING
Arizona Scenic Drives
Back Country Byways
California Scenic Drives
Colorado Scenic Drives
New Mexico Scenic Drives
Oregon Scenic Drives
Scenic Byways
Scenic Byways II
Trail of the Great Bear
Traveler's Guide to the Oregon Trail
Traveler's Guide to the
  Lewis and Clark Trail

WILDLIFE VIEWING GUIDES
Arizona Wildlife Viewing Guide
California Wildlife Viewing Guide
Colorado Wildlife Viewing Guide
Florida Wildlife Viewing Guide
Idaho Wildlife Viewing Guide
Indiana Wildlife Viewing Guide
Montana Wildlife Viewing Guide
Nevada Wildlife Viewing Guide
New Mexico Wildlife Viewing Guide
North Carolina Wildlife Viewing Guide
North Dakota Wildlife Viewing Guide
Oregon Wildlife Viewing Guide
Tennessee Wildlife Viewing Guide
Texas Wildlife Viewing Guide
Utah Wildlife Viewing Guide
Washington Wildlife Viewing Guide

PLUS—
Birder's Guide to Montana
Hunter's Guide to Montana
Recreation Guide to
  California National Forests
Recreation Guide to Washington
  National Forests

The Mountain Bike Way to Knowledge is through William Nealy

No other great Zen master approaches William Nealy in style or originality. His handwritten text, signature cartoons, and off-beat sense of humor have made him a household name among bikers. His expertise, acquired through years of meditation (and some crash and burn), enables him to translate hard-learned reflexes and instinctive responses into his unique, easy-to-understand drawings. Anyone who wants to learn from the master (and even those who don't) will get a good laugh.

Mountain Bike!
A Manual of Beginning to Advanced Technique

The ultimate mountain bike book for the totally honed! Master the techniques of mountain biking and have a good laugh while logging miles with Nealy.

Soft cover, 172 pages, 7" by 10"
Cartoon illustrations
$12.95

The Mountain Bike Way of Knowledge

This is the first compendium of mountain bike "insider" knowledge ever published. Between the covers of this book are the secrets of wheelie turns, log jumps, bar hops, dog evasion techniques, and much more! Nealy shares his wisdom with beginner and expert alike in this self-help manual.

Soft cover, 128 pages, 8" by 5 1/2"
Cartoon illustrations
$6.95

From Menasha Ridge Press
1-800-247-9437